A Franc

A Franciscan Odyssey

Father Lucjan Z. Krolikowski, OFM Conv.

Translated and adapted by Dr. Gosia Brykczynska

To Dear Lisa
with blessing

fr. Lucjan Krolikowski

Published by

William R. Parks

Stanwrite@aol.com

www.wrparks.com

The cover:

Private audience with Blessed Pope John Paul II, 1978

Contents

Translator's Note

Translating a book as rich in content as this manuscript could never be just a mechanical task. I was asked to undertake the translation of Father Królikowski's autobiography precisely because I could relate so well to the unfolding story and shared with the author a common culture, faith and membership in the Polish scouting/guiding movement; and I am bi-lingual. I knew some of the people the author referred to and I had also spent some time working in the USA! The book refers to my own family experiences as much as to the fate of the author and the many orphaned children he encountered along the way. At times it was a difficult and emotionally draining task and I had to be extremely disciplined to continue with the work. But the work was also very rewarding.

For linguistic and cultural reasons I have decided to be as faithful as possible to all the names of the people mentioned. A name, especially a first name is unique to an individual and even if a Christian name has an English language equivalent e.g. *Rysiek* is a diminutive of *Ryszard*, that is, Richard, that particular individual was still always known as *Rysiek* not Dick. Besides, indiscriminate translations of first names can have the undesired tendency of obscuring the intrinsic otherness (and therefore distinctiveness) of these individuals. I do appreciate however that Polish names can prove to be a mouthful for the average Anglo-Saxon. Likewise I have kept wherever possible the linguistic inflections encountered in foreign place names, as this is a matter of cultural and linguistic accuracy. Also, I have left unchanged (in the first instance) the names of places that Father Królikowski had passed through, even if today these places are known under entirely different names. Lastly, I have tried to clarify where practical and necessary some of the Polish cultural and historical references which Father Królikowski mentions, but others, although present in the Polish text of the book, I have omitted entirely as they could confuse more than help someone reading it in English. All biblical quotes are from the Revised Standard Version (1965). It remains to be said that this edition of Father Królikowski's autobiography has been adapted for an English-speaking readership.

Finally I wish to thank John Revell for his superb help in editing and proof-reading the text and Moya Jolley for her helpful comments on reading the manuscript.

Part I

A country whose name is Poland

The first word belongs to God

Human life can only be seen in its true light from a distance. I am achieving this distance only now, when I am almost at the end of my life. This is because only now have all of its events come together to form a single image, similar to a jigsaw puzzle formed from many coloured pieces of cardboard. God and the angels have always enjoyed perfect perspective; the perspective which I am only now beginning to acquire is allowing me to see clearly the ways of Divine Providence; to become convinced that for God there is no such thing as coincidence; thus even my faults, imperfections and sins which I have committed through my own volition God has turned around to my spiritual benefit through love of me. God presents Himself to me as a Sculptor, who foreseeing my life's imperfections, has capitalised on them in order to shape my very humanity when I submit to His will.

I am convinced that God loves me from the beginning of time; that He has planned my birth at this particular time on our planet; that He has designated these and not any other parents for me. He has decided that I should see the light of day in Poland, that I should grow up in a thousand-year old Christian culture and that I should speak Polish. I am increasingly becoming aware that God has indeed made me in His image and likeness, and that it is His wish to sanctify me, and for me to reach such perfection as I would have had if our first parents had not sinned. That is how I see myself from the perspective of time and in the light of the Bible.

In my childhood life appeared to me as a collection of events; and that is how many non-believers deprived of the light of faith still see their lives – right into their old age. I, on the other hand, from the very beginning of my consciousness, possessed that minimum of wisdom imparted through the Christian faith that my life is in the hands of God, and that God has a specific plan as regards my life and that He wishes that I should co-operate with Him in that plan.

I first saw the light of day on 7 September 1919. According to the Japanese on the day of my birth I would have reached nine months of age, since they count the age of a person from the moment of conception. I am sure such calculations must be more logical and pleasing to God. I spent the day of my birth into the physical world in fear and trepidation before the great unknown now that I had left my mother's womb. But the good Lord ordered that on his behalf I was to be welcomed into the arms of my beloved mother. In that way love was to be my first human experience. Our family house stood less than a hundred metres from the parish church, so shortly after my birth I was taken there to be baptised. I became a child of the church and incorporated into the Mystical Body of Christ of which He is the head and we are the members. I consider it a sign of divine providence that I was born on the eve of the feast of the nativity of the Blessed Virgin Mary and that I was baptised in a church under that title; in this way from the very beginning of my life I consider myself a child of Mary.

The village in which I came into the world is called Nowe Kramsko. Its history goes back almost to the beginning of the Polish state. The land had been given to a Western order whose missionaries were kindling the Christian faith on Polish soil. The very name of the village suggests that in those days the place was a significant trading centre. During the Second World War the village was unjustly put under German occupation in spite of the fact that the inhabitants of the village and surrounding areas were all ethnic Poles. My mother's brothers took part in the Wielkopolska Uprising to secure these lands for Poland and my mother added the names of these uncles to my daily prayers.

I have vague recollections of those faraway times, based on family stories; soldiers in our yard and constant commotion. For participation in the Wielkopolska Uprising the Babimojska lands (which included the village of Nowe Kramsko) were decorated with the military honours of the Grunwald Cross.

I don't know if my father Stanisław Królikowski was around when I was born. My father was called up into the German army, but managed to get over to the French side outside Verdun and then joined the newly formed Polish army led by General Józef Haller. I remember how on some anniversary he went with his army friends to some reunion in France. From a photograph I also remember him in his full German dress uniform with his pick helmet. Another photograph of my father places him in Berlin, fashionably dressed in a suit, hat and with an elegant walking cane. I never asked my father about particular events in his life as I was too small to contextualise the unfolding events of the Great War.

My father came from southern Wielkopolska, while my mother Victoria, née Tomiak, came from Nowe Kramsko. They were married in the church where I was baptised and where after many years I celebrated the Holy Eucharist on the occasion of both my silver jubilee and golden jubilee of priesthood. My father was a baker by occupation and had a bakery and pastry shop. He was the kind of person whom everyone found relaxing; humble, careful about his appearance, frugal with words and with a smile for everyone. He loved us all, there being apart from myself, my sister Władysława, who was four years older than I and whom we called Władzia, and then my brother Czesław, always called Czesio. I was next and after me there was my younger brother Marian, whom we called Maryś.

My father ruled the house fairly with dignity and cheerfulness. Because he worked many hours at night, during the day he would often take a snooze with his pipe still in his mouth. My mother was the picture of goodness and patience – she was everything to everyone (I Corinthians 9,22). In the fourth commandment the Lord God orders us to honour our father and mother not only to love them. Today I understand why this is so. It is as if God "loans" children to parents keeping at all times His full rights to them. Therefore, after God, for the child, the parents are the closest and most important beings; they are the most recognisable gift from God. Through them He gave us life, but they helped God shape our characters and bring us up, mainly through an exemplary Christian life. I will never be able to pay them back for all that they did for me. After God I consider my mother to be the dearest and most beloved person I have had.

Three years after the end of the war and as a result of harassment from the Germans who could not forget his participation in conspiratorial fighting for a free homeland, my father sold his property in Nowe Kramsko which by then lay within the boundaries of Germany. In company with several of my uncles who were also involved in the independence movement he left with his family to settle in free and independent Poland. My cousin Bronek Munko gave me a book in which were listed reports by the German secret police about the activities of Polish patriotic associations. From these reports it would appear that my father was treasurer of the association, which explains why the German police were following him.

In the land of my fathers

At the conclusion of the First World War the German currency was devalued and my family suffered considerable financial losses because money for the bakery and food warehouse lost its value. We finally settled down for a longer period of time in Krotoszyn in Southern Wielkopolska, having lived for short periods in Leszno and Rawicz. In one of those towns I went to a kindergarten, which in those days was called a *crèche.* The kindergarten was run by an order of sisters. I mention this because of a particular experience that I had. My mother would take me every day to the kindergarten along a path which crossed a park. For many months of the year the park was full of plants, flowers and the sound of birds. To this day I can recall the hymn, *All ye May-tide meadows praise [the Virgin]* which we used to sing in the *crèche.* All this contributed to my conviction that the world was a Garden of Eden. But one day this feeling of enchantment was shattered – and this is how it came about. My mother escorted me right up to the door of the *crèche* and telling me to go inside quickly, immediately took leave of me, possibly having some appointment to go to – probably to see the doctor. But the surrounding beauty of nature enchanted me. In the park a little boy of my age was building sandcastles. I ran up to him. He gave me a spade and soon we were both playing in the sand. After some time the mother of the boy, who was sitting on a bench, asked me, "Little boy, where is your mother?" Only at that point did I remember about the *crèche* and I quickly ran back to it. I explained to the sister what had happened. The sister decided that I had played truant. In order to ensure that this truancy would never be repeated she put me into a dark utility cupboard – for buckets and brooms – located under the stairs. The darkness terrified me. I was wailing and choking from crying. The enchantment with this earthly paradise was shattered.

In our family life we did everything together. We would go for walks and pick mushrooms and while we were still quite small our parents would take us for picnics to clearings in the woods and by the lake-side. My father would place us on the handlebars of his bicycle, or our mother would carry us in her basket, tied to the front of her bicycle.

Family photograph, Back row, 1st R; Krotoszyn, 1930

"And in one's soul the magic of youth ..."

(From the scouting song: *How lucky for us...*)

Already at the age of eight I had become a scout. I thank my parents to this day that they were inspired to instil in me the ideals of the scouting movement at such an early age. For the rest of my life I have been guided by my favourite scouting song: *He who once has scaled the heights, and touched the clouds with his forehead, will forever long for those heaven-touching mountains.* Scouting has given me a wealth of experiences, which I treasure to this day as some my most precious memories – troop meetings, sing-songs, exercises, rambles, stalking, summer-camps. The most evocative memories however come from camp-fires and within these the telling of tales and yarns by the camp commanders, presentations by the scouts, ad hoc theatricals, improvisations and clowning around. If in the vicinity of our camp there girl guides were bivouacking, we would invite them to our camp, especially to attend our camp-fires.

Scouting essentially taught me to love God and my country; it developed in me a sense of brotherhood, encouraged co-operation and competition and a sense of leadership. Later, in the wider world, every encountered scout and guide, regardless of their race, nationality or language were considered to be my brother or sister. The acquired scouting virtues spontaneously facilitated making contact with them. I considered it a point of honour not to smoke or drink alcohol and I respected the scouting code as a form of important way-marking for young people. I especially liked the instruction that *a Scout loves nature and tries to get to know it.* I really loved nature which surrounded me on all sides. In this way I had my eyes and heart open to everything; the Lord God, people and the world.

The boundaries of my experiences and competencies were expanded thanks to camps and scouting trips. It was during these activities that I learnt to swim, row, build shelters and to keep a journal in which I noted down my experiences, both happy and sad. I would illustrate the text with coloured pencils. I developed such an appreciation for painting that later I thought I should undertake a career as a painter. I was often singled out for the neatness and rich content of my journal. Very quickly I became self-dependent, since like everyone else I darned my own socks, washed my underwear, worked in the kitchen and helped the cook. On my sleeve I wore my badges. The pride of every scout is his Scout's cross. In Poland I got to the rank of Eagle Scout and once abroad I obtained the title of Scout of the [Polish] Republic. In a word, I discovered myself through the scouting movement. Everything that was good and beautiful and noble became the goal of my aspirations. Saint Paul would add *and what is pleasing to God.* But at that time I was not mature enough to appreciate everything that I encountered. During this time my faith was fairly traditional, superficial and not particularly deep.

In spite of this, to a large extent it was precisely scouting which prepared me to endure the hardships of exile in Siberia, army service, wanderings as a refugee and the undertaking of responsibilities at an early age.

My brother Czesio also belonged to a scouting troop but he was not drawn to such an active life, while Maryś from the start was a sickly child and my mother preferred to keep him at home. In Krotoszyn all three of us went to the local primary school, called a public school, followed by a general multi-departmental high school.

My sister Władzia attended a high school and wore a beautiful pleated blue skirt with a white blouse with a huge sailor's collar and a navy-blue felt cap on which were embellished in gold-embroidered letters G.K. – *Gymnasium Kołłątaja* (Kołłątaj High School). We liked to tease her that the initials stood for *Głupie Kozy* – or silly goats! Władzia belonged to both the girl guides and to the Marian Sodality. In the summer she went off to camps. She inherited from her mother a beautiful strong singing voice, thanks to which she filled our home with either scouting or religious songs. Her favourite hymn was the hymn of the Sodality of Mary - *I have sworn allegiance to my Queen, and from now on I will serve only her. I have also taken her as my mother and placed all my trust in her. I swore to her, I swore to her, at the foot of the altar I swore to her, that all my life long, I will live for her, I will love her and I will honour her...* I quote here the words of the hymn as they formed the agenda of my sister's life. Whether the hymn is sung by Polish girls in Lebanon or in Africa, in Canada or the United States, in the past or today, it always makes my eyes water. No doubt I associate the hymn with my beloved sister.

Władzia took piano lessons, while Czesio took violin lessons, thanks to which he was later accepted into the army orchestra. I also wanted to learn to play an instrument but my parents could not afford such a "joke" – as they would say. My father promised me that when I passed my matriculation exam he would buy me an instrument. I was so fond of music that every Sunday I attended the garrison Church in Krotoszyn, where Czesio accompanied the choir, and after Mass the Fifty-Seventh infantry regiment would organise a parade together with the orchestra. I would always stand close-by, eyes fixed on the orchestra looking at the musicians, especially my brother; after which I would escort them to the barracks.

I would also go carolling with my brothers and friends. My mother and sister made us costumes for the three kings, the devil and angel. We would visit homes of officials where wealthier families lived. We were greeted eagerly wherever we went, and upon occasion invited in, especially where there were children. At one apartment on the third or fourth floor we rang the door-bell for a long time as we thought we heard the sound of coins. It turned out that the owner of the apartment was bent on getting rid of us and as soon as the doors opened our skulls were subjected to blows from his belt. We fled down the stairs and banisters as if on wings. That unpleasant episode discouraged us from visiting the homes of officials. On the other side of the road were the soldiers' barracks. So by now, not so much to get "donations" as to bring some "cheer" to the soldiers, we decided that we would go there – to replicate for them the atmosphere of their family homes. For a long time the sentry did not want to let boys dressed like us into the compound, but the commander (presumably a good Catholic) ordered him to let us in. I never imagined that we could give so much joy to the soldiers.

One more memory from life in Krotoszyn. One of our teachers was prone to spanking us liberally for any old offence. This must have been a relic from his time in German schools, where punishing school-children by beatings was required by law. The teacher used a cane and would tell the child to lift up his hands and bend down to the floor, shouting at the same time, "lower, lower still". When the "delinquent" touched the floor with the tips of his fingers, he was then showered with blows. If he straightened up too quickly, he would hear, "Once more... lower, lower still..." In the winter the boys would burn the cane and in the summer they would break it, until one day the teacher started to carry it home in the sleeve of his coat.

Classroom photo, 1928, Back row 5th from L; Krotoszyn

Forty years later

Forty years had passed since those days, when I returned to my native land from Canada for the first time. My siblings and I decided to visit old haunts and in particular the "old doghouse" that was our school. Władzia especially wanted to see her gymnasium, and in the linden avenue, not far from the Protestant church, the house of her German piano teacher. As we were considering what to do next, we noticed on the opposite side on the road a grey-haired man, whose tread and stiff sleeve reminded us of our teacher from primary school. My brothers and I stopped dead in our tracks. Could that be our old teacher? But why did he have a stiff sleeve? We sent Maryś to do some spying for us. He was speaking for a while with the presumed teacher and nodded for us to come over. Yes, this was our old form teacher. In the process of stories and memories we mentioned the case of the canings. Someone asked the question, "Do you still wear a cane up your sleeve?" "Yes, I do." "So that means that you still teach?" "Yes, I still teach!" "Who and where?" The answer took us completely by surprise: "Well, those scoundrels – the police and the militia. The authorities send them to evening school to obtain a diploma of completion of primary school. Without that they cannot remain in the ranks of the militia."

"And you cane such louts? They allow themselves to be caned? Don't they complain to their bosses? Are you not afraid to teach the armed militia and secret police who are so despised by society?"

The teacher was lost for words for a while, but did not lose his self-assurance, and replied – "Let them try to complain… They are afraid they might not get their diploma, and would then lose their jobs. I'll only add, that none of my old pupils has ever come back to me to complain that a couple of spankings had hurt him."

I thought to myself: People who were spared the rod when they were young get it from life later on – and very painfully at that.

In the stronghold of King Mieszko I and King Bolesław Chrobry

I don't know why my parents moved from Krotoszyn to Poznan. It was a bigger and more beautiful town, with a history going back a thousand years to King Mieszko I (930-992) and King Bolesław Chrobry (966-1025). My father once more opened a bakery and my mother ran a food store. They worked really hard but in spite of that we often lived from hand to mouth.

In Poznan I joined the Association of Catholic Youth and I continued to attend the departmental school, but it took me a long time to get used to my new school and friends. One of my class-mates started to bully me during class breaks. Although I was of a placid nature I was forced to fight a duel with him. The class split into two camps. After lessons we went out of town to the military shooting range. The class divided their support, some were for me, some for him. However, I was stronger and better built than he, and so I won. After this fight, he started to seek my friendship and since he lived close to me I consented. We would go to school together but he had a bad influence on me. He took away my positive outlook on people and the world.

Enchanted by the Spirit of Saint Francis

My family had a subscription to the Franciscan monthly *The Knight of Mary Immaculate,* which was published in Niepokalanów. Often it contained articles by Father Maksymilian Kolbe. I enjoyed reading his articles and I even took part in some of the competitions on religious subjects. Once or twice I even won books as prizes.

From the time at Krotoszyn I had harboured in my heart the thought of entering a monastery. It was a calling to consecrated life and not to a profession or craft or occupation. In fact I was thinking more about life in a monastery than a particular calling to the priesthood. I did not tell anyone about my desires, not even my mother. I had no idea what order to enter or indeed how to go about it. But Father Maksymilian was steering my thoughts towards the Franciscans. Saint Francis's life-style was in keeping with my love of nature, poverty and humility. But it was God who prepared the way; and it was He who did the calling and who made the way-marks easy to read. I was soon to be convinced of this.

One day Władzia came back from school with great news; in the old Market Square she had met Uncle John, who was a friar from Niepokalanów and who had come to Poznan with an exhibition of Japanese missionary artefacts. He was not really planning to visit us as setting up the exhibition and manning the stand required his constant attention and care and for that reason he did not even tell us he was going to be in town. It was a rainy day. In the old Market Square Władzia noticed in front of her two friars, one of whom was limping slightly. My sister knew that our uncle had some slight residual defects after a childhood illness, but she was not sure who it was as she could not see the friar's face. She decided to take a risk, and gently touching his back with her umbrella, whispered, "Johnny, is that you?" (The friar was her uncle, but he was our mother's youngest brother and the difference in age between him and Władzia was so small that for Władzia he was always known as Johnny.) And yes, it was, and of course he could not refuse the invitation.

After he dismantled the exhibition he came over to our house. During the conversation which followed I asked my mother if she would speak on my behalf with uncle, since I wanted to enter the Minor Seminary for the Missions at Niepokalanów. My mother was greatly surprised at this, but I could tell she was happy with this news. Everybody was amazed and asked my father for his opinion, and he replied, "If he is sure that he will find happiness following that road, may God bless him. Let him go."

My mother did not hide her joy. Maybe she had even been secretly praying for a vocation for me, who knows? Later she confided in me that the very thought that as a priest I would be praying for her when she died filled her with happiness. Władzia, who wanted me to reflect a bit more on my vocation, jokingly said, "You can barely open your mouth and you want to be a priest?" But my uncle who was a friar from Niepokalanów and knew the entry requirements explained them to us in detail.

It was 1935, and I was fifteen years old. My uncle left and after a short while a letter arrived from Niepokalanów informing me of my acceptance to the Minor Seminary.

I can still recall in my mind the farewell scenes. Before sunrise I left the house, having first kissed Maryś goodbye, while he was still sleeping. My father was waiting in the street in his white baker's smock and hat. There was no time or energy for talk, and words stuck in my throat. I was escorted to Poznan railway station by my mother and sister. I pulled alongside them a wheeled wicker laundry-basket into which their loving hands had carefully placed my monastic "dowry". We walked in silence; it was only years later that I got to know the French proverb - *Partir c'est un peu mourir* (To part is to die a little). I had no idea that for my mother it would be such a sacrifice, and I had no idea at that time that I would only see her four more times in my life, on visits from Niepokalanów.

Later in life, after finishing the novitiate and taking monastic vows it so happened that I did not return to Poznan but went straight to Lwów to study theology. The next day the Second World War broke out. Where life was to take me afterwards I will explain later, but from that time forward I was never to see my mother again, even though she lived for many years. She died in 1956 but by then I was living in Canada. However, I was not allowed back into Poland, which was under a Stalinist regime at that time, for a variety of reasons, but mainly because they had taken away my citizenship. I recall as a young boy talking about death with my mother. I told her then that I did not wish to see her dead and God answered my prayers. But the physical death of my mother is not what is most significant for me, as she is constantly alive in my heart.

When the train pulled out of Poznan railway station and the dearest people in my life disappeared from view, I started to calm down. I don't remember if I made conversation with anyone or if anybody asked me questions. But I will never forget the sound of the wheels rhythmically hitting the rails on the joins, flashing past telegraph poles and the sight of the wide open landscape of the Polish lowlands. This was my first solo trip into the world and I was afraid of what the future would bring. The constantly changing kaleidoscope of shapes and colours was taking me ever closer to my goal. My heart started to pound in my chest as the train pulled into Szymanów Station not far from Warsaw. To the left of the station I recognised the buildings of the Niepokalanów Monastery from pictures in *The Knight of Mary Immaculate.*

A group of pupils from the Minor Seminary greeted me at the station in their newly acquired deep tones; their voices had just broken. Among them stood out Leitholz, who had a coarse tuba-like voice. They asked me what my name was and where I had come from. I told them that I came from Poznan; but every lisped "s" or "z" amused the seminarians. Leitholz was roaring with laughter. Up until that point no one had pointed out to me my lisping, and somehow I got away with it. Lisping is often considered an endearing oddity in a young child. But there at Szymanów station I was made aware that I would have problems on account of my lisping and that if I did not correct this fault I would be made the butt of jokes.

In the Junior Seminary, Back row 3rd from L;

Niepokalanów, 1935

Niepokalanów – Homestead of the Immaculate Mary Mother of God. Behind the entrance gate the visitor is immediately greeted by a statue of Mary Immaculate. From first setting eyes on it I fell in love with this dwelling of the Immaculate Virgin Mary. Its creator Father Kolbe was in Nagasaki, Japan, at the time, where he named the newly built monastery there Mugenzai na Sono (Garden of the Immaculate).

I felt Maksymilian's spirit in Polish Niepokalanów from the moment I entered it. This was no ordinary monastery; it was an entire town with over seven hundred brothers, several priests and about one hundred and fifty seminarians. One could compare the complex to the Benedictine Abbey of Cluny in France, established in the eleventh century and which played such a big role in re-invigorating the church in Europe. Niepokalanów, as it turned out, prepared the Polish nation for the shock and unspeakable sufferings of the Second World War. Poverty was evident everywhere – in the barracks-style buildings, rough-sawn timber benches, tin plates in the refectory, acorn-coffee, slices of bread with jam, and potatoes with sour-milk. But the spirit of poverty was confined mostly to the buildings – how cosy but also how functional they were. In the winter they were warm and in the summer cool. Slag insulation had been poured into the space between the wooden walls; the outside walls were plastered of course. Ever since my time in Niepokalanów, I have always felt uncomfortable in reinforced concrete buildings, not to mention in marble edifices, especially if they are built not as dwelling places but to store banknotes or documents.

Another characteristic of Niepokalanów was the silence, only broken by the prayers of several hundred inhabitants who would go to the chapel in shifts, as determined by their work. Often, we seminarians could hear drifting from the open windows the rhythmic scanning of the words of Saint John *God is love; who abides in love lives in God and God in him* (I John 4,16). That sentiment became my yardstick and animates my soul to this day.

Niepokalanów was among other things a publishing house, and it produced *The Knight of Mary Immaculate, The Little Daily* and other journals and books. For that reason when one approached the buildings with the printing presses, linotypes or typewriters one was greeted by the sound of monotonous buzzing. In fact, Father Maksymilian compared the monastery of Niepokalanów to a bee-hive – calling it the Hive of the Immaculate, as the inhabitants were like industrious bees of Mary the Queen. He also had a special name for Niepokalanów – a heavenly oasis in this of vale tears.

On the little streets it was always quiet; and passing friars would greet each other with the sweet name of "Mary". Along the streets and beside the houses there were trees and flower beds and huge borders. The Italians have a saying that flowers are the smile of Our Lord. After all, God created us for happiness and joy – and Niepokalanów was bathed in that smile.

Father Maksymilian used to say that Niepokalanów was the work of the Immaculate. He considered himself to be her unworthy instrument, so whenever he could he tried to play down his contribution to the work. He unswervingly trusted Our Lady and would always remain composed, while others trembled over the fate of Niepokalanów.

The provincial of our order often expressed his concern for Niepokalanów should Father Maksymilian die. Who could continue such an enormous undertaking? The concerns of the superiors were not without good reason, since from the time of Father Maksymilian's studies in Rome he succumbed regularly to bouts of tuberculosis. The disease had progressed so far that after one particular stay in a sanatorium in Poland, the Father Provincial sent him away for convalescence to a quiet monastery in the countryside and he instructed the local superior to buy a plot in the cemetery because young Maksymilian "...will not last much longer". But after each period of remission and restoration of his health he would return to his work, to his dream of Knights of Mary Immaculate and to his publication of *The Knight of Mary Immaculate* in Kraków, later in Grodno and from 1927 in Niepokalanów.

When I came to Niepokalanów I could not believe that Father Maksymilian had created it all in seven years. He started building Polish Niepokalanów in 1927 and three years later, in 1930, he founded the

Japanese Niepokalanów. Barely a month after landing in Nagasaki he produced the first issue of *The Knight* in Japanese – *Seibo No Kishi* - with a print run of ten thousand copies. How did he manage to do that without knowing the language in a foreign country so culturally different from Poland? The Japanese language has 145 characters. Father Maksymilian wrote his articles in Italian since that was the only language that the translator knew. The rest of the work was done by Japanese printers and typesetters recruited from among religiously apathetic workers and even atheists. To the question, "How did you do it?" Father Maksymilian would give an answer that not every reasonable person would agree with, namely: "Everything is guided by Our Lady. It is her work." Saints have a different way of thinking from ordinary mortals.

Father Maksymilian saw himself as merely her tool; but the tool was indeed extraordinary. When Raymond Kolbe – for that was the name he received at Baptism – entered the novitiate, a team of high school teachers and Franciscan Fathers would analyse the qualities of each entrant. When the time came to discuss the predisposing qualities of Raymond, his teacher of physics and mathematics advised that he should not be shut away in a monastery but sent to a university. In his opinion he had the mind of a genius. When he set the youngster an exam question he had difficulty keeping up with him, for example when with lightning speed Raymond calculated the necessary level of force required to overcome gravitation in order to send a rocket to the moon! Father Provincial - Peregrine Haczela - agreed that Raymond was indeed an extraordinary young man, unlike any other that the Franciscan Province had ever encountered. He predicted however that Raymond could also become a genius in the spiritual domain, that is, a saint. So they gave him as his monastic name Maksymilian, from the word *"maximus"*, the greatest. Father Provincial Haczela did not make a mistake. During one of his seminary retreats Maksymilian wrote in his notebook, "I have to be a saint, and the greatest one at that." He wanted to be a saint through the greatest love of God and people. Like a child, he put his trust in Mary, asked her to guide him and entrusted her with everything.

In 1936 Father Maksymilian returned to Poland from Japan for the provincial chapter meeting. Meanwhile, his Japanese doctors advised his Polish superiors that they should keep him in Poland since the climate in Japan was not good for his health. But Maksymilian had every intention of returning to his beloved Japan. He said that he wished to lay his bones to rest in the Far East. Maybe he thought that it was there that he was to receive a martyr's crown in accordance with Our Lady's promise in his youth.

Sometimes one has the impression that for saints everything comes easily; that heaven moves all obstacles out of their way. But it's not like that. The martyrdom of Father Maksymilian began at the time of his ordination; it was simply spread out. His real martyrdom was due to tuberculosis. He also experienced episodes of discouragement, for example when he received the news about the death of his blood brother, Father Alfonse, to whom he had entrusted Niepokalanów before he left for Japan. Trusting our most Holy Mother and the determination to become a saint – in fact a great saint – would always put him back on the right track. He knew that the essence of sainthood was love, and that love is always generous.

The provincial chapter elected Maksymilian as the Father Superior of Niepokalanów. This news was accepted with great joy by the whole community. And I who was at that time a member of the community watched with my own eyes the incredible expansion of Niepokalanów under his leadership. I witnessed the putting together of the latest model rotary press that had been bought in Germany. It printed *The Knight of Mary Immaculate,* folding it into a booklet, stapling it together and even overprinting on each copy the address of the subscriber.

Once the monthlies came off the press the brothers packed them into sacks and took them to the railway station. I also witnessed the building of the radio station. I even heard of plans to use our sports field in the near future as an airfield in order to facilitate the distribution of *The Knight* and *The Little Daily* – the cheapest newspaper in Poland. This was because some malicious people kept interfering with its distribution to the more outlying places in Poland. Planes were to be bought and a few brothers even started taking flying lessons. This magnificent expansion was stopped however by the outbreak of the Second World War.

The apple of Father Maksymilian's eye was the Junior Missionary Seminary. He dreamed of building many monasteries such as Niepokalanów all over the world. His motto was "Through the Immaculate Virgin Mary to the Sweetest Heart of Jesus". In order to accomplish such an endeavour there was a need for missionaries, hence his concern for the seminary.

Father Maksymilian would come over to us for talks and took part in picnics in the Kaminowska Forest. He played chess, he would tell us tales about his work in Japan and would ask questions like "What is the word for *mountain* in Japanese?" Smiling playfully he asserted that we all knew the word very well. He would give us to understand that it was the opposite of the Polish word for mountain, finally telling us himself, *Jama,* as in Fuji Jama! This was a play on the Polish word *jama* which means abyss or cave.

After his time as a missionary he was left with a beard where the superficial external hairs were black while those underneath were red. We asked him how it came to be that his beard was in two colours? Again, playfully, and winking at us he would explain – "Well, it's like this. In the monastery they ran out of tea. So I helped the brothers out of a bit of bother by brewing tea with my beard; but when I put it into the boiling water it lost some of its pigment."

Niepokalanów Junior Seminary, Front row 2nd from L, 1937

"He who once has scaled the heights..."

I remember well the Polish scouting song beginning with the words *He who once has scaled the heights, and touched the clouds with his forehead, will forever long for those heaven-touching mountains...*

In the junior seminary for the second time in my life I had the opportunity to be involved in the scouting movement; and this is how it came about. Father Maksymilian wanted to harden us up in order to be prepared for the rigours of missionary life by setting up a scouting troop in Niepokalanów. The Provincial Father Anselm Kubit approved the project on 25 April 1937 and this was duly recorded in the monastery bulletin *Echo of Immaculate Mary.*

In order to establish this scout troop my superiors sent me on a month-long course for Scout Masters not far from Nowogródek in Eastern Poland on the river Niemen. These areas are superbly described by our national bard Adam Mickiewicz in his epic poem *Pan Tadeusz.*

...Those little wooded hills, those fields beside
The azure Niemen, spreading green and wide,
The vari-painted cornfields like a quilt,

The silver of the rye, the wheatfields' gilt... [Translated by K McKenzie 1986]

During the camp the spirit of the bard supported us. We sang the song *"Za Niemen, Za Niemen"...* completely differently over there. *(Beyond the Niemen, beyond the Niemen! Why won't you leave your heart here? What is pulling you to those places beyond the Niemen? Is the land more beautiful there or are there more flowers in the meadows, or are the girls prettier, that you long so much to be there?)*

Naturally, we visited the family home of the poet Mickiewicz in Nowogródek and touched as if it were a relic the parapet from which he fell as a child. In the prologue to *Pan Tadeusz* he gives thanks to God for saving his life:

...O Holy Maid, who Częstochowa's shrine
Dost guard and on the Pointed Gateway shine
And watchest Nowogródek's pinnacle!
As Thou didst heal me by a miracle
For when my weeping mother sought Thy power,
I raised my dying eyes, and in that hour
My strength returned, and to Thy shrine I trod
For life restored to offer thanks to God... [Translated by K McKenzie 1986]

We also took a trip to Lake Świteź, immortalised by the bard in the poem *Świtezianka*. We recited it walking along the shore of the lake and later we sailed on the lake, until all of a sudden from behind the wall of woods which encircled the lake a storm hit us. While in the locality of Wilno (Vilnius, the capital of today's Lithuania) I visited the city. I also went to the Marian Shrine of Ostra Brama (The Peaked Gate) which is located in the gatehouse itself, and I visited the historic cemetery in Rossia, where next to the grave of Marshal Józef Piłsudzki's mother is the urn with the Marshal's heart.

I will not describe the course itself although the activities were varied and educational. However, one thing I do want to mention. We were sent out in a radiating fashion into the countryside for a couple of days to study the way of life and work of Polish and Belarus peasants. The peasants treated us as if we were princes. Hardly any of the peasants had ready cash, and so when it came to First Holy Communion celebrations or the wedding of a daughter, they would take out a loan with the inn-keeper. It would then take them years to pay off the loan, selling their produce to the inn-keeper at unfavourable rates. I must also mention here that I was examined for First Aid by a young master scout, Doctor Wiktor Szyrynski, with whom my life was to become entwined again in Lebanon, Egypt, East Africa and eventually in Canada – and always to do with scouting matters.

After my return to Niepokalanów three scouting units were established and half the members of the junior seminary signed up for membership in the ZHP (*Związek Harcerstwa Polskiego*) – Association of Polish Scouts. We even organised a Sports and Scouting Day at the monastery! The programme included not only sporting activities but also an enormous camp-fire with singing and folk-dances from the mountain region and the scout-master's yarn. One of the more memorable photographs of Father Maksymilian shows him on a picnic in the Kampinowska Forest surrounded by scouts; I am standing next to him. We are all dressed in scout uniforms complete with our four-cornered military-style caps.

I also remember one rather unpleasant episode from Niepokalanów and the questionable anti-heroes of the event were boys from my class. Brother Julius confiscated our football; and we were the most senior class at the seminary. Although we engaged in various sports football was our favourite activity. We would play after lessons. This collective punishment for a prank by one of our class-mates – we didn't even know what it was – shocked us. Behind the closed classroom door we took the decision to go on a hunger strike. But a rebellion by boys aspiring to be future priests seemed to the rector of the seminary to be a scandalous and reprehensible act. In order that we would not be accused of lacking religious fervour we joined the younger classes in the chapel, having waited for them to finish eating in the refectory. Publicity about the strike grew; days passed. Meanwhile nobody realised that we were being saved from starvation by cakes! It just so happened that a few days before the strike several scouts were working towards their Bakery badge. The friars had allowed the boys access to all the ingredients necessary for baking cakes and to the ovens. When the rolls and cakes came out of the oven I approached the friar in charge of the bakery and asked if we could take some of the produce back to our scouts' hut since after our exercises and games we were often quite hungry. During the strike the baked goods which had been put away in the scouts hut cupboard saved us from hunger. Naturally, our superiors did not know anything about this secret form of nutrition and they were terrified that we might become ill. We heard rumours that the rector was considering sending the entire class back home as a warning to the younger boys.

Finally the case went to the highest authority for adjudication. To our utter amazement Father Maksymilian managed to resolve the rebellion in just half an hour. He asked one of us to give him an account of the case. He wanted to know whether and to what extent we felt culpable. Then, with perfect calm and a fatherly smile, he reminded us of the reason why we were there. But he did not reprimand us. He knew that collective punishments were immoral. Neither did he subvert the authority of Brother Julius or the rector of the seminary. He finished with the words, "Get back to your lessons, the ball will be returned to you." The rector of the junior seminary was not a well man, but he did not forget our outburst and when we went on our holidays prior to starting our novitiate he sent letters to some of the parents suggesting that perhaps they should not send their precious sons to the novitiate as they did not seem to have a vocation. But they all returned and several of them went on to hold senior positions in the order. The rector who was participating in the inaugural Mass for the start of the novitiate must have been mightily surprised to see us there. Today, in spite of everything, I look on the strike somewhat differently, thinking about the scandal we must have created for our younger schoolmates.

At a scout camp

A year of religious formation

The novice master was Father George Wierdak. As an educator and counsellor he possessed all the required attributes of a good mother and father. He immediately got to work on sorting out my habit of lisping. He put me on the carpet saying, "You cannot be a priest with such an impediment." He designated one of the seminarians – Dziuba – to work with me. I would sit with him in front of a mirror and watch where he placed his tongue as he spoke, and then like Demosthenes I would attempt to equal his oratory. The novice master forbade the other novices to make fun of me during lessons and he had enough tact not to ask me to perform publicly until I had corrected my speech defect.

The master managed to stamp out of me my stubbornness and selfishness. These faults were quite evident during games of volley-ball. The novice master would call out my name "Brother Zbigniew!" – a name which had been given to me in the novitiate – and he would proceed to serve in such a way that I could not return the ball. I would then become quite angry with him. After the game however he would take me aside and tenderly rebuke me for my outburst of frustration and anger. He also introduced the function of a "guardian angel". Every one of us had such a protective helper and was a "guardian angel" for someone else. I was astonished at how many character flaws and speech faults my "angel" pointed out to me. Some silly expressions like *I'll be damned*, I would repeat without thinking.

We were taught how to pray the Latin breviary, discussed the life of Saint Francis, studied the rule of Saint Francis by heart, became acquainted with the history and constitution of the order, learnt Gregorian chant and moreover were introduced to the principles of good manners which we would recite by heart. One such rule still echoes in my mind: Everybody deserves to be shown politeness, but to everyone in a different way.

The cause of a great sensation at the time was a musical instrument which I had received from my father as a reward for finishing my secondary education. My father kept his promise although I had completely forgotten about it. He sent me a guitar. I get rather tearful at the very thought of it. The novice master was even more surprised by the gift than I was and said, "But this is an instrument for lovers", as such was its reputation at the time. So I asked the master, "What should I do with it?" He replied laconically, "Send it back to your family."

At that time I experienced a crisis in my vocation caused by my over-focusing on my faults and sins. To be a priest you need to be someone better, I heard in my soul. I was afraid of discussing this matter with the novice master so I wrote him a letter, even though our rooms were next to each other. I slipped the letter under his door and he used exactly the same communication method for his response. I found the letter on the floor of my room. The crisis immediately dissipated when I got to the quintessence of the note – *Misericordias Domini in aeternum cantabo* (Psalm 88,2) – the Latin verse for the psalm "I will sing forever the glory of God's mercy". I grew to love and appreciate this maxim even more many years later when Saint Faustyna Kowalska, the apostle of Divine Mercy, appeared in the life of the church.

At the end of the novitiate and the taking of temporary vows for three years on 29 August 1939 I had the joy and privilege of making them in the presence of the superior of Niepokalanów – Father Maksymilian – and many other brothers and priests. The figure of Father Maksymilian is visible on our group photograph, which is one of my most treasured possessions to have survived the turmoil of war.

Niepokalanów – Homestead of the Immaculate Virgin – my beloved spiritual cradle. I thank God for my vocation and the Mother of God for her protection. Thanks also for the chance of a lifetime to be included in the radiating circle of sanctity which surrounded Father Maksymilian. *"Noblesse oblige"* (nobility obliges service... as the French would say.) Many years later when Pope John Paul II canonised him some Jewish people accused him of anti-Semitism, and I felt some bitterness towards them since in such a great soul there just wasn't a shade of anti-Semitism. When an article, written by one of the lay editors, appeared in *The Little Daily* criticising the Jews, Father Maksymilian advised the author to write in such a way that the Blessed Virgin Mary herself could sign her name underneath the script – and with both hands at that! Moreover, during the first days of the Second World War Maksymilian took in 1,500 Jewish fugitives, housing them in the monastery and at the same time sending the brothers out to raise money for food to feed them.

The following day, 30 August 1939, after making our vows we prepared ourselves to leave Niepokalanów in order to study philosophy in Lwów. One could sense war in the air. On wireless sets one could catch the singing of *"Die Fahne hoch, die Reien sind geschlossen..."* (Banners up and ranks closed...) booming out from German transmitters. For several weeks trains with soldiers and military equipment had been heading day and night towards the Western borders; while at Szymanów railway station the friars were distributing Miraculous Medals of the Immaculate Conception of the Blessed Virgin Mary, which were to protect soldiers going to the front from danger.

On 30 August our group of seminarians set out for Lwów. The railway station in Warsaw teemed with civilians and military. By the following day we were in Lwów, and on 1 September German airplanes bombed all the major Polish towns without declaring war. The Provincial Building next to our monastery also became a target. People were killed; while the wounded were taken to our cellars. Grievous news reached us concerning the war.

It was impossible to study in such circumstances, and we rarely heard a full lesson. Neither could we eat in peace. In view of this situation the Father Superior told us to leave Lwów in pairs and to reconvene on the Hanaczów Grange in the Wołyn district. The estate served as an economic back-up for our monastery. After one of the bombing raids, Rysiek Gruza and I, still dressed in our habits, slipped out of the monastery. We managed to reach the suburbs of the town when the air-raid sirens warned us of the next attack. We should have gone down to the nearest shelter, but instead we started walking faster in order to get out of town, as we noticed that the German planes were heading towards another district. The security forces tried to stop us, as our religious habits provoked their suspicion because there had been several reports of German spies dressed as priests having been intercepted. Therefore the annoyed security officers, with their bands of office across their shoulders, pushed us into the shelter which was already full of women, children and young people. They started to look for our identity papers – and of course we did not have any papers on us, which only increased the level of suspicion against us. Fists were clenched and angry looks were thrown in our direction. Seminarians or not, we would have been ripped apart if it were not for a simple woman who started to shout, "They're Franciscan *centenarians*. We've seen them in church." Another added, "At the procession."

We continued on our way to Hanaczów. German pilots were bombing towns and villages, machine-gunning thousands of refugees along the roads and fields. In this situation we decided to avoid Hanaczów and continued towards Halicz, where we also had a monastery. Day by day the situation was getting worse. At the entrances to villages stood groups of Ukrainians armed with pitch-forks and knives. From smaller units of Polish soldiers they confiscated their horses and commandeered their carts and provisions, but seeing our habits they did not pick on us.

Rysiek and I, coming from the Mazowsze and Wielkopolska regions, were not familiar with the problem of Ukrainian nationalism. We were made aware of it by Polish farmstead owners who would give us shelter for the night. They tried to keep us for longer, perhaps to give themselves more courage. The orchards and gardens rendered a bumper harvest that year, but we continued onwards avoiding villages and Ukrainian farms, travelling along deep ravines.

While crossing a particular river we availed ourselves of the help of a Ukrainian, who was carefully observing us all the time. We finally managed to reach Halicz-on-the-Dnieper without too many mishaps, but just before the town we got a foretaste of what was to follow in the near future. From under a bridge a young officer-cadet jumped out. His unit had been defending this troublesome structure and having caught sight of us he started to ask us urgently for news from the front, because he had lost contact with his commanding officers. When we finally got onto the bridge a group of Jewish militia with red arm-bands was standing there.

Next day which was 17 September 1939, the Red Army crossed the Eastern borders of Poland, announcing to all that it was coming as a friend of the Polish people. Nobody knew at that point about the secret pact between Stalin and Hitler for the new partition of Poland which had been signed a month earlier. In spite of that everyone knew the true motives of our historic enemies. In a short time Soviet tanks appeared on the streets of Halicz. For Rysiek and me this meant that we ought to go back to Hanaczów. We travelled by night on a train carrying tanks of crude oil destined for Lwów which was under siege from the Germans. The horizon was illuminated by the glow of burning villages. After a few hours the train halted in an open field. The driver was afraid to go any further, while from afar we could hear the deafening cannonade of the artillery. The head of the local village council put us up on beds of straw in his own home. During the night his son suffered an epileptic seizure, but we thought that it was the Ukrainians who had attacked the village and were murdering everyone.

Assault on the Franciscan farm

In the morning we left on foot for Hanaczów. On arrival we found that our Franciscan farm had been attacked by Ukrainians from the neighbouring village. From morning to night they looted everything that they could; horses, cattle, pigs, fowl, carts, grain and farming tools; they also ransacked the house. Ukrainian children carried away in buckets squealing piglets that had been torn away from the sow. On the farm, apart from the stable lads, there were a sickly priest, a housekeeper and ourselves. We stood in the middle of the yard not knowing how it would all end. After the desecration there was nothing for it but to make our way to the Polish peasant huts in Hanaczów and ask for a place for the night. One peasant agreed to take us in but we did not accept his offer of hospitality as he remarked to us, "When the Ukrainians were plundering could you not have brought at least one cow to me?"

We were taken in by two women whose husbands were still on the front. Not long after, we were filled with trepidation when like locusts Soviet tanks appeared on the dirt roads. In order not to draw ourselves to the attention of the secret police (NKVD), we decided to disguise ourselves as farmhands and offered our help in digging up potatoes. After work we all gathered into one hut where a meal was prepared for us. Usually we sat down to a huge bowl of *pierogi* - dumplings. It was the local custom to eat the *pierogi* by hand but for us *centenarians* they managed to find two forks. The young girls were embarrassed to reach for the *pierogi* with their hands, so in order to put them at ease, we would often turn around and face the older farmers. The older farmers would congregate in our hut in the evenings; and the topic of discussion was always the war. People shared their experiences of what they knew or saw; and it was the men with the most vivid imaginations who invariably got to have their say. One of them began recounting a story about the size of the Soviet tanks. "You're standing in the middle of the track and this tank lumbers towards you. Iron gates open up and another smaller tank rolls out, and from that one a third, and the last one is a real miniature. I tell you, it was easier in Sodom and Gomorrah than it will be for us." Another one was telling us how all the Soviet planes sparkled in the sunshine, as if they were made of silver.

Both of our kind-hearted housekeepers would share with each other observations about us. The woman who lived in the house where Rysiek Gruza stayed was full of admiration for him as she told my landlady, "My *centenarian* just sits there and prays and prays." I overheard this conversation so I asked Rysiek how he had become so holy all of a sudden? He replied, "I found a copy of Rejmont's *Peasants* in the house and I can't put the book down." The Polish novelist Władysław Rejmont (1867-1925) had won the Nobel prize for literature in 1924.

Shortly after that the Germans handed over Lwów to the Soviet Union. Relative peace descended. Our superiors called us back to our studies. I felt sad to leave behind these exceptionally kind and devout people. Later, when Rysiek Gruza and I were sent into the heart of the USSR, our contact with them automatically came to an end. Many years later, after our agonising suffering in Siberia, which I will tell you about in the next section of my memoirs, we got to hear the terrible news about the mass slaughter of Poles in Wołyn. In 1943 gangs of Ukrainian terrorists from Bandera, the OUN (The Organisation of Ukrainian Nationalists) and UPA (Ukrainian Insurgent Army) and other nationalists massacred around 120,000 Polish people living along the Eastern borders of Poland. Many Ukrainians from mixed marriages also died in the massacre because they refused to take part in the slaughter of their Polish wives or husbands. I read somewhere that the Hanaczów families were also rounded up and bestially murdered. After these massacres all traces of Polish life in the area were eliminated; and their homes were set on fire.

A difficult life after our return to Lwów

It was difficult to get down to studying after our return to Lwów. One of our professors insisted that we memorise the entire material by heart – not from a book but from his lecture notes – and studying for exams meant we didn't get much sleep. The new Soviet way of doing things didn't help much either. In the early hours of the morning, right after prayers and meditation, we would get stuck in long bread queues in order to make it on time to the first lecture. So as not to draw attention to myself I grew a moustache.

To make matters worse, the new Communist authorities took away half of our building and placed psychiatric patients in it from Kulparków Hospital. The more disturbed patients would rush into the church during services making a huge commotion. Everywhere Communist rule was increasingly evident. Polish shops and warehouses were plundered and the goods sent deep into the Soviet Union. Grand pianos were taken from private homes; and from churches the more famous organs. From our church they took not only the organ but also the organist, apparently to Leningrad, where they made him reassemble the instrument in an Orthodox church that had been turned into a museum of atheism. Mostly we felt the lack of shoes. Leather was taken away in wagon-loads, probably to make shoes for Soviet soldiers.

The authorities demanded that every inhabitant of occupied Eastern Poland accept Soviet citizenship. For the seminarians this posed the threat of conscription to serve in the Red Army. Our religious superiors left the decision to us. Three of us immediately said no, Rysiek Gruza from Warsaw, Wiesiek Kotarski from Torun, and myself from Poznan. We did not want to lose touch with our families who were now under German occupation. We reported to the appropriate office, in order to be sent back legally to our Western monasteries, and to maintain contact with our families; but that move proved to be a mistake. We really believed that the Soviet authorities wanted to show good faith by reuniting families. After registering in the office the NKVD (the Soviet secret police) started to visit our monastery under the pretence of looking for arms. Our superiors realised that they were controlling our movements and checking-up to determine if we were still there. At every visit they checked the list of residents.

In June 1940 we finished our philosophy course and after a week's break we were to start studying theology. Usually when seminarians finished the philosophy course they would go to Kraków to study theology, but that plan fell through because of the partition of Poland by the Germans and Soviets. I spent the week's holiday with Rysiek Gruza on the Franciscan farm. The superior became extremely concerned when he found out that the NKVD had come round to our monastery again. From then on he insisted that we slept in the barn on the hay. Upon our return to Lwów the Soviet authorities informed us that if we wished to avoid being arrested we had to take out temporary identity cards. This was because in a police state the checking of documents is a common occurrence.

Imprisonment

We believed in the rationale for possessing such documents and so one day, very early in the morning (so as to be able to get back for classes in time) we went to the militia headquarters on Kurkowa Street to sort out the formalities. It was to turn out differently. The number of people trying to obtain such documents rose with each passing hour. We recognised some young religious sisters who had changed out of their habits. The heat started to be felt although we were only lightly dressed in trousers and shirts. There was no food and nothing to drink. Around noon a Soviet official came out of the commissariat and accused us of blocking the pavement. "Where are your manners?" he shouted at those standing in line by the wall. He told us to assemble in the commissariat courtyard and wait there for our documents. Once inside, he slammed the gates behind us and bolted them shut. We were in a trap. There were about two hundred of us. We already knew about the deportation of civilians, usually whole families, by Soviet authorities in the occupied Polish lands. The first such wave of deportations was on 10 February 1940 in the middle of a severe winter. The second was in April and ours in June was to be the third. From the whole of the Soviet-occupied Eastern Polish territories Poles were arrested and deported. During the space of one year over a million-and-a-half people were sent into the interior of the Soviet Union, including about 300,000 children.

Meanwhile, in the courtyard a selection of the people was conducted according to a previously agreed plan. Some people were freed, among whom were the religious sisters, but we three were kept behind. One of the sisters came up to us and said that all three of them wished to stay with the people and to be of help to them. We rejected this beautiful Christian response, since we did not even know what the immediate future held for us and we were not certain that we would not be separated. Hours went by. The courtyard was bursting at the seams, as there were more and more people arriving. People who had come in the morning were placed in rooms in the Commissariat. Wiesiek went in first and seeing an open window immediately jumped out of it and hid in the bushes.

Late that evening, Rysiek and I were taken to the Commissar. We could not believe our eyes, when in front of us we saw Father Superior Rafał Kiernicki and Wiesiek. They had brought some clothes for us and some food for the journey. Wiesiek told us that he had surrendered to the NKVD to share our fate, as he would not have been able to enjoy his freedom if he thought that he had managed to escape but that we had not. The fate of Father Rafał Kiernicki was to become quite tragic. He was imprisoned in Soviet labour camps and after being released, he became parish priest for Lwów Cathedral. The authorities however took away his rights to perform his pastoral duties. He started to work as a night watchman in the town park and later as a porter, while performing his priestly role in secret. Ultimately, Pope John Paul II elevated him to a bishopric.

Around three o'clock in the morning they transported us in lorries to the railway station. People always hide evil deeds, and night-time is considered most appropriate for such activities. Lwów was asleep; and it would not be till the morning that it would find out about our deportation. In Poznan, none of my nearest and dearest even had an idea that I was leaving my country under guard. Would I ever return? Would I survive the ordeal? God alone knew my fate.

An extremely long goods train stood in a siding, into which more than a thousand people were to be squashed. Soviet convoy officials stood guard by the wagons and saw to their loading. Inside the wagons, in the dim light, we could see to the right and to the left two-storey bunks. In the middle of the wagon stood a *parasha*, that is, a pail for faeces; in other wagons there was only a hole cut out in the floor.

There were small grilled windows in the roof of the wagon; those who were fortunate enough to stand next to them could see the towns and villages which we passed - the fields and forests - and would try and guess where we could be. The thoughts of we three seminarians ran to our families and religious community. Our only encouragement was that this capture involved only us and not other members of our families. We did not have to see the sufferings and humiliation of our loved ones. We would recall our fellow brothers in the community and our professors. Meanwhile Rysiek Gruza would lighten up the tense atmosphere with jokes, reminding us that we did not need to learn by heart the lectures of Father Albert for exams.

They squeezed us into the wagons like sardines in a tin; and we got to know others more by sight than through any talk. Almost by instinct, from the very beginning we learnt to keep silent, not to trust even ourselves. They forced into our wagon some Jewish people from Silesia and two young prostitutes – one Polish and one Jewish. We were surprised that they were also picking up Jewish people.

It was getting dark, and when we crossed the Eastern borders of Poland a painful sigh went up from our hearts. We said farewell to our country with tears in our eyes and the singing of *Jescze Polska nie zginęła, póki my żyjemy* (the first words of the national anthem of Poland "Poland has not died so long as we are still alive"). And so we carried away into an unknown world a bit of Poland, our beloved country, to whom we were grateful for a thousand years of Christian culture. We were to expand her boundaries wherever our wandering life was to take us – if we ever survived. According to the words of the poet Adam Mickiewicz, Poland would become more precious to us with every passing day, the further away we were from her. Such were the thoughts of youth, who believe in ideals.

I am sure that all of the deportees had similar reactions – that similar thoughts came to them also – Why? Why was our normal living routine so brutally altered? Why were we visited with such misfortune, separated from our homes, country, the Holy Mass, church services, religious literature, the possibility of going to confession? Why had this misfortune come not only to me but also to my friends, the whole country, to so many nations? There was only one answer: *Misterium iniquitatis* – the mystery of human wrongdoing. God respects human freedom of the will so much that very often he does not intervene; if that were the case He would have to be constantly entering into the affairs of men, straightening and sorting things out. There would be no end to it. But fortunately He loves us from the beginning of time; we are His children. He has the power to turn around every misfortune – personal, familial and national – into goodness and a blessing.

Those who reciprocate His love will have to put aside any thoughts of revenge or retaliation and *"overcome evil with goodness"* so that the perpetrator may finally come to his senses. When will this happen? It might be that I will no longer be present on this earth, but I have to believe in goodness and love. Without them life would not have the slightest meaning. God patiently waits for our enemy, in reality our brother, to reform himself and live a life of happiness in His kingdom of love, peace and justice. Meanwhile, evil people will try to oppress and destroy us; or they will try and turn us into *"homo sovieticus"* – the Soviet man. What that really meant we as yet had only a murky idea, and were to find out later.

Part II

History repeats itself

A journey into the unknown

None of the deportees had a map with them and so the journey was into unknown territory. The train did pass towns and villages along the way but at such speed that it was difficult to make out their names; the general direction however was to the East. It seemed that even the operator of the train did not know our final destination for at each major station where the train would slow down he would receive a letter. We surmised that he was receiving further instructions as to the direction of the train. We reached Penza, not far from Kuibyshev (today's Samara), at the southern end of the Ural Mountains. In ancient times this was a gateway for invading tribes to enter Europe. It was from here that in antiquity hordes of Germanic tribes – Goths, Franks, Vandals and others – infiltrated from Asia. For the first two days we had nothing to eat. They probably thought that people had brought supplies with them from Poland – but of course many people were taken not from their homes but from the street. They started to feed us during the train's nightly stopovers. This was probably for two reasons – so that we would not realise where we were and because they were afraid that we would escape. After a few days the train began to stop during the day; they would unbolt the doors and put down a bucket of soup. Nothing else.

During the stopovers, crowds of unruly children would be running around between the wagons expecting some bread from the travellers; but they were to be disillusioned. Our fate was no better than theirs. We were being sent to camps and they were homeless, usually orphans of murdered parents, or whose parents were also sent to labour camps. The militia relentlessly chased them away; but they would hide under the wagons or they would go stealthily to other platforms. There were so many of these children in the whole of the USSR by 1935 that Stalin ordered that all children over the age of twelve should be punished for "hooliganism". They were sent to correctional camps and when these became overcrowded they were simply murdered by machine-gun fire. It

42

was during this time that the Moscow-based *Pravda* newspaper published pictures of Stalin with a small girl sitting on his knee, holding a bouquet of flowers for the *Father of Nations.*

To our amazement the transport was rerouted from Penza in a north-westerly direction. We even started to hope that maybe the war had come to an end and that we were returning to Poland. We were taken to the Russian capital, Moscow. The NKVD was sending so many deported exiles from occupied territories to its camps that either the places prepared for us were not ready or the strategists had miscalculated; and so we waited for two whole days on railway sidings for a decision to be taken. Meanwhile, Muscovite Jews came around checking to see if there were any of their religion also held captive among us. On the opposite platform stood another goods train carrying Lithuanian families; however they were allowed to take with them kitchen utensils, cows, goats and dogs.

We were incredibly embarrassed at the need to avail ourselves of physiological necessities – especially in the presence of the two women who were travelling with us. The fact that a blanket was held up as an improvised screen for that moment in no way assuaged our embarrassment. Medieval scholastics used to say: *Naturalia non sunt turpia* – things pertaining to nature are never dirty; but they can be embarrassing and respecting that instinct of shame is a testament to the level of one's culture. We cheered ourselves up with the words of Christ who said, *"not what goes into one's mouth makes one unclean but what comes out of one's mouth"* – slander, cursing, filthy language – profanity which was wounding to our ears and our hearts.

Direction – the White Sea

From Moscow our train went in a northerly direction towards Vologda and the White Sea. We had been travelling for over a week now, and in spite of our attempts at hygiene we caught lice. But it would have been worse, were it not for one of our travelling companions – Mr Józef Grabiec, a neat forty-year-old gentleman, who carried a lot of weight with us. He would correct anyone who did not pay proper respect to matters of order, hygiene or the use of civilised language. Mr Józef and his friend Roman were people after our own hearts and so a friendship struck up between us. As we were seminarians, who were not particularly experienced in the ways of the world, Mr Józef was a godsend. He rescued us from many a trouble; but throughout the entire time of our captivity we never found out what his occupation was back in Poland.

Along our route northward the transport of prisoners would stop at small and sometimes really tiny, empty, stations where wagons would be separated from the train and just left there. The wagons with our group stopped at Tarza in the Nyandomsky area of the Arkhangelsk (Archangel) region. Here, huge sleighs pulled along by steel ropes attached to tractors on caterpillar tyres, awaited us. We were rather surprised by this as it was the height of summer. We only realised what the enormous caterpillar runners were for when we entered the forests. Our camp was separated from the railway station by swamps, and the road to it was constructed from huge pine logs, which would sink deep into the swamps under the weight of the sleighs and people. The tractors zig-zagged over the slippery tree-trunks deep into the Siberian taiga. Geographically, Siberia takes in all the forested lands from the Ural Mountains to Kamchatka, but for Poles the term "Siberia" also includes the European forests in addition to the Asiatic ones, due to the thousands upon thousands of Polish citizens who were sent to them under Tsarist rule and later on under the Red Dictatorship. Siberia occupies an area of land larger than the whole of the USA, and its forests constitute a huge and renewable natural resource.

Siberian taiga

The Siberian taiga continues to enchant me with its majestic beauty in spite of memories of the hunger and poverty which I experienced there. Above all, for me the taiga was a sign of the presence of God; of His love and other intangible attributes, including His humility, but also His almighty power, divinity and goodness. Among all those earthly wonders, I never doubted that I belonged to Him; that He was close to me and was with me and would never abandon me. Thanks to this awareness, even in my darkest moments I still had joy and peace in my heart. Majestic woods and impenetrable forests substituted for churches. After all, steeple-shaped pines and spruce were once the inspiration behind masons for Gothic cathedrals. Saint Bernard of Clairvaux was of the opinion that he learnt more from forests than from books. The mystique of the forests encouraged one to pray, giving praise and thanksgiving to the Lord. An Orthodox monk once wrote that *only silence can fertilise speech.* The thoughts of God brought comfort and courage to my sad heart and reminded me that there is no need to be afraid of those who can kill my body but only of Him who can send one's body and soul to hell (Matthew 10,28). Apparently these words of Christ were paraphrased by Józef Beck (a pre-war Polish Minister of Foreign Affairs) applying them to his own situation when he found himself in Romania following the fall of Poland. A Soviet agent tried to persuade him to co-operate with the Soviet government. The minister rejected the temptation stating that Hitler killed the body but Communists were killing the body and the soul. Killing the soul meant transforming a prisoner into a *"homo sovieticus"*. We were to be convinced of this truth when the Soviets would say to us that "any thoughts about God, the church, politics, history, culture even love – you can leave with us. Your only concern is where to obtain the next slice of bread."

Camp Tarza

In Tarza we were greeted at the roll-call assembly point by a stern looking young NKVD commandant. He allowed us to disperse and examine the barracks which we were to inhabit. To our utter horror we discovered that they were already inhabited by armies of starving bedbugs. From then on, we were to wage war with them every night. A list was drawn up of who was to go to which barracks. A group of Silesian Jews, who had shared our miseries with us on the train journey, approached Mr Grabiec with a request that they might join the barracks which would be assigned to the five of us by the commandant. Mr Grabiec chose several of them – as many as there were free places – and for the next seven months we formed a harmonious and close-knit unit.

Work brigades were formed and each unit was assigned a section of the forest for felling. The work brigades were constantly penetrating ever deeper into the forest. We were assigned a Russian foreman – Gladkov – an enigmatic character. He looked sick and worn out. He suffered from asthma but persisted in smoking rolled cigarettes which he made from tree leaves wrapped in dirty newspapers. He was not a prisoner but worked alongside prisoners. He declared himself to be a Communist. He tried to explain to us that although we then had to work in sweat and blood from morning to night the time would come when machines would do all the work. Future generations would be working only one or maybe two days a week; we would be living in a Garden of Eden. Outside the camp Gladkov had a wife and a ten-year-old daughter, but he never talked about them or himself. We suspected that at some point in the past he was sent to the camp as punishment for some anti-Soviet crime and after his sentence was finished he was forbidden to return home, and therefore stayed on marrying a local woman. This was a method which the Soviets employed to colonise Siberia since few people wanted to settle there voluntarily, even during Tsarist times. It was felt imperative that Russians should colonise Siberia because if they failed to do so it would be done for them by the peoples of overcrowded China.

After some time another Russian, Puminov, was assigned to our work brigade. He too was a married free-man. He was an incredibly kind-hearted, simple, country bumpkin. From Siberia he was conscripted into the army fighting during the Bolshevik-Polish War of 1920. He recounted to us how he gave himself up rather than attempting to flee when the Red Army was hastily retreating. Like all Bolsheviks he had a Communist mania on the subject of the Polish bourgeoisie. He said that when they were led through the streets of Warsaw the bourgeoisie would come out of their houses to look at them. He was held in captivity on the Western side of Poland, where the snow barely covered the ground. For a native Siberian such a land appeared strange.

I will never forget the Siberian forests. The standing timber consisted mostly of pine-trees, but there were also fir-trees, spruce, larches and birches. I got to experience all the logging and forestry jobs, as a member of our working brigade, to which various Poles from various professional backgrounds were also assigned. Our work varied but it all centred around felling trees, processing them and transporting them to an open-air depot. We used circular or broad tree-felling saws and axes. We would fell the pine-trees and then cut them up according to the specifications. Larger branches and boughs, the litter of needles and leaves we would burn in bonfires which would still be burning when we left for the night. In the winter the flames of the fire enticed us to warm our hands while in the summer they transported us back to our homeland and allowed us some time to daydream. The twinkling of the embers created a reflective ambiance.

Rysiek Gruza would take the tree logs to the timber depot - called *zashek* - where logs were piled high one on top of the other. For this work he used a special sleigh with a beam placed on top of it. To this beam he would attach three or four several metre high tree-trunks, with their ends dragging behind the sleigh, impeding the transportation. This work was murder not only for the driver but also for the horse. The skinny nag, fed on a rotten diet, would look behind her first before she would pull the load to see if the burden was beyond her capabilities. If the horse decided that the load was too heavy, even if the driver would prod her with a rod, the animal would not move. The driver wanted to take as much timber to the *zashek* as possible since his food ration was calculated as a percentage of the fulfilled quota. Once, a horse collapsed and died on a driver. During the night the prisoners dug up the corpse and ate it, which was a severely punishable offence on account of food poisoning. The logging depots filled up fairly quickly, but because of the swamps the logs could not be taken to the railway station before the winter when the wetlands would freeze over. On one occasion I was taken to help with *nagruzanye* – the loading of logs onto train wagons. The temperature was minus forty degrees Celsius, and it felt even more in the wind. Our noses, ears, and fingers turned white in no time, and we had to be careful to avoid the loss of feeling in our extremities.

Wiesiek, who was the youngest seminarian of our threesome, showed such linguistic talents that he was employed in the administration block. He learnt Russian just from listening, since we had neither a dictionary nor a newspaper, not to mention writing paper and pencils. After a few months he spoke the language fluently. He grew a beard which lent him a bit more gravitas, and so the Russians assumed he was the oldest and called him *starik* – old man.

In the summer, during the polar nights, some of the brigades were taken to bring in the hay, also harvesting grasses and water reeds as the entire area was marshland. Rysiek Gruza would go with them. The greatest trial for these reapers was standing all night in the water amongst countless mosquitoes, who attacked mercilessly on the hands and face.

Gulag Archipelago

Our camp was not a particularly large one, consisting of about a thousand men and a handful of women, and the camp discipline was rather undemanding. We were not surrounded by watch-towers or barbed-wire but by marshes and wet-lands. We would hear occasionally carried on the wind the sound of hacksaws and axes made by other work brigades from other areas. We deduced from this that we must be located in a sea of *gulags* – labour camps.

Alexander Solzhenitsyn (1918-2008) called this phenomenon an archipelago of *gulags*. By education, Solzhenitsyn was a physicist, and by vocation a writer. During the years 1945-1956 he was a prisoner in a Soviet labour camp, making him a renowned authority on the Soviet penal system, writing about the *gulag* archipelago in several books. In 1970 he received the Nobel prize for literature but in 1974 had his Soviet citizenship revoked and was deported to West Germany. He settled in the USA and eventually returned to a post-Communist Russia in 1994.

As I already mentioned our camp was considered one of the lighter ones – and the very thought of these other camps where whole armies of prisoners were kept under the constant surveillance of armed guards gave us the creeps. According to Solzhenitsyn, over fifty million men and women worked in these labour camps amid organised violence, brutality and cruelty. Many died from hunger, the freezing cold, emaciation and disease. Their stay in the camps was a prolonged martyrdom, in contrast to those in Nazi camps, where in a relatively short period of time people were gassed and burnt in crematoria. In Nazi camps every prisoner had his own file with the documentation carried out with German precision; meanwhile the Russians attempted to obliterate all evidence of their crimes.

Gladkov's Brigade

In the beginning Gladkov reserved for himself the job of felling the trees, but because of his asthma he was not supplying us with enough trees to fulfil our quota, so he chose me to be the second logger. I was 21 years old at the time, healthy and strong. Gladkov explained to me the system of segregating the trees, and which tree was destined for which purpose. Those trees that were to go to the saw-mills were referred to as *pilowochniks* – sawyers. Others, which were shorter and intended for use as railway sleepers, were called columns; and those destined to be support beams down the mines were referred to as *rudstojki*. Trees that were healthy, slender, straight and without knots were earmarked as ship-masts, and for the building of ships, boats and airplanes. Wood that was referred to as resonating was considered to be good for the making of musical instruments. Because of the softness of their fibres, birch trees were used for the making of cotton spools. Tall, healthy, tapering pines called *shemyenne* – seed-bearers – were left in the clearing to reseed the new forest. The sight of a falling pine is something really beautiful to behold, and when a tree came tumbling down with a loud crash spreading out its beautiful splaying crown, Gladkov would proclaim, "it flies like an angel but falls like the devil".

Gladkov took advantage of my youthful strength so that increasingly it was I who felled the trees with my axe and saw, while he rested. One winter day we returned to the camp which was five kilometres distant, passing a forest clearing where the fallen snow lay chest deep. The horse was to pave the way for us to follow, but he could not get past the snow-drifts as his broad chest was only compacting the snow even more. Gladkov designated me to break up the frozen snow-drifts with my axe, commenting, "Young man, we'll make a stakhanovite out of you yet". I felt aggrieved by this, mumbling to myself, "I'll give you stakhanovite". Alexey Stakhanov (1906-1977) was a socialist miner who was famous for his prodigious industrial output. He gave the name to the Stakhanovite movement.

Gladkov gave himself a productivity rate of 200%; assigned to me a rate of 110%, and to all the rest 90%. We considered this to be unfair and we complained about him to the regional head forester – Kirylov. We adapted the Communist slogan of *one person taking advantage of another*. Kirylov obviously had a bone to pick with Gladkov because he readily supported us. Gladkov defended himself referring to his knowledge of the forest and logging. I told the forester that I also had the same knowledge and that the brigade could function just as well without him. We were left on our own and everyone was allotted the same rate – which did not really mean very much as the camp shop was poorly stocked. Very rarely would we see cotton padded jackets or trousers or waxed boots. The first refusal for these goods was given to party members, then the stakhanovites, followed by Soviet citizens and at the very end – prisoners. The easiest thing to buy was eau-de-Cologne. Well may you ask what use it had for us? The Russians used to buy it on account of its alcoholic content. They drank it instead of vodka oblivious to the fact that their mouths smelt of cheap perfume.

A cashier on horseback, from the head forester's office, would bring our pay to the camp, his money bag slung over his shoulder. We associated his arrival with the hope that tomorrow would be a bit better – but on the whole the bag with our pay was always half empty as the money was already paid out somewhere along the way.

Stakhanovites

The camp authorities expected us to fulfil our production quotas, but no one actually accomplished these since they were unrealistic. To demonstrate to us that this was not the case they brought in three Russian stakhanovites, as strong as Ursus from Henryk Sienkiewicz's famous novel *Quo Vadis*. Henryk Sienkiewicz (1846-1916) was awarded the Nobel prize for literature in 1905. The stakhanovites were not assigned to any quarters so they ended up in our barracks sleeping on the large brick stove which had no doors, only a gaping hole. We burnt charred pine-chips in it until we had a roaring fire. We joked that we would burn the stove down in honour of Stalin. Because the stove was so hot the stakhanovites experienced really deep and heavy dreams and they swore in their sleep the way only Russians seem capable of. They would leave for work before sunrise and return from the forest two hours after we did. They would use mechanical saws; and they were fed better, with more bread and an extra portion of sausage and maybe some sugar. They also received public praise on the anniversary of the October Revolution. Just as suddenly as they appeared, they disappeared, no doubt to work in another camp.

Practical ways to survive

In order to preserve our health and energies we had to find ways to show that we had fulfilled more of our quota than we could realistically manage. Thousands of work brigades intuitively came up with the same solutions in order to survive. The Communist state forced us to engage in slave-like work, beyond our strength, in inhuman conditions, for derisory wages. Therefore, the methods of self-preservation which we employed in this situation were entirely justified and in keeping with a Christian ethos. Our sabotage against the Soviet Union consisted of going out nightly and cutting off a small round piece of wood which had the logging seal on it from those tree trunks which had already been handed over to the foreman and marked as that day's quota (according to cubic metre of timber). The next day we would hand that trunk in again – as newly felled that day. This way, five to ten (and sometimes even more) large tall trees would increase our cubic metric output and save us from charges that we were evading work.

We used this ploy especially around Jewish and Christian holidays. When the Jews had their festivities the Catholics worked harder than usual to make up for their absence and we handed in more of the re-stamped timber, and during the Catholic holidays the Jews reciprocated; but we had to be vigilant so that the guards did not figure out what we were doing.

No doubt the foreman, a simple kind-hearted man, knew what the prisoners were up to in order to preserve their health and energy. We surmised that he too had been a prisoner and now was working in the forestry department. We had reached that conclusion because he was very taciturn and when he could he would try to help us. Various methods of preserving health and energy were common practice in all the *gulag* archipelago. Barely half of the annual reports from the various forestry departments tallied with reality. The short-fall in production was usually blamed on the forest rangers who would be sent to the labour camps for a few years, but they left with a smile, stating "today it is us, but tomorrow it will be you who will be sent to the camps".

How were we fed?

Our daily ration of food consisted of one ladle of porridge, brought to us all year round in the forest at noon-time in huge thermos flasks, and delivered on a sleigh; and in the evening a bowl of soup and 600 grams of bread. There was never enough bread and it was as hard as a rock. We suspected that they put wood-shavings in it, while the soup had already been gone over by the Russians and only a few cabbage leaves were left floating in the liquid. There was never any fat or pieces of meat, fruit or vegetables or even a pinch of sugar. In order to avoid contracting scurvy we would nibble on grasses and suck their juices, while in the summer we would collect wild berries and raspberries (if the bears had not got to them first), and in the autumn mushrooms. Some, in the hope that it was beneficial, rubbed powdered bark into their soup.

Mr Grabiec was responsible for saving our lives as quite by chance he was assigned to work in the stables. For some reason the horses became ill, and it was impossible to work in the forest without the horses. A *felshar* (a physician's assistant) was called in but he was young and inexperienced and did not even know how to take the temperature of a horse. The horses were kicking so much that it was impossible to take their temperatures. The camp authorities began to look for someone among the prisoners who might know about the care of horses. Mr Grabiec reported himself to the authorities; the horses recovered and they even took on a better appearance as Mr Grabiec knew how to look after them properly. We were really amazed; who could Mr Grabiec have been in Poland? However, his knowledge about horses allowed him to keep his job working with them. Many times in the evening he would bring us some oats to share with us. When hunger really got to us we would crunch the oats with our teeth, trying to fool our stomachs. Every evening I would collect my bread and divide it into three portions - one for the evening, one for the morning and one for noon-time – but more often than not hunger would get the better of me and I would eat all my portion of bread that very same evening. Among other reasons for doing this was a fear that the bread would be stolen. Today, as I write this account, I cannot recall what it was like to be really hungry any more.

Conditions of health and hygiene

We lived in appalling hygienic conditions. Almost no one had a change of underwear, and soap was worth the price of gold so it was effectively impossible to wash oneself properly or to wash one's clothes. It was a miracle that so few of us got ill. In the event of sickness the camp authorities did not provide a physician or medication – but there were exceptions to this. One summer day, working in the timber yard, I fell ill with pneumonia. The world was whirling around in my head and I was soaked in sweat. Mr Grabiec advised that I surreptitiously return to the barracks. As I dragged myself through the forest my way was blocked by the camp commander on his horse who started to shout at me, "Slacker, where are you sneaking off to? Get back to work." I replied that I was swaying on my feet and did not have the energy to work. He kicked me in the chest and assured me that they would check out the illness in the evening. Should it turn out to be fictitious he implied there would be nasty consequences for me. When the work brigade returned in the evening they sent a *felshar* to me with four witnesses to attest to the existence of the illness. One Russian witness after another checked the thermometer and left. I was saved by my work mates who administered *banki* to me. This is a form of Russian folk medicine consisting of placing heated suction cups onto a person's torso. But my mates used tin cans of various sizes as suction cups for this purpose, and I thought that I would be split apart alive, as some of the cans were far too big. I was ill for a long time and to this day I have a shadow on my lungs. Mr Roman, the friend of Mr Grabiec, returned from work one day, squared his shoulders and declared to us all, " Humans are stronger than steel." Indeed, our stamina in respect to work and hardships and our resistance to infections was remarkable.

Sara

One day, when I was ill, a Jewish cleaning-lady named Sara came to our barracks. Seeing how the officials had treated me during my sickness, she snivelled a little, and told me the story of her life. She came from Kraków where she was a member of a secret Communist youth group. On hearing that the Second World War had started and that the Red Army had entered Poland, she ran away from home in the night, to join the "liberators" of the proletariat. She was merely a naive eighteen-year-old labourer. On the far side of the River San she encountered some Soviet youths who were greatly surprised at this turn of events; they assumed she would have been much more likely to try to get to the West and escape the Communist nightmare. She wanted to sacrifice her young life for the good of the revolution – how could they understand her idealism? They handed her over to the NKVD who sent her to a clothing factory where she sewed uniforms for the Red Army, but the work conditions were dreadful. Her eyes were opened then to the realities of

Soviet Communism. Once, while she was standing in line for sugar the all-seeing NKVD spotted her in the queue. She would have waited in line for an hour of more as the queue was quite long, but the informer who spotted her turned to the people in the queue and told them to let Sara get her sugar without having to wait, since in bourgeois Poland she had been denied sugar. Sara felt tears welling up from such humiliation. After several other similar incidents Sara decided to return to Poland, where the Soviets now occupied Lwów. When she got off the train in Lwów she was immediately arrested and sent into the heart of the USSR.

Ministering to spiritual needs

In the camp everyone prayed the best way they could. I spent Christmas Eve 1940 alone in the forest. Shortly before we were due to return to the camp from the clearing, I managed to slip away from the fire-light and I stood in front of a snow-clad Christmas tree which was growing a short distance away. I united myself in my thoughts and in my heart with my family in Poland. This act of homage to the Baby Jesus from the heart of the taiga did not last long, but it was so profound and so full of nostalgia that I have never experienced anything like it before or since. I felt I was secure in the hand of God.

In our barracks we decided to celebrate Easter all together, and we decided that sharing with each other the traditional hard-boiled egg seemed the most important symbol. But where could we get an egg? Even *one*? No one in the camp kept hens. The only person who could help us was an old Russian who vaguely remembered celebrating Easter at home, before the Russian Revolution, and who lived outside the camp. The man in question guessed that we wanted to celebrate Easter and agreed that he would give us an egg on condition that he could be present at our celebrations. In the evening, having returned from the forest, we covered the windows with blankets. The service was led by Wiesiek Kotarski, and a tiny picture of Our Lady of Częstochowa framed in pine branches hung up on the log wall served as our little altar. We started with a prayer and an Easter Hymn. I was kneeling close to the door, and next to me hunched over and terrified was the Russian benefactor of the egg. The Word of God was read out by an elderly schools' inspector, Mr Bem. Tears started to flow – a sign of our spiritual unity with our families in Poland and our martyred country, but also with those in exile, in labour camps and on the front. We hadn't even got to the moment where we were to share the egg and give each other greetings when we heard the sound of the camp commander's boots. We heard them thudding as he passed over the walk-way which was made of planks put down on the boggy soil. Had someone informed about the service? Had someone betrayed us? I looked over at the huddled Russian but there was more fear in his eyes than in ours. The door was pushed open with great force and the silhouette of the camp commander stood in the doorway. He ordered us to stop singing while with a thunderous gaze he looked around us to locate the ring-leader. We sang even louder not getting up from our knees. The NKVD officer started to make his way towards Wiesiek who was kneeling under the picture of Our Lady, past the crammed faithful, guessing that he must be the instigator. Having finally reached him, the officer caught hold of his collar, lifted him up onto his feet and ordered him to follow him. He took Wiesiek away for interrogation and we were very worried about his fate. Wiesiek returned to the barracks after midnight and from the door-way shouted out, "Right folks! From now on in my presence keep your mouths shut under lock and key, and no more joking about Uncle Stalin or Communism. I signed up that I would be an informer and I will be denouncing you... for a bigger slice of bread." Every week he had to go to "confession"; so we were careful about what we said in front of him, not because he would really get us into trouble but so that he could have a clear conscience when he said he did not see or hear anything untoward.

Marxist "catechist"

On one occasion, when we returned from the forest to our barracks an indoctrination officer came to us to teach us about religion. The sight of the young, elegant officer contrasted sharply with the poverty of the camp, the prisoners with emaciated bodies, and dirty, unshaven faces. Nobody was paying any attention to him, as everyone was busy with their own concerns and resting. Trying to draw attention to himself and engage us in a discussion he shouted out, "There is no God". Silence. Someone was putting bark-powder into his soup in the hope it would save him from scurvy, while someone else was slowly chewing on his saved-up bread rations savouring the taste. Most of us were just resting on our bunks. The officer, obviously disappointed, shouted for the second time, "There is no God". Again silence. The officer looked around at our faces, to see at least a glimmer of interest – it looked as if in these circumstances no one wanted to take up the discussion, and certainly not with him. For all of us this was a sacred topic close to our hearts. Again silence, which was broken however after a while, by the prisoner closest to him. Calmly, in a voice full of conviction, he said, "But there is a devil". This completely threw the officer off guard and in a considerably humbler tone he said, "Well you see, I have not covered that problem yet". Whereupon he turned on his heel and left the barracks quietly. No one ever commented on that episode. The truth spoke for itself.

One should not joke - it is forbidden

After some time the camp commandant realised that he would not obtain much information from Wiesiek, so he assigned an informant to us, a former student from Lwów University, a Jewish man who had a strong dislike of Poles. Not suspecting anything, we would make fun of anything Soviet in his presence. For example, on the lid of a Russian box of matches there was a picture of the Soviet insignia of a hammer and sickle. Surely we said they could find better symbols – since a sickle is the symbol of death and a hammer is the symbol of hunger. Or we would joke that a Russian pilot flying over Moscow noticed a queue of people standing in line for some provisions. The length of the queue intrigued the pilot and he reversed the plane following the queue until to his utter amazement it reached the Finnish border. He returned to the capital and hastened to the queue, where he found out that they were waiting for bread, whereupon he was no longer surprised. Now and then the repertoire of jokes would increase. The laughter and scorn would help to relieve the terrible nightmare of the daily life in the camp and would help restore our psychological balance. Mr Grabiec would often ask Rysiek, Wiesiek and me to stop telling jokes, and as a warning he would throw pebbles at us, at the same time winking at us. I wondered many a time who Mr Grabiec really was.

One morning, at the crack of dawn the commandant of the camp and an officer burst into our barracks, while the windows were guarded by armed soldiers. The commandant went from bed to bed throwing off the blankets and looking us straight in the face. To the five Jews in a row, he shouted, "Get up, take your belongings and go". One of them called Teichman had managed to collect some pieces of soap which was an incredible treasure in the camp as one could exchange these for bread. Teichman wanted to take them with him but the commandant shouted at him to throw them away, pointing to a box with bits of soap. We were terrified when the commandant approached the corner where we five Poles slept. My heart was pounding. If only we are not separated, I thought. But the commandant went past us leaving us in peace; but he took the five Jews. Maybe they went to another harsher camp, or to the prison that they kept threatening us with. We never saw any of the five again, not even later in the army formed by General Anders. We suspected that the student-informer, himself a Jew, grassed on his own people. The Communists managed to arouse in him some sympathy for their ideology promising him a prosthesis for his amputated leg. He did eventually get it, but apart from that his fate did not particularly improve. He sold his humanity for a prosthesis.

Hitler's attack on Russia in 1941 awakened our hopes that Communism would fall. Maybe the people would even manage to reject the scourge if only the Germans treated them in a humane way. We even thought that the camps along the route (Moscow – Vologda – Archangelsk) would be freed by the German army. We considered every larger boom which we heard coming to us from afar as evidence of the approaching front. Some of the Russian prisoners enlisted in the Red Army and went to the front, as this was a way to obtain their longed-for freedom.

Clearing the forest

We began to feel the effects of the war. The Soviet authorities fearing that there might be a break in the delivery of foodstuffs to the camp ordered us to dig up the tree-stumps from the forest floor and to plant potatoes. This was an additional drudgery that we had to perform after we came back from felling the trees. The polar nights made the work somewhat easier. The most talented in this craft was again Mr Grabiec. From the planted potatoes grew small, green, bitter tubers.

We were not informed about how the Red Army was managing with the Germans but we did hear rumours that Hitler's armoured divisions had laid siege to Moscow, and others that they were moving towards

Leningrad (St Petersburg); in other words, that they were not that far from us. The Soviet army was losing people, equipment and ammunition. Among many other things, the Soviet military enterprise needed more timber to construct planes, ships, rifles and so on. The head forester allocated Rysiek Gruza and me to a special job cutting down the young pines that had been left by the work brigades as seedlings towards the new forest. It was a beautiful sight to behold – each pine-tree standing erect like the Paschal Eastertide Candle or an elegant princess against a blue sky. In accordance with Gladkov's saying, under our axes and saws the pines fell down like angels while their crowns shattered like devils.

Freedom for the Poles

It was while we were working on the forest clearings that we were freed. The Red Army was suffering successive defeats, which we did not know about at the time. Stalin had declared a Patriotic War in order to mobilise everyone who could move. He re-opened any surviving Orthodox Churches and started to print Bibles. He was also forced to free the Poles from the camps. This act of liberation he derisively called an amnesty, having forgotten that he had also deported children.

News about this 'amnesty' was brought to us by a Russian who lived with his family outside the camp. The old man ran across the fields and clearings waving his arms in the air for joy. It was a strange sight since he was always so restrained. He brought us the happiest most-prayed-for news, "You are now free". He told us about the signing of the treaty between the Polish Prime Minister, the head of the Army Sikorski and the Soviet leader Stalin. On the basis of this treaty the Soviets resumed diplomatic relations with the Polish government and all the Poles imprisoned in the Soviet Union were to be immediately freed. We returned to the camp where we found that in front of the commander's headquarters many of our countrymen had already gathered. Soon we marched in front of the NKVD building singing the national anthem *"Poland has not yet died so long as we are still alive..."*

In our barracks we debated what we were to do with this freedom. Where should we go? Almost everyone was of the opinion that we should head south, where it was warm and there was no need for a padded jacket or winter shoes. But above all, that is where there were countries with abundant food supplies. There were even suggestions that we should go to the Ferganska Valley across the Urals, which the Soviets considered to be a type of Florida. Groups of like-minded people started to form small cliques and we three seminarians chose Mr Grabiec as our leader. Roman also joined us out of friendship to Józef Grabiec. Both of them presented us with an enigma; we still didn't know who they had been in pre-war Poland.

The NKVD Commandant changed his approach to us and advised us to stay put in the camps on account of the continuing war activities and because we would have at least guaranteed bread rations. He was tight-lipped about the formation of a Polish army on USSR territory but he did intimate that the Red Army would gladly accept us, and would then pass us on to the Polish forces when those were formed. He also said that our barracks would be occupied by German prisoners-of-war. We didn't listen to his advice and we decided to leave the camp. But not everyone left. Sara, the Jewish woman, had started to go mad. She would sit forlornly on her own, hair tousled, head lowered – the very image of sadness. For some time she had been manifesting signs of psychiatric illness.

We received a ration of bread and a few roubles for the road. In front of us was a new unknown stage of our life. We were leaving the taiga, a silent witness of our misery.

Polish men in Siberia making their way to join the Polish army, 1941

The Utopian experiment: *"homo sovieticus"*

How can I summarise this short but eventful period of my life, encompassing the invasion by the Red Army of Poland on 17 September 1939, the deportation into the interior of the Soviet Union, life in the labour camp and encountering godless Communism? What had I experienced and what had I understood?

Firstly, the Soviets did not succeed with their hellish experiment of transforming prisoners and exiles into *"homo sovieticus"*, that is into Soviet citizens of the world. Neither in the Soviet Union nor later in China, Cambodia or Vietnam was a new world created and a new person who wouldn't need God and disowned his native history and culture. According to the Communist ideologues – Marx, Engels and Lenin – Communism was to satisfy all human needs. It is hard to believe that this inhuman ideology, this curse reaching back to the eighteenth and nineteenth centuries, first in Europe and then spreading out all over the world (as the writer Vittorio Messori comments in his book *Such is Life*) was to be the beginning of new times and the realisation of a kingdom of justice on earth, as our Brigade master Gladkov tried to explain to us at length. He tried to convince us that paradise would be established on earth – as he put it – by hard work and consciously created for future generations. Every one of us experienced in our own being that this was an illusion, a Utopian dream. Communism was incapable of changing people, let alone making them better. Quite the opposite; those who gave in to the system became even worse. Communism suffered a defeat many years before the fall of the Soviet Union and its satellite states. It suffered a defeat above all in the Gulag Archipelago, in every camp and hamlet.

In the life of the camp there was one experience which gained high ratings and huge value – and this was suffering – which was more of a spiritual than physical nature. At the moment when we gained our freedom physical sufferings dispersed like burst soap bubbles or a bad dream, even though life as a free person was still one long struggle to obtain a slice of bread. But God turned our suffering into something good. As with a plant the sun, rain and winds contribute to its growth and maturing fruit, so for us suffering became a catalyst for greater spiritual advancement. Christian charity deepened towards all people, especially the most disadvantaged and poor, even to the extent of loving one's enemies, especially the most immediate. I wished that they would shake off the enslavement of their minds which godless Communism had thrown them into. I wished that the great and beautiful country which is Russia would return to God and His commandments. As for myself, I did not wish to lose the experiences I had gained or to forget them or to exchange them with someone who had had an easier life. I consider this stage of my life as an interesting and educational adventure. The events I experienced at the camp I considered to be God's wrath but also God's grace. God helps us to forget sad and evil events while remembering the good ones. From the many gifts I received I will always remember the picture of the taiga, the rustling of the leaves in the forests heavy with the fragrance of resin, while at night the sight of the northern lights and the twinkling stars, of which there were more than in any other sky. For me all these wonders of nature were a silent witness to the presence and love of God. In my soul I carry that mysterious silence through which God speaks to us.

Part III

Polish Armed Forces in the Soviet Union

A taste of Soviet freedom

The railway station at Tarza, where we waited for any train to stop that would take us South, consisted of an empty shelter. On both sides of the railway tracks were forests. As we waited by the shelter we observed long transport trains with timber passing through without stopping. Night came, then another, then a third. We began to be affected by hunger and although we ate berries and mushrooms foraged from the forests these only upset our stomachs. The problem was that we were missing a staple ingredient – bread. On the third day, to our utter amazement, we heard voices reaching us from afar but from a different direction than our labour camp.

We decided to go in that direction. In a huge clearing that had been turned into a field, women were digging potatoes. Among them was a little boy – no more than seven years old. Our group of five, without making itself known to the women, delegated me to approach them in order to beg for some food. Watching me approach, the women, who were mostly young, stopped working and lent on their hoes. They asked me how I got there and who I was. I replied that I had just been freed from a labour camp with four others and that we had not eaten anything substantial for three days. They motioned to the boy to give me some potatoes. He brought me some in a hat and I took it from him. At that point one of the women cried, "That's a Jew, don't give him any". The boy immediately reached up and with a punch knocked the potatoes out of the hat; they rolled between our legs and my tears started to well up at the thought of my hungry friends. But another woman asked for more information. I told them that I was a Pole, and that after the occupation of Eastern Poland by the Soviets, thousands of Poles were deported into the interior of the Soviet Union. My story gained a sympathetic hearing with the women as they had suffered a similar fate. They told me they were Ukrainian. During Stalin's man-made famine, engineered in order to force fathers and sons to agree to the collectivisation of farming, millions of people died of starvation and thousands of others were deported northward during the harsh winters. Adults cut down trees and built barracks while children and the elderly spent whole days huddled around camp-fires. Many simply died.

After this sad exchange of information I collected the scattered potatoes, and together with my friends we baked them in a camp-fire. A day or two later, we managed to get on a train which by some miracle had stopped at the station.

Vologda

In front of us lay the great expanse of the beautiful Russian landscape and in our ears were the words of the Russian folk-song which we had heard so many times – *My country is wide and boundless, Full of forests and fields and rivers; And I don't know of any other land, Where a person can breathe so freely.* A beautiful country – but one turned into an inhuman landscape by Communism, so we would alter the last line of the song to *Where a person slowly breathes their last breath.*

In Vologda at the first big station, everybody was told to get off the train. It was not going any further south. Moscow was under siege from German armoured tanks. In spite of our jackets and trousers being singed by flying cinders we posed as combatants and managed to create some sympathy with the Soviet soldiers, so much so that we were able to sit in front of the windows in their common-room. The Red Army soldiers were full of enthusiasm, ready to set off and kill the Germans immediately. They asked us for news of Hitler's hordes. They sang and danced Cossack-style till late in the night to the accompaniment of balalaikas.

Meanwhile hundreds of freed Poles from the labour camps were descending on Vologda railway station. They were camped out on the platforms hoping to connect with some transport. Families were in a pitiful state with children asking when they could eat while mothers, accustomed to such requests, just gazed ahead with a stony detached look. We managed somehow to push our way onto a train that was going Eastward in the direction of the Ural Mountains, which divide Europe from Asia. It was a long and tiresome journey as many Russians were also evacuating to the East. I managed to find a place for myself on a luggage rack right up by the ceiling and I would come down from my perch every now and then to feast my eyes on the sight of Soviet officers holding in their hands bread-rolls spread with butter and lard. I rehearsed in my mind various ways of asking them to share a morsel of this food with me. But I did not have the courage, because I might pay with my life for such effrontery. At stop-overs we would make do with boiling water, which warmed our empty stomachs and intestines, giving us the impression of having eaten fully. At every station there would be a tap with boiling water, a left-over from Tsarist days when samovars were in common use and everyone travelled with their own supplies of tea.

On the boundary of Europe and Asia

Finally we reached Sverdlovsk (Yekaterinburg) in the Urals, a main railway junction between the East and West, Vladivostok and Moscow. After numerous Polish uprisings, military wagons would pass this way with insurrectionists on their trek to the East. It was much later however, that I found out that it was in this area, at the beginning of the Bolshevik Revolution, that Tsar Nicholas II was brutally murdered together with his whole family, servants and even their dog. We had told ourselves that it would be easier to find something to eat in Sverdlovsk, and so we designated the vast railway station as our headquarters. As night descended, passenger activity ceased and the waiting room emptied out, only to be taken over by hundreds of ex-prisoners and refugees who seemed to emerge from the woodwork. They lay down on the stone floor, spreading themselves out on benches and in all the station's nooks and crannies. On the first night I found a place for myself high up on the plinth of a huge statue of Lenin striding with raised fist – or maybe it was Stalin! There was a penetrating cold rising from the floor as in this elevated terrain winter was already beginning its onslaught. Everybody huddled together as closely as they could, like puppies. If someone didn't have enough room they would put their heads on the stomach of their neighbour, or their legs on the nearest available body. One could actually see the lice crossing over from one body to the next.

In the middle of the night, the sleep of these wandering refugees was broken by the cleaning women who unceremoniously pushed the people out of their way. But as soon as they had passed the spaces were filled up again with bodies. A particular inconvenience of this nightly arrangement was trying to crawl out from under all these bodies in order to relieve oneself. Once you had left your sleeping place it was impossible to return to it, as it was immediately taken over by the mass of other sleepers. One needed to find a new sleeping place; and going on all fours it was necessary to push aside the sleepers, which of course was accompanied by grumblings, swearing, hissings and groans, especially if you stepped on someone.

Most of our time was spent in the search for food. Since it was autumn, the locals had already gathered up the produce from their gardens, nonetheless there was still sufficient left behind for us – the roots of a kohlrabi, an overlooked potato still in the ground or rotting fruit. No one chased us away from this foraging. One day however we decided it was time to return to civilisation and we went to the cafeteria with the intention of equipping ourselves with cutlery. Up till then everyone carried around with him a mess-kit attached to his waist with a piece of string, from which one could drink soup, while porridge or millet would be taken up in one's fingers straight to the mouth. I am ashamed to write about it now, but at the time the intention was praiseworthy as we really didn't want to be considered as savages any longer; but the endeavour was unsuccessful anyway. The waitresses became aware of the missing utensils and immediately closed the doors and called in the police. We were horror-struck but thankfully in the ensuing confusion we managed to kick the cutlery under some empty tables and leave the cafeteria unobtrusively.

An adventure in Chkalov

We managed to board a train going south along the ridge of the Ural Mountains. But the conductress realising that we were fare-dodgers threatened to report us to the police at the next station. We resolved this overall unpleasant situation by breaking our journey and disembarking from the train at Chkalov (Orenburg); which was basically motivated by an attack of hunger. The Ural mountain range was coming to an end and in front of us stretched the Bashkir and Kirgiz steppes, the gateway through which barbarian hordes passed on their way to conquer Europe. This was also an area of many labour camps and settlements, a land drenched with the sweat and tears of Polish political exiles, such as the insurrectionists of the 1831 and 1863 uprisings, and again of Polish civilians during World War II.

Evening was approaching. We held a strategy meeting in a park close to the railway station, and I was chosen to stay put and look after our bundles while the other four went into town in search of food. A tramp came and settled down on a bench opposite me, and without speaking we kept our eyes on one and other. Night fell and fatigue and hunger started to get the better of me; so I lay down but for fear that I might fall asleep I arranged the bundles under my back. There wasn't much in them - a letter from my mother, a change of underwear, a family photograph and that was it; but for us in captivity they represented priceless treasures. For a long time I struggled against sleep. My friends returned at dawn, and I was woken from my sleep with shouts of "Where are our bundles?" Instinctively I looked over at the opposite bench; it was empty. I was filled with sadness not so much for the lost items but for shame that I had let my friends down. I was also angry at myself. Rysiek Gruza, who always looked at things in a detached way, patted me on the shoulder saying, "Don't worry about it. The most precious gift we can give our mothers is managing to get back to our family homes. Think about it; only now can we really say that as sons of Saint Francis we are truly free and unattached to earthly things." How this freedom was to help us we were shortly to find out, when we pushed our way onto another train; travelling again without a ticket.

Buzuluk – hub of the Polish army

Directed by uniformed Polish soldiers whom we met along the way, we finally arrived at Buzuluk, a small town with wooden buildings on the Samara River, a tributary of the Volga. We had made an excellent choice since this was the headquarters of the Polish Army in the USSR under the leadership of General Władysław Anders. At this time other army units situated in the neighbouring towns of Totskoye and Tatishchev were just beginning to be formed. To the very end our two companions-in-misery Józef and Roman, did not disclose to us who they had been in pre-war Poland; they simply went on to these other camps. We suspected that they may have been high-ranking policemen. We three religious stayed together in Buzuluk. I use the word "religious" here for the last time as we had formally ceased to be friars. Our three-year temporary vows had run out in the taiga as there was no one there to witness our final vows. But we continued to be tied in spirit to the Franciscan order and to the clergy, so we asked the head of the army chaplaincy what we should do in such a situation. He threw up his arms saying, "I don't have enough priests for the army and you're concerned with lectures, books and a place to study. Enlist in the army!"

The army was in the process of being organised, and living conditions defied any comparison with twentieth century civilisation. We slept on straw and apart from bread we ate only herrings. In order not to become demoralised and to show solidarity with the local population we were advised to go out into the countryside and help the women with the harvest as all their men-folk had gone to fight at the front.

Help with the harvest

About twenty young soldiers were directed to go on foot to the village of Aleksandrovka. At the entrance to the village a young woman barred the road and demanded to know if we had permission from the NKVD to move freely around the area. Simultaneously a Soviet security officer appeared from nowhere and took over our command. Leading us along the main track he sent us in pairs to the farmsteads, not even asking permission of the women. Rysiek and I landed up with an old woman who immediately sent us off to a steam bath to be deloused. She was genuinely afraid of us. She did not know who we were or how long we would be staying with her or what our purpose was for being there. Throughout she maintained a sepulchral silence.

The old biddy lived in a small room with a kitchen, where she spent most of her time. At night we would stretch out to sleep under the window. Only when our voices grew silent for the night would she quietly get into her bed. She would rise before us. She led a miserable life, living on steamed squash. We won her over by bringing back potatoes, carrots and beetroot from our work on the collective farm and even some wood for fuel, which we obtained under cover of darkness. The wood had to be chopped up immediately and the sawdust cleared away; the logs were stacked along-side the wall and hidden under earlier mouldering logs as the next day the forester would look around the enclosures for the looters.

It turned out that our work in the fields was pointless. All methods of transport had been taken over by the army for hauling military equipment and troops to the front and bringing back the wounded, so the on-forwarding of wheat, potatoes, carrots and beetroot failed to be done on schedule. We were therefore told to dig temporary shallow trenches and to cover the collected vegetables with a thin layer of soil. We never did transport the vegetables on to their destination, as we had to leave to go back to Buzuluk. Meanwhile a harsh winter was approaching.

A few weeks later we received through the military base in Buzuluk some supplies of butter, sugar, chocolate and even some devotional objects, which were sent from England via Archangelsk. News of these gifts spread like wild-fire among the villagers, and the women begged us for little crosses, medals and holy pictures, in return for which they brought us their priceless treasures – bread and butter. However, we did not take anything from them, giving away the holy objects as gifts. The women were mostly young and could not have remembered religious freedom under the Tsar. The fact that religion had not died here but survived is testimony to the faith of previous generations who transmitted it in the face of great persecution. From that time on, the attitude of the villagers towards us changed significantly. We were even invited to the community centre for their dances, and while we did not decline the invitations, we felt so fatigued by life in the labour camps and by work in the fields that we really were not in the mood for dancing. We sat on benches placed along the walls, heartened to see such energetic women. They sang and played on the balalaika in time to the beat of the dance and poured out their sorrows in songs about living in the shadow of Soviet reality. I remember the words of one song about a train journey – *We waited three hours for the train and finally went on foot*. On one occasion the foreman of the fishery drank too much, and with his tongue loosened by liquor he started to recount what he didn't like under Stalinism. The next day, at the crack of dawn, the NKVD took him away for questioning.

When our landlady found out that the three of us had been deported from a seminary she found the courage to talk to us. From the bottom of a wicker basket she produced a yellowing Bible, whose pages had tattered corners. She recounted how Lenin and Stalin considered the

Ukraine to be the most reactionary republic because it opposed collectivisation of farming. After many attempts Stalin broke the opposition of the *kulaks* (Ukrainian farmers) by starving them. He ordered that all their wheat should be taken away from them, and the punishment for hiding grain was unthinkable. Thousands of Ukrainians were deported to Siberia and the fight against the farmers ranged over several years, from 1929 to 1933. On some of the most fertile soil on earth, people died of hunger. Our landlady recalled that some people simply lost their minds. Some would hide in ditches and pull down corpses of children from passing carts in order to eat them so that they and others could survive.

Our old granny had a daughter who was a fanatical Communist and who lived in a nearby town, sewing uniforms for Red Army soldiers. On Sundays – her day off – she would come home. On finding out that we were Polish and in order to annoy us she would get out her balalaika and sing army songs about how the Reds triumphed over the Poles. In return we sang her songs about Polish soldiers plundering Moscow.

Life in Buzuluk

After a few weeks we returned to Buzuluk. All the rank-and-file soldiers who had enlisted were sent to basic training camp from which they would subsequently be directed to various officer-training schools. Already great gaps were apparent in the officer ranks. The office of the chief-of-staff drew up a list of professional and reservist officers who had been taken prisoner at the beginning of the war. It was some time later that the news spread about the murder of 25,000 commissioned officers and reservists – mostly from the upper social classes – in the woods of Katyn, Kharkov and Mednoye.

In the barracks that I was assigned to there was no room for me on the plank-beds, so even there, as at our landlady's in Aleksandrovka, I lay down to sleep each night under the window. But it was not a particularly comfortable spot as day and night there was constant traffic along the narrow passage. After a few nights of such nomadic existence my fate radically changed; and the reason for this was a small copy of the New Testament which had been given to me by Father Francis Pluta, the army chaplain, because I was his altar server. I read it on all possible occasions. A book, and in particular a Polish religious book, was a rarity in that godless land where for years Bibles – even transcribed pages from Bibles – and liturgical vessels had been suppressed. Those who possessed them fell under a cloud of suspicion and this was to continue for years.

The sight of me reading this book intrigued a boy from an upper bunk-bed. He jumped down from his bed, sat down next to me, introduced himself as Rysiek Jędrczak and asked, "What are you reading, mate? What book is that?" I told him I was reading the New Testament and he asked if he could borrow it. He read it enthusiastically and in gratitude he gave me a chunk of sugar to suck to appease my hunger. He worked in a Soviet warehouse unloading sacks of sugar. After work, together with our boys who worked there, he would tie up the leggings of his trousers above his ankles to smuggle lumps of sugar in them. Sucking on these lumps of sugar augmented the calorie deficiencies of our meagre diet. Rysiek gave me even more pleasure when he invited me to his upper bunk, to which of course all the others had to confer and give their consent as they had to squeeze up to make room for me. The Bible had united Rysiek and me forever – and in spite of following different paths during the war and in later post-war wanderings we met up again many years later quite by chance in the Grand Theatre in Warsaw. By then he was living in England in London and I was in the USA. It transpired that our friendship survived and it continues to this day.

The army in Buzuluk organised a theatre, in which popular pre-war actors used to appear. I used to help behind the scenes with the setting up of stage props. One evening, just before the curtains were to be raised, I noticed an actress biting her nails because of an attack of stage fright. I was amazed at this sight and I asked her, "You have been acting for so many years and you are still afraid?" To which she replied, "Until I actually stand on the stage I always tremble with fear. I want to be in the best condition possible and give them my all." Deep inside me I thanked her for that insight, and from that time the memory of that event motivates me to pursue perfection, even in the smallest of everyday things. Meanwhile, I had already received encouragement for perfection in spiritual matters in the seminary from the words of Jesus Christ, *Be perfect as your Father in heaven is perfect* (Matthew 5, 48); as countless saints - canonised and unrecognised - have also heeded.

On Christmas Day the city hospital informed the chaplain, Father Pluta, that there were Polish corpses that needed to be taken to the cemetery. Father Pluta asked me to help him with this task. In a dirty wooden hut, on the bare soil, lay a mound of naked frozen bodies. The Soviet nurses opened the doors and waited for the two of us to start moving the bodies onto the waiting horse-drawn cart. But we hesitated a moment, taken aback by the pagan way in which the nurses were treating the dead - in this instance our fellow Poles and victims of exile and life in labour camps. The sight of the dead was an almost daily occurrence for us, but we were even more astounded when the impatient nurses started to move the bodies themselves. One would grab hold of the feet of the dead person and another would take hold of the hands and with a swinging motion they would throw the body onto the cart like a sack of potatoes. Later, together with Father Pluta, we followed the cart making our way to the Soviet cemetery, which was covered in stakes bearing a red star. There were only a few Orthodox crosses; how courageously families had had to fight to have a cross put on a grave. A shallow pit had already been dug. We were left on our own to bury the bodies, and we transferred them to the void. Then Father Pluta said the prayers for the dead. With the aid of pickaxes and spades we covered the grave with frozen sods of soil. We did not have a cross or a sign with the names of the dead to mark the grave, which caused us great distress. Perhaps someone made up for these omissions later.

After the Christmas break our basic training course was moved to Kotubayka, where the temperature on occasions could drop to minus sixty degrees Celsius. The leader of the course was Captain Hassan, a Polish Tatar, an honest man, exceptionally hardened and much loved by the soldiers. He had a routine of jumping out of his dug-out every morning and without any clothes rolling in the snow for a few minutes, after which he would come inside and dry himself off with a towel. He was a picture of health.

In my dug-out there were several soldiers. Even inside, the frost could be felt in spite of the stoves which kept going out, especially at night. The most unpleasant occupation was the so-called flea-hunt. Every morning, all of us would sit naked on our bunks, our clothes spread out in front of us, and shivering from the cold we would diligently search for fleas. We gave them names depending on their size and markings on their backs - Battleship, Soviet tank, Crusader etc. Later an inspection officer would come around and check up on the effectiveness of our work. I completed my basic military training course in Kotubayka and was then assigned to the artillery officers' academy, while Rysiek was sent to the engineering corps academy and Wiesiek to infantry officers' school.

Evacuation to Asian republics

In January and February 1942 the Polish army was evacuated from the Volga region to the northern Asian republics of Kazakhstan, Uzbekistan and Kyrgyzstan. The journey in crowded goods wagons took place during violent snow-storms. With a whistling sound the freezing wind blew into the wagons through cracks in the thin walls. Huddling together, we sheltered from the cold, and the water froze in our mess-kits. During our stopovers, we tried in vain to obtain government coal to heat the wagons. Driven by hunger, some soldiers tried to catch dogs who, sensing danger, would run away from them as fast as they could, their tails tucked between their legs. At one station, while the train was being transferred onto different rails using the pretext that an axle of a wagon had broken, a whole wagon of provisions from England was stolen. Our officer training school stopped for a short while in Jangi-Jul, in Uzbekistan in the vicinity of Tashkent. This little town was chosen as the headquarters of the Polish Army in the USSR. I witnessed there the unloading of trains with Polish children, often orphans. The nurses would support them under the arms, almost carrying them from the trains to the lorries. They were so emaciated – veritable skeletons. But they were proud and they attempted to walk on their own.

The town of Jangi-Jul was located in a region where cotton grew and was encircled by two rivers, the Syr-Dar and the Amu-Dar. During our stay there, due to the presence of sub-units from officer training schools, men were deployed to guard huge bales of cotton. As I stood by them on guard, with my machine-gun in my hand, in spite of myself my thoughts would invariably return to the Siberian forests, where so often we lacked cotton trousers and padded jackets. Meanwhile here there were whole fields of cotton bales - dirty from the rain - covered with tarpaulins. This was typical Soviet disorganisation; lack of competent planning and logistics.

After a short stay in Jangi-Jul, the Artillery Cadet Officers Training Academy of about 150 cadets moved to the Fergansk Valley in Uzbekistan, to a place called Kara-Su. We were split into two platoons, one battery designated as anti-aircraft and the other as a terrestrial unit. From windows in the school we could see in the distance the panorama of the town of Osh, lying close to the Chinese border. Kara-Su in the local language means Black Water, and the word *kara* can be found in many expressions, for example, Karakorum (a mountain range), Karakalpaks (ethnic people living predominantly in Uzbekistan) and Karakuls (a breed of sheep whose lambs are born with a characteristic curly woollen coat, also known as Persian lambs or Astrakhan sheep). In the region of Kara-Su there is an abundance of water as many rivers and fast streams (with freezing waters) flow down from the Pamir Mountains, which are over seven thousand metres high. For centuries the Uzbeks have built networks of canals which water their gardens and fields.

Stationed in Jalal-Abad, not far from Kara-Su, was the Fifth Division of General Borut Spiechowicz, from whom we received our equipment and gear. In no time we began to have drill, and in addition exercises, lectures, anti-aircraft/tank activities, sessions at a tiny shooting range and route marches, even up to the Chinese border.

We were schooled to be officers. But by nature I am quiet and rather self-effacing, which made it difficult for me to develop those attributes which a future leader should have if he is to keep discipline among his soldiers. Orders given by me did not motivate the soldiers; my voice did not inspire them. My commands were not given in a sufficiently booming and determined voice. So that I would come out of my quiet cocoon of "friardom", they made me issue commands to soldiers from a distance of one hundred metres or more - until I got it right.

Every now and then we would go out to the firing ranges in the foothills of the Pamir Mountains, the highest peak of which is 7,495 metres above sea level, and used to be called Stalin's Peak. After the death of the dictator it was renamed Communist Peak. Shepherds from the collective farms were informed about our exercises so that they could move thousands of sheep and rams to safer pastures. A few hours before the main column started out on the day the school was to march to the shooting grounds for exercises, an advance-guard on horseback would leave to check out the terrain, mark the various divisional positions with flags and determine the location of the hypothetical frontline. On one occasion this function fell to me, but I had never in my life ridden a horse. All my rural friends knew about horse-riding, but I, whether from a false sense of shame or ignorance, had not reported this particular lack of competency. I thought that the most important thing to do was to sit on the horse and hope that it would then simply carry me on. How I was to be disillusioned! We walked the horses through the sleeping town of Kara-Su in order not to wake up the inhabitants, but as soon as we left the town behind we accelerated to a trot – and then a gallop! The horse could sense my clumsiness and he was confused especially when we needed to cross a ditch. The hour-long ride was a sheer torment for me, and I ended up being saddle-sore so that I could barely walk.

For the cannons we used horse-drawn yokes as the Soviets had not yet provided us with tractors. The horses who were well looked after and in excellent form caught the eye of a passing Uzbek. He suggested the exchange of his wretched nag for one of our horses, and to make up for the somewhat uneven exchange, he offered to add to the bargain a beautiful girl; it could have even been his own daughter sitting on that downtrodden Arab horse. The Soviets forbade trade in humans but nonetheless some surreptitious activity still went on. The very idea of such a proposition resulted in an outburst of laughter and ribald comments among the soldiers.

When our cadet cannon-rigs ran onto the exercise fields, it took only a few minutes for the batteries to open fire. During one such exercise, a volley of shots was deliberately sent in the direction of a herd of sheep. The soldiers quickly brought the sheep back to the camp, and anticipating an ensuing Soviet inspection of the camp, hung up the animals with rope in an ice cold mountain stream. Sure enough, the next day an NKVD horse patrolman came to inspect the contents of our pots; he looked around perfunctorily and left. Later, from time to time, the cooks would pull a sheep out of the stream, cut it into little pieces and throw them into the soup. The desert terrain was home to an abundance of scorpions. Once, while washing myself in the morning, I almost dried myself with a towel that had a scorpion hiding in it.

On the firing range we were taught through simulated exercises to maintain constant fire at a tank while attempting to take it over. One day while I was manning an observation position on the front line with a group of my friends, an army chaplain suddenly appeared, a Captain Kulikowski, who was notorious for his bravado and somewhat ill-considered actions. He loved riding about in various army vehicles and relished the presence of danger. He asked whether he could be permitted to give the command to the artillery divisions stationed about 15 to 20 kilometres away to open fire. Such violation of the rules was not allowed in the army and was no doubt punishable, but we were in Soviet Russia, and apart from our own division no one else was armed. (Here and there discipline may have been lacking.) The chaplain was so persistent that the instructing officer wrote out orders for him which he was to read over the radio to the firing units. A moment later we heard the metallic sound of flying artillery shells and we knew that they would explode close by; therefore we instinctively dropped to the ground. Shrapnel fell all around us like hail-stones. Fortunately no one was hurt. It later turned out that the commanding officer in the artillery unit did not take into account the level of the land or the varying gradients of the terrain. After all, we were shooting in the mountains. In relation to our observation point the cannons were positioned on a much lower plane. Apparently an investigation was launched into the incident.

Weather permitting, our Sunday Holy Mass would be celebrated in the open air. Each service was attended by a delegation of NKVD officials; and like mannequins they would stand and sit down throughout the entire Mass with their hands in their pockets, without removing their work-men's caps. Separate from the rows of our soldiers and at a slight distance from us, we could see the hesitantly-gathered Uzbeks who were hungry for religious freedom and conscious that at the altar we were enacting a service to God. When we left the area to go to Iran, the army corps of engineers who were dismantling the camp found out that there had been arrests of the civilian population as a punishment for attending our Masses and as a means of intimidation there were even deportations.

The Chaplain-in-Chief Bishop Józef Gawlina came from London to visit the Polish army in southern Asia. The officer cadets greeted him by the camp-fire with a rich repertoire of speeches, songs and funny sketches. The camp-fire atmosphere was marred by a sad prank involving a cadet who insulted the bishop by comparing him to a meteor in an astronomical sketch in which the bishop was supposedly fleeing fighting Poland in 1939 as fast as he could. This was actually not true, since the bishop was evacuated from his country with the rest of the Polish army on the specific orders of the supreme Commander in order to be able to take up the continuing fight against the occupiers – German Nazis and the Red Soviet Union.

Throughout our entire stay in Kara-Su, we witnessed the arrival of haggard Polish families from Soviet Republics, near and far. They turned up at the Polish orphanage which was located close to our academy, in the hope that the army would at least look after the children. I once witnessed a touching scene. A muscular Uzbek on an Arab horse which was harnessed to a donkey carrying a Polish woman and a bunch of children rode into the camp. He became so attached to them that he could not bring himself to go back to his village. He camped out for three days close to our army tents and awaited the return of the children from the nursery school in the mulberry grove, in order to be able to talk and play with them. When the moment came to say goodbye he took each child into his arms, kissed them and gave them a hug. Leaving them several jars of honey, he departed, spurring on his donkey. He was so overcome with emotion that he could not bear to turn around, while the wailing children tearfully said goodbye to their benefactor and protector as they waved their hands. Meanwhile Father Zabluski, chaplain to the orphanage and nursery school, took over the care of the mother and her children.

I was really moved by this display of the Uzbek's attachment to the Polish children since the locals were rather prejudiced towards Polish nationals. The reason for this was that the Polish Army in the USSR was supposed to be fighting against the German army together with the Red Army, but we were miles from the front line. And the Uzbeks, who were after all descendents of Genghis Khan, held that against us.

Historical ties

In time however, the Uzbeks changed their approach to the Poles. They found out about the partition of our country and the subsequent loss of our sovereignty, about our faith in God and that our only wish was to regain our country's freedom.

We found ourselves stationed in a land full of history. In the fourth century BC Alexander the Great conquered Samarkand. In the eighth century AD Genghis Khan was so taken by the climate and rich fertility of these lands that he established Samarkand as the capital of his empire, which stretched from Korea to the Persian Gulf. It was from here that he sent out his chieftains to Europe; all the way to Poland, or Lechistan as they called it. In high school I learnt about this "state on horseback". After Genghis Khan the next great warrior was Timur (known also as Tamburlaine the Great). At that time the Tatars, infamous for their raids on Polish lands, were considered to be a Mongol people. A particular Tatar raid on Kraków in the thirteenth century led to the legendary episode of the bugler in the tower of the Blessed Virgin Mary Church. He had just started to warn the townspeople of the impending raid when he was hit in the throat by an arrow in the middle of his bugle-call. To this very day, in commemoration of that event, the music of the bugler is broken off suddenly when it is played from the church tower, every hour on the hour.

Two legends

It was in Uzbekistan that our Polish legend of the bugler met up with a Mongolian legend. This came about in a strange way. The Uzbeks asked buglers from Lechistan – Polish soldiers – to sound the bugle-call in the market square in Samarkand. The Poles readily agreed to do this. On the appointed day the market square and adjacent streets were filled with crowds of local people. The crowds waited in silence while the buglers were arranged facing the mosque, in which Timur the Great was buried. The Polish buglers played the reveille, then a call to assembly and finally the *Mariacki* church bugle-call. It made such an impression on everyone that they dispersed to their settlements, in reflection and silence; more especially as it was also the time of Ramadan. This event as retold by an officer acquaintance of mine has also been recorded in a book by Xavier Pruszynski.

There is also another legend uniting Uzbeks and Poles. When I was in the Artillery Officer Training School in Kara-Su I got to hear about a visit paid to our commanders by some Uzbek elders who showed them a breast-plate with an engraving of the Blessed Virgin Mary which their ancestors had brought back from Lechistan (Poland), either as a war trophy or as a relic. The Uzbeks have their own legend concerning this breast-plate and the Tatar archer who caused the death of the Lechistan bugler as he warned the townsfolk of the impending raid from the church tower. Apparently the Tatars returned home without their leader, as he had died fighting. Their spiritual leaders explained to them that the death of their leader and their defeat was due to a punishment from heaven, and with this punishment came a prophecy – that the Mongol nations would fall into captivity, but that they would regain their independence when soldiers came from Lechistan and their horses drank of the waters from the local rivers, and their buglers played that same bugle-call once again in Samarkand.

Both legends have an interesting connection, as if constituting two links joining the two nations together. I am not sure how much is truth and how much is fantasy; but surely there is a measure of truth woven in.

I recall that my friend and Jesuit cleric, Józef Janus, underwent a profound experience. At that time in Uzbekistan he was a soldier like me, later studying theology with me in Beirut. I quote from his recollections of the time: "We were stationed in Guzar in Uzbekistan. We arrived in an army car at Karkin Batash (in Uzbek this translates as Death Valley). The Bolsheviks had set up an orphanage there for Polish children liberated from Soviet camps, most of whom were orphans. Long mud huts baked dry in the sun served as dwelling units. Typhoid, malaria, dysentery and scurvy reaped a daily harvest. At that moment an ox-drawn cart loaded with the naked bodies of six children went past us on its way to the cemetery. It represented that day's harvest. I don't know how many children there were in the orphanage, but there were around forty healthy children – that is, children who could stand up on their own two feet unaided. The rest did not even get up from the ground (they did not even have camp beds); they were waiting for their turn when death would take pity on them. The entire orphanage of several thousand children was in reality a hospital – a mortuary. I consider myself to be a self-styled "tough guy"; I cried neither in prison, nor when I was beaten or given the death sentence; I did not cry when I buried my nearest and dearest, not even when I buried my father; and I have personally conducted over seven hundred burials. But on that occasion I could not control myself, in spite of the fact that I was in uniform. Around us stood forty louse-infested skeletons. Living corpses. Some thin, some swollen; but all covered with sores from vitamin deficiencies. They looked at us with glassy eyes, burnt lips smiling, behind which we glimpsed their toothless ulcer-covered gums. They radiated an atmosphere of death. The sight of those bare-foot, half-naked children on the endless desert plain amongst the vipers, scorpions and thousands of malaria-carrying mosquitoes froze the blood in our veins at the thought of their impotence and innocence. When those living beings, so damaged by life, started to sing in their hoarse and aching voices, 'From our pain and effort Poland will rise and live...' somebody behind me exclaimed in an awesome whisper, 'Jesus and Maria'. I bit my lips so hard they started to bleed. I started to weep out loud. In fact no one could control himself and no one was ashamed. We couldn't stand that sight. We were overcome with a paroxysm of pain."

How often from the mouths of Polish children, women and soldiers – those liberated from prisons and labour camps – went up the prayerful hymn:

O Lord who art in heaven, lend to us your hand of justice,
We call to you from so many parts, for a Polish hearth and Polish arms.
Crush the sword, O God, which has lashed out at our country
Allow us to return to our land. Let it become a fortress full of new
strength:
Our Home – our land.
O Lord hear our complaints, hear this wanderer's song,
From the banks of the Wisła, Warta, Niemen and Bug – the blood of
martyrs is calling out to you...

Stalin was livid with rage that the Polish civilian population was leaving its places of exile – the collective farms and factories – and was making its way down south in search of the Polish army. In order to put a stop to this influx of people he forbade the army to feed them. But how could Polish soldiers refuse a piece of bread to starving Polish children? Therefore the Polish army, including our officers' academy, took upon itself the task of providing rations for the civilian population, sharing with them our soldiers' rations, which Stalin was constantly cutting back.

A tragicomic event took place in the tents when it came to the collection and distribution of bread. In our tent, and almost certainly in all the other ones too, the division of bread bordered on an almost religious ceremony. The most senior officer cadet was given the privilege of cutting the bread and weighing it on make-shift scales devised from tin cans and strung together with thread. Everyone took part in the allocation of bread in the capacity of observers. Eyes sparkled as they focused on the scales. A terrible hunger, left over from our labour camp days, still pre-occupied us. Sometimes, in spite of this precise clinical division, the last person to get his share just received scraps.

As a result of my slow starvation it was not unusual for me to sway on my feet during exercises. Once, during military exercises my eyes glazed over to such an extent that I leaned on a cannon which to an artillery-soldier was a sacred object. The officer leading the exercise told

80

me to apologise to the cannon for this act of disrespect. I had to jump around the cannon three times while squatting and holding my heels. Finally I had to kiss the cannon's gun-carriage.

I am grateful to the army for a great deal and I think every young healthy person should pass through the military mangle, but I would not want to be a professional soldier. Sometimes the corporal who was conducting the drill humiliated the cadets, amongst whom were some, who for obvious reasons were a lot more senior in profession than he, for example lawyers, judges, professors and entrepreneurs. Even a small mistake during drill would provoke an outburst from the corporal such as, "This is not a university, you need to think here." And when he noticed a button that was not done up, he would shout, "You're all naked" until the guilty person realised that he had a wayward button on his uniform.

The time was drawing near for General Anders to leave for Persia – now Iran. The first transport had already left in April 1942. Our academy was to leave in the second wave in August of that year, together with the Fifth and Sixth Division. We were extremely excited, but also fearful that Stalin would withdraw his consent for us to leave, as relations between him and General Anders were becoming increasingly strained. If the Red Army had carried out the victory in Stalingrad at that time, it is possible that we would have been held back. It was rumoured among us that our leaders were considering the possibility of getting us through to the free world via the Afghanistan or Iranian border.

Meanwhile the Artillery Officer-Training Academy finished the year in a state of great excitement. I do not have many memories of that time. I received my graduation diploma with a poor mark, not because I was not good soldier material but because even from my high-school days I was always weak in mathematics – a crucial drawback in the work of an artillery officer. Lack of adequate food, a condensed programme and an accelerated course all played their part in my capacity to learn. We later found out that we were supposed to take the place of the murdered officers in Katyn and similar places.

Finally the dreamt-and-prayed-for day arrived, when we left through the Kizil Kum desert for the base-port of Krasnovodsk, the embarkation point from which ships carrying the Polish Army, civilians and children were to leave for the Persian port of Pahlevi (in today's Iran and now called Bandar-e-Anzali).

But our joy was not without sorrow, as only seventy-eight per cent of the army and thirty-eight per cent of the civilian population – over half of which were children and youngsters – were leaving that inhuman land. We had no idea how many of our countrymen had died and how many Stalin would not release from the labour camps. After we had left for Iran another secret was uncovered. After we had embarked, the commander of the base in Krasnovodsk, Lieutenant Colonel Sigmund Berling, a legionnaire and chief of staff of the Fifth Infantry Division, deserted and put himself at the service of Stalin. Apparently he became offended that he was not promoted to the rank of General. He received this promotion from Stalin, who instructed him to form a new army under the name of the Tadeusz Kościuszko Division. During its formation it had around 170,000 soldiers, among whom was our third colleague from the seminary Wiesiek Kotarski. It's not clear how he joined up, but we suspect that he was led astray by the NKVD, like many other soldiers, as he did not say goodbye to us. The Kościuszko Division fell victim to Stalin's evil plans. Unprepared for action, the division suffered huge losses at the battle of Lenino, where they did not receive the promised Red Army tank or air support. The division was saved from complete annihilation by the intervention of the Communist activist Wanda Wasilewska, who managed to convince Stalin that when the Soviets reached the Polish border the Red Army would not be able to draft any Poles into their army unless there was a Polish army accompanying them. I remember that apart from the Fifth Division he deliberately held back from arming other divisions, as a pretext to sending them to the front with the intention of having them slaughtered, as they were the remaining witnesses of the atrocities in the Gulag Archipelago. As to Wiesiek Kotarski we heard rumours that he died not far from Warsaw during an attempt to cross the Wisła (Vistula) River. Meanwhile, Polish sentiment awoke in General Berling when he stood outside burning Warsaw during the 1944 Uprising. He decided to expedite aid and assistance without the permission of Stalin, for which he fell from grace and his military career came to an abrupt halt.

We thus said goodbye to the Soviet Empire which according to Lenin, Trotsky and Stalin was to become a paradise for the conquered nations and was to take over the whole world. Communism was to take the place of religion, especially in the sense of matters spiritual, and Christianity itself was to be reduced to a type of secular religion. In accordance with the views of the Age of Enlightenment Communism rejects the concept of original sin and asserts the notion that humans come into the world in total innocence, and that the spread of evil is due to ignorance. But the time will come, say the Soviet Communists (including Brigadier Gladkov from our labour camp) when science will dispel evil. There will be no need for prisons, armies and courts of law, and people will have loads of free time because machines will do the work for them. Then freedom, love, justice, peace and happiness will rule supreme.

For us who saw the building of this earthly paradise it was clear that behind this Communist Utopia stood Satan, of whom Christ said that from the very beginning he was a killer, a liar and the father of deception (see John 8, 44). The builders of this earthly paradise believed Satan and so everything they do is deceitful – proletarian governments, the newspaper *Pravda,* the brotherhood of nations, science, history, art and finally the title of Stalin himself as the *Father of the Nations.*

During these adverse times of captivity and oppression a support for us all was the Catholic faith – as much for those who escaped from the Soviet paradise as for those who were unable to leave with us and go to Iran and the free world, or return to their country. We asked ourselves the question, how long will it take for the world to see through the appalling lies of the Communist system and free itself from the charms of its
false Utopia?

Lucjan Królikowski and H Szymanski, in the Polish army, 1943

Part IV

The Near East: Towards the Priesthood

Freedom

We docked at the Persian port of Pahlevi. It was a sunny day, but even if it had been overcast our feeling of freedom would have brightened it up. We were all filled with a sense of euphoria. We were free at last from the misery that had engulfed millions of people under Bolshevism. We had only been two years in that inhuman land but it felt like a never-ending ordeal. The Soviet ship which had docked in the port became a symbol of that sentiment; everyone ran ashore as if their life depended on it.

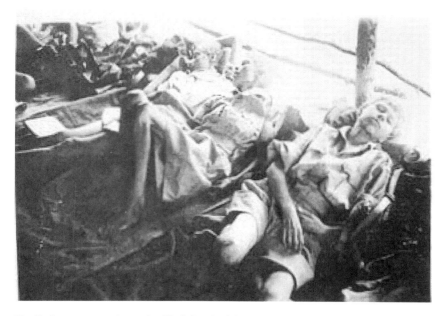

Polish youngsters in Pahlevi, 1943

I remember one particular scene. Everyone had already left the ship and a young woman with two daughters was the last to walk down the gangway. Half way down she stopped, as she heard the whimpering of a child coming from the coal-hold of the ship. She called out to her compatriots standing on the shore, "Whose child is that?" And after a while, "Does anybody claim that child?" Stony silence. Could it be that the child's mother felt that if she returned to the ship it would sail away, as had happened numerous times with the transportations, when a train would suddenly move off separating sons from their mothers and daughters from their families. The woman called out again, but again no reply. She then went back on board the ship and after a short while came out carrying in her arms a child covered in coal dust, smelly from unwashed clothes and no doubt full of lice. But still nobody claimed the child; he was obviously an orphan. Some good Samaritan had managed to smuggle him on board the ship, maybe even a Russian – a secret enemy of Communism. I happen to know the ending of this story. The boy was called Eugene Rusin and he ended up in a Polish orphanage in East Africa and I brought him later to Canada.

Polish children in Pahlevi, 1943

The civilian population was allocated to several camps around Teheran; the children and some of their families went to Isfahan. After a while they were sent around the world, mainly to Africa, India and New Zealand.

Dates and a swim in the sea

The artillery units were camped in tents not far from Pahlevi. On the beaches the local people were selling pomegranates and dates. I had never eaten these types of fruit before. An aroma of sweetness came from the dates. Suddenly a feeling of hunger overcame me – that overpowering sense of need which forces one to grab food while it is there because it may be gone tomorrow. I spent my entire soldier's pay on a bag of dates – and immediately ate them all. As a result I cannot look at dates to this day! Fortunately fatty foods were not being sold on the beaches; as being unused to such foods, this could have resulted in intestinal torsion – as had occurred with many civilians, especially children, who were dying day after day. Testimony to this death rate was the newly-erected cemetery in Teheran.

One of the pleasures of freedom was swimming in the Caspian Sea. With some encouragement from one of our leaders, our group of officer-cadets hurled themselves into the sea. We swam out for a considerable distance so that the tops of our tents disappeared from view. We were at the end of our endurance, and we still needed energy to return to shore, but we were dare-devils as only young people can be. Everyone wanted to show off his strength. However, after the Soviet hell, we lacked sufficient energy for such feats. I returned to shore more dead than alive.

The final delousing

One day it was announced that there would be a universal war declared on the lice which we had brought over with us from the Soviet paradise. This time the delousing was a pleasant yet radical affair. We took off our coats, uniforms and underwear which we had worn in the Soviet Union and put them on a pile to be burnt. We then went into huts with showers where paramedics with scrubbing brushes brushed out the nits (that is, the eggs of the lice) from our hair. After bathing we went through to the other side of the provisional baths collecting on the way a set of clean new underwear and a British uniform. And so little by little we freed ourselves of all that was Soviet.

However, after two days, when everyone else was luxuriating in the freedom from lice, I felt an intruder crawling across my back. By its movement I knew it was a louse. I was terrified that my commanding officers would leave me behind in Iran to undergo quarantine, while the rest of the army moved on to Iraq. So I decided in the greatest of secrecy to deal with the louse myself. I tightened my shirt really well, so that the parasite could not wander off anywhere else. I went out far into the desert so that I could no longer see the row of tents. It was no easy feat to find two stones in the desert, but when all was ready for the execution I slowly took off my taut shirt and finding the intruder – who was naturally of Soviet origin – put him on one flat stone and with the other delivered the fatal blow. I inspected my underwear, especially the seams, to check that no eggs had been laid. There were none. I returned triumphant like a warrior from a battlefield, but for the next few days I was vigilant in case a sibling should turn up.

Soviet propaganda

Our sense of security was shattered when we found out that Soviet soldiers were stationed in Iran. We heard rumours that Soviet officials were spreading false information about the Polish army and civilian population to the effect that the Soviets had taken in the Poles, who were running eastward ahead of the German onslaught – the *Blitzkreig*. Traces of Soviet propaganda could be found everywhere in the Near East. These lies found favourable acceptance among those who had already been primed by Communist indoctrination, which claimed that Communism was a faith which would replace all hitherto known religions and social systems.

Until we left Iran I could not sleep because of fear. I even had nightmares in which I was pursued by a red ogre and I would then grow wings soaring above rooftops and between houses. I was plagued by such dreams for over a year.

Along the ancient Babylonian road

Finally, like the Bedouins, we rolled up our tents and crossed the desert into Iraq. Every now and then we would come across a German bunker, from which we concluded that even before the Second World War, Hitler was preparing to secure sources of Iraqi oil, vital in the conduct of modern warfare. In the south along the coast of Africa, Marshal Rommel was forcing his way towards Egypt; while in the north Hitler's armies were pushing towards the Caucasus. Had the German armies in the Near East actually met up and decided to close their pincers, Polish forces may well have been used in that arena of war. The allied forces certainly considered this as a possibility – or so I think. If Hitler ever had such plans then they were well scuttled; Field Marshal Friedrich Paulus became bogged down in Stalingrad losing ignonimiously, while Rommel was ousted from Africa.

I had always associated Iraq with the ancient history of Mesopotamia, the cradle of Sumerian civilisation which lived and worked there thousands of years before the Bible was written. The two rivers – the Tigris and Euphrates – encircle the huge country, turning it into a fertile oasis. After the fall of the Sumerians their cultural heritage and civilisation was inherited by nomadic Semitic peoples who poured in from all sides – Assyrians, Babylonians, Canaanites and many others. They all lived side by side in a melting pot. Finally the Greeks and Romans took over the cultural legacy from them. From my lessons in ancient history I was reminded of events and cultural monuments in that land – the Biblical flood and the building of Noah's Ark, the hanging gardens of Babylon, gigantic building projects like the Tower of Babel, the discovery of cuneiform script and the beginning of literature with the Epic of Gilgamesh and Hammurabi's code of laws.

You can imagine then our disappointment when our vehicles actually drove into Iraq – the so-called ancient fertile oasis of Mesopotamia. We encountered a desert and piles of ruins – all that was left from ancient palaces, libraries and other once splendid edifices. Parts of these ancient buildings were even used to construct shabby domestic dwellings. Obviously, the present day Arabs could not even build irrigation systems as serviceable as the ancient Sumerians, Babylonians or Assyrians. Today there is almost no trace left of these jewels – the pride of the Chaldeans (or Babylonians).

Creation of the Second Corps

A part of the Polish army was stationed near Baghdad, today the capital of Iraq, not far from the ruins of ancient Babylon. The artillery units were stationed to the north of the capital in Khanaqin and Quizil Ribat. In Iraq the army was re-organised in preparation for the invasion of Italy. The Carpathian Riflemen Brigade under General Stanisław Kopanski, already famous for its engagements in North Africa with Rommel's Afrikakorps, joined up with the rest of the army which came from the Soviet Union. From all these units the Second Polish Corps was created under the overall command of General Anders.

During the stopover in Iraq, several thousand soldiers of Jewish descent deserted to go to Palestine to fight for their country which their ancestors had lost two thousand years before. Our commanders turned a blind eye to this escape; the deserters were neither punished nor were they pursued. Some of the Jews however remained faithful to Poland, among them my friend Alexander Dandig from my officer-cadet platoon in Kara-Su.

Mesopotamia and Abraham

The desertion of Jews reminded me of a previous incident involving the Jewish peoples in Mesopotamia around four thousand years ago. Generally the whole history of the Jewish nation overlaps with the ancient history of Assyria and Babylon; as that land was the country of Abraham who was born in Chaldean Ur, the capital of the Sumerians, not far from today's Persian Gulf. From there, Terah with his three sons (one of whom was Abraham) and with Abraham's beautiful wife Sara, struck out to the north of Mesopotamia, settling down in Harran. It was in Harran that God changed the name of the protoplast of the Jewish nation from Abram to Abraham and gave him His promise that he would become the father of nations. He also gave him ownership of the land of Canaan – Palestine.

Tower of Babel

The Bible mentions the construction of the Tower of Babel which according to the Jewish writers of the Bible was a symbol of human pride, although we know from general history that the Tower of Babel was not the only such building. Assyrians and Babylonians constructed such buildings in every large town and they were known as *ziggurats*. They served several functions: a religious function as the seat of God, a scientific function as an observatory of the stars and finally a social function as the tomb of a king.

According to some archaeologists, these structures were attempts at establishing a contact between heaven and earth. I am especially reminded of this latter proposition when reading the story of the Patriarch Jacob, the grandson of Abraham, who while on his way to Mesopotamia – the land of his ancestors – had a strange dream. In his dream he saw a ladder, the top end of which touched the skies while the other end was resting on the ground. And as the Bible relates, the angels of God were going up and down the ladder. Then God stood in front of Jacob and said, "I am Yahweh, the God of your father Abraham and the God of Isaac." At this, Jacob woke up from his dream and cried out, "I did not realise this before, but truly God is in this place." Jacob then became very frightened and he said, *This is none other than the house of God, and this is the gate of heaven* (Genesis 28, 17). Could that have been an unusual pre-empting of the prophet Isaiah's statement *O that thou wouldst rend the heavens and come down* (Isaiah 64, 1)? In another place entirely, Saint Benedict compares our life on earth to a ladder which the Lord raises up to heaven; here the two uprights of the ladder represent our body and our soul, that is, the spiritual and the corporal aspects of our being.

Jews in Babylonian captivity

The Israelites are a "nation which remembers". They remember well the two major deportations of their ancestors in the fourth century before Christ. Nebuchadnezzar II, the Babylonian King, burnt down the city of Jerusalem and its temple taking into captivity King Jeconiah and his entire family, the court and all competent artisans and craftsmen, even the prophet Ezekiel. Since the land of the victors was far more fertile than Palestine, life in exile was not too burdensome. The Jewish exiles were not deported to concentration camps as were the Poles during World War II by the Soviets on the orders of Stalin. The Jews were allocated dwellings in the heart of the capital city and in other places around the country.

The author of Psalm 137 recalls:

By the waters of Babylon,
there we sat down and wept,
when we remembered Zion.
On the willows there
we hung up our lyres.
For there our captors
required of us songs,
and our tormentors, mirth, saying,
"Sing us one of the songs of Zion!"

The psalmist is obviously recalling the Sabbath day during which the exiles in accordance with customary law were resting, having gathered along the banks of the canals. But how much more tragic sound the words of the Polish hymn composed in exile during WWII: *O Lord who art in heaven... hear this wanderer's song. From the banks of the Wisła, Warta, Niemen and Bug – the blood of martyrs is calling out to you.*

Jewish colonies prospered splendidly in Mesopotamia. So much so, that when, sixty years later, Cyrus (the Persian Caesar) declared an edict allowing the Jews to return to Jerusalem, many of them chose to remain in Babylon preferring a peaceful and lucrative life over a problematic future in the promised land. But apparently while around fifty thousand people did return to their homeland others continued to work and prosper in Mesopotamia, as is recorded in cuneiform script on stone tablets.

Christian associations with Mesopotamia

Christianity also has connections with Mesopotamia. The wise men from the East, who followed the star to Bethlehem in order to pay homage to the newly-born King of the Jews Jesus Christ, probably came from Mesopotamia where astronomy was well developed (see Matthew 2, 1-2). During the Descent of the Holy Spirit in Jerusalem, there were also present pious Jews from Mesopotamia (see Acts 2,9), probably descendents of those who had been exiled. Before the destruction of Jerusalem by the Roman army the apostles left the city for Antioch, as

Christ had instructed them; and from there they went in all directions spreading the Good News (the gospel) about salvation. The apostle Thomas made his way to Mesopotamia, which was close by.

The presence of the Polish army was an attraction for the Iraqis. During mealtimes multitudes of neglected children – urchins in rags with flies circling their sunken eyes – would approach the camp kitchen and our tents for *baksheesh* or alms. It was considered useful for adults to carry a rifle or even a field gun. One night the sentry on guard alerted the sleeping camp that one of the cannons was slowly moving although there were no people or animals near it. It turned out that some Arabs, hidden behind a hillock, were pulling it along on ropes. The chaplain to the tenth heavy artillery regiment lost his red knee-high boots; the gendarmerie located them in a neighbouring village.

We were stationed next to the Indian army, and the Indians would come over to us to play volley-ball. The British however forbade us to fraternise with them – as they were still at that time a British colony.

Rysiek Jędrczak

In Khanaqin, as part of the re-organisation of the army, I was assigned to the tenth heavy artillery regiment. I shared my quarters there with a chief warrant officer who could not advance further in the army as he had not completed his matriculation examinations (even before the war). For this reason he bore a grudge against officer-cadets who had passed their matriculation exams and who therefore had no impediment to their army career. However, he became friendly with me since I would regularly hand over to him my ration of alcoholic beverages. But it sometimes happened that he got his own back on other officer-cadets, like my engineer friend Rysiek Jędrczak.

One Sunday Rysiek drove over to visit me from Habbaniyah on the Euphrates, not far from Baghdad, to find out if I had signed up to do theology studies in Beirut in Lebanon. I was so shocked and puzzled when he asked me about this that it took my breath away.

"What are you talking about?" I asked, not believing my ears. He explained that in all the regiments a letter had been read out to the following effect: "Anyone who has started his seminary studies in Poland and who still wishes to continue them, can report to the Chaplain-in-Chief Bishop Józef Gawlina who is staying for a short while in Baghdad. The army needs priests." In our regiment the chaplain Father Kulikowski had not read out that announcement and when I later reproached him about this he replied, "I thought that you had chosen a military career for yourself."

But I had never given up my original intention and I told Rysiek that I still wanted to be a priest. Encouraged by this information he said, "Well, sit down then and write to Bishop Gawlina requesting to be accepted by the seminary and I will deliver the letter to him in person immediately as he is leaving for London tomorrow." "Hold on," I said, "I cannot just do it like that. I have to do things via the official channels: from the commander of my regiment to the commander of the whole artillery division, then to General Anders who formally accepts the petition and then he presents the request to the bishop." "But that way you will never get anywhere with your studies! Don't do things the formal way – the bishop is leaving for England tomorrow! Sit down and write." Realising the exceptional nature of the situation, I sat down and started to compose a letter.

While I was writing the letter, my room-mate, the chief warrant officer, surreptitiously offered Rysiek (who was a teetotaller) something to drink. He must have been mixing some drinks behind our backs because a short while later Rysiek collapsed on top of the bed having completely blacked out and he was in no shape to deliver the letter to the bishop. I was at a real loss as to what to do. I waited for over an hour, after which I lifted my friend off the bed and led him out into the desert to sober up. I had to lead him by the arm, as occasionally his legs would buckle under him. Moreover, the sand made walking difficult. Two hours passed by but Rysiek still did not know who or where he was. It started to get dark. I led my friend onto the road. I managed to stop an open lorry full of young soldiers returning to Baghdad from leave. The driver was an Indian. I asked the soldiers if they could lift Rysiek up onto the lorry by his arms while I pushed his rear-end. By now it was completely dark.

94

Then I heard a loud thud. Rysiek had fallen to the floor of the lorry like a sack of potatoes.

Several days passed. There was no answer to the letter. I assumed that Rysiek had been in no state to deliver the letter to Bishop Gawlina. But a short while later, on my way to the officers' mess, the regimental secretary – also an officer-cadet – stopped me and said, "You've made a real mess of things." I immediately guessed it was something to do with the letter. No doubt the bishop's reply came through official channels, but I pretended not to understand what was going on. I asked him to explain himself. And he replied half-jokingly half-seriously, "You really behaved like an idiot – they'll put you into prison."

It was a Sunday so the regimental commander had not yet checked the post. I begged my pal to tell me the content of the letter. It appeared from Bishop Gawlina's letter that he had accepted me into the Beirut Seminary in Lebanon, but in the margins of the letter was a note added by General Anders, "The cadet has circumvented formal channels – check out why?" The Chief of Artillery of the Second Corps, General Roman Odzierzynski added to this his own comment, "If the cadet is at fault – punish."

The next day the platoon commander informed me that he had to present me to the colonel for a disciplinary hearing, stressing, "Take a handkerchief with you so that before you enter the colonel's tent you can clean the dust from your boots. We are in the desert." From the stern expression on the colonel's face I surmised that the meeting was not going to be particularly pleasant. The colonel started his reprimand saying:

"Officer-cadet, you teach soldiers to obey army rules but break them yourself."
I clicked my heels together and said, "Yes Sir."
"Does officer-cadet realise the consequences of such lapses in discipline?"
I was only too aware of the potential consequences, and so once again I put on the appearance of military humility, "Yes Sir."

I sensed that he was embarrassed for me in front of the generals. He had been humiliated and his pride as an exemplary commander had been challenged. But he had reason to be disillusioned; our regiment had already gone through re-organisation and was ready for battle. The loss of a cadet made a significant gap in the cadre numbers. Suddenly, he changed his tone and said in a friendly voice, "Officer-cadet, I also am a Catholic. I wish you God's overall blessing on your new path in life."

It was not till much later that I found out about a project in Iraq to provide theological studies in a seminary which was to be run by Dominicans in the town of Mosul. But this project collapsed when the Jesuit fathers in Beirut agreed to take us into the university in Lebanon.

For some reason Rysiek Gruza, my companion in the Soviet Union and now an officer-cadet in the Engineering Corps, also failed to get his application for theological studies in on time, and so the two of us found ourselves together in a transit camp waiting to leave for Lebanon. Even there I had an adventure. During bathing I had managed to contract scabies. I even thought that the devil must be pursuing me and was trying to stop me from becoming a priest. Since it was a Sunday again, the doctors' clinics were closed. I became terrified that the transport to Lebanon would leave without me, but after I explained my predicament and said that I needed immediate help, a sympathetic nurse gave me a quarter of a bottle of some liquid medicine. In order to get rid of the parasite thoroughly I rubbed it on my skin so hard that I acquired abrasions and the soldiers around me could not sleep because of the caustic fumes.

Fulfilment of my dreams

Finally, an army lorry was located which would take the group of soldiers to Palestine, and it also took the two of us who were detailed to go to Lebanon. It was the early spring of 1943 and we travelled down the Trans-Jordanian Highway along the oil pipelines. The scenery consisted of desert, the air was shimmering from the heat and several times we saw mirages – illusions of oases surrounded with palm-trees. When we drove into Palestine I understood why the Jews, who had been wandering in the desert for forty years after their release from Egyptian captivity, were convinced that they had reached a land flowing with milk and honey. Everywhere it was green, with banana, olive, mulberry and orange groves and vineyards. The orange trees were almost brushing the ground under the weight of the fruit. In the first little town which we passed a Jewish milkman, having spotted the eagles on our forage-caps, cried out to us in Polish, "Heads high lads!"

Lebanon

Lebanon, to which we were heading, fascinated us but we knew little about it. We only knew a few extracts from the Bible and Polish literature. We knew a verse from The Song of Songs, *Veni de Libano, veni* (4, 8) and from our knowledge of Polish literature we knew that Juliusz Słowacki had travelled in Lebanon.

We arrived in Beirut by train from Haifa at 2 o'clock in the morning on 17 March 1943. Hospitable English soldiers put us up for the night in an excellently equipped transit camp. The sleeping town of Beirut – with its houses, villas sheltering in the shade of pine-trees and illuminated in the pale glow of the moon – evoked a magical and exotic atmosphere. In the morning we made our way to the Polish consulate to find out the whereabouts of other seminarians who had arrived a month before us. They showed us the way. Finally, we arrived at the buildings of the French University of St Joseph.

Now years later, writing these memoirs, I know that the name Lebanon comes from the Semitic word *luban* (meaning white) from the snow-covered peaks of Mount Hermon and Mount Jabal Şannįn. Mount Hermon is covered with snow all year round. We were impressed with the city of Beirut, one of the oldest cities in the world, even older than Rome. Its history goes back several thousand years before the birth of Christ. As a backdrop to the city are the gently rising mountains of Lebanon in whose folds nestled villages and the odd sprinkling of small white houses with red tiled roofs. Shortly after our arrival seven Polish settlements were established over an area of thirty kilometres, encircling the capital like a wreath. They were inhabited mostly by Polish civilians and the Poles from Siberian labour camps who had come over from Iran – about six thousand people all together. The names of the settlements sounded like something from the *Tales of the Arabian Nights*: Ajaltoun, Baabdat, Bdadoun, Beit Chabab, Roumieh, Zouk and Ghazir.

Perfect Franciscan charity

At the university we were warmly welcomed by the rector, a tall slim man, Father Jacques Bonnet-Eymard. He informed us that the majority of seminarians were staying at the Retreat House in the Al-Ashrafia district of Beirut, which was a quarter of an hour's walk from the university; while four Jesuit scholastics were living at the university itself. Meanwhile, with the permission of the superior, he had placed the two of us in a Franciscan monastery not far from the college. We mumbled something about the Franciscans not necessarily being from the same branch as we were, that they might be reformed – in brown habits – or even Capuchins. We were Conventual Franciscans and we wore black habits. The rector dismissed our concerns stating that we are all sons of Saint Francis and he personally escorted us to the house during the siesta. We waited at the monastery gate for quite some time, and when the sleepy brother at the gate caught sight of the rector he ran off to call the superior. The rector and superior talked amongst themselves for quite a while in French, but at that stage we did not understand the language; after which the rector departed leaving us in the monastery. The superior received us cordially, taking us to musty cells which had not been in use for ages, and moving aside the shutters, threw open the windows onto the gardens. Immediately the room was filled with warm fragrant air and our spirits rose. We tried to establish contact with the superior, who was a Spaniard. We decided to try Latin, but our partial loss of memory after Soviet incarceration and his melodic Spanish pronunciation made communication difficult. We settled for miming and gesticulation. I showed him a photograph, which I had managed to smuggle out with me of the celebration of our vows, on which was our beloved Father Maksymilian Kolbe, the founder of Niepokalanów. We thought that upon seeing the photograph no more words would be necessary; and that we would have a cordial reception.

However, I gazed speechless at the change which overcame the superior's face – from being sympathetic to one of anger. His focused eyes were trying to make out our black habits on the photograph. Suddenly he threw up his hands in the air and exclaimed in French, "*Faux Franciscains*"! We did not know what the word *faux* meant, as only later were we told that it meant false. Pointing with his finger at our suitcases he showed us the door and personally led the way to the monastery gate, mumbling to himself as he went "*Faux Franciscains*". Even as he accompanied us on the street he was shouting at us "*Faux Franciscains*" so we distanced ourselves from him so that people would not think he was referring to us. Anyway they would not have made that connection with us since we were still wearing our army uniforms.

The Spaniard took off at a trot to the university and we followed him. Once in the building, while he was talking to the rector, we went and sat down in the waiting room. We were rather amused by the whole event, and no doubt Saint Francis would have considered the episode evidence of *perfect joy*. After a quarter of an hour the superior flew past us down through the hall and ran onto the street. Then the rector approached us, and embracing us warmly, said, "The Franciscan brothers have rejected you but we Jesuits accept you with our whole hearts".

The villa in Al-Ashrafia

We were escorted to a villa in the quiet district of Al-Ashrafia, which was mostly inhabited by Armenians. The villa was run by Father Góralik, a Jesuit refugee who had managed to get to the Near East via Romania after the fall of Poland. The Polish alumni greeted us with shouts of approval, for just as soldiers are united by fighting at the front so we were united by our shared Soviet sufferings. Although we belonged to various religious groups, congregations and dioceses we formed a cohesive and friendly whole.

The villa was actually a retreat house situated in a large garden, with many splendid trees and flower beds, surrounded by a high wall. Dates, figs, oranges and grapes grew there. The garden consisted of several avenues, a few fountains and a swimming pool which also served as a water reservoir. Every so often the water was let out and channelled to the furthest corners of the kitchen garden.

Epilogue to the Franciscan episode

Some time passed after the episode involving Rysiek and me at the Franciscan monastery, but the story about it reached the ears of the apostolic delegate for the Middle East Archbishop Rémy Leprêtre. Apparently he ordered the superior to be sent back to Spain immediately. In his place his successor invited us to live with them in the monastery, but we declined the offer because by then we had become friendly with the other seminarians in the villa, and besides which we felt much freer to come and go.

The Second Corps had given leave for us to do our studies, with the intention that we would go back to serve as chaplains in the army, so we kept our military privileges, such as using the army shop of the NAAFI (Navy, Army, Air Forces Institutions) and our military uniforms which meant we could take army transport around the countries of the Near East.

The new Franciscan superior, also a Spaniard, invited us to dinner, which he called a "dinner of reconciliation". He invited many Lebanese guests, but I don't know if the guests were aware of the true purpose of the banquet. Rysiek and I rose to the occasion, we drank wine, ate fruit and while talking gesticulated even more than usual. Afterwards we were led out into the garden where the father superior photographed himself with the two of us under the trees and by a well. These photographs were later given to us as a gift, on one of which was written *Reconciliation des Péres Franciscains* with the signature of the superior.

It was on that occasion that we found out what had been the reason for the previous superior's refusal to accept us in the friary. During the Spanish Civil War (1936-1939) the Communists had captured a group of

Catholic civilians and clergy. They were all lined up against a wall to be shot. Among them was the Father Superior from Beirut. One of the Red officers recognised him as his old professor and spared him his life; but the sight of the execution squad ready to take his life had affected the nerves of the friar. From then on he kept suspecting the presence of disguised Communists everywhere. As we were in uniform he probably took us for such undercover Communists. I need to add here that during the Civil War in Spain the death toll amounted to 13 bishops, around 4,000 diocesan priests and many seminarians, and around 7,000 priests from various congregations and their associated communities. Among the dead were a countless number of lay Catholics, who were murdered for simply wearing the miraculous medal or attending Mass or hiding a priest.

Jesuits

All the seminarians would leave the villa for our lectures in our cassocks. Rysiek and I put on diocesan cassocks because our Franciscan vows had expired in the Siberian taiga, but after four years of theological studies we were accepted at the seminary with full diocesan rights.

The University of St Joseph was the only Catholic university in the Near East of that calibre of academic standing. Some of the professors were world-renowned. The teaching staff consisted mostly of Jesuits from the Lyon province in France, people of great culture and intellectual competence. Father Ferdinand de Lanversin, was the Vice-Chancellor, a lovable and humble man; an aristocrat in all senses of the word. He lectured in Dogmatic Theology as did three other priests, Fathers Michel Doumit, Aloysius Escoula and Jean Mercerian. Fathers Charles Abela from Malta, and François Galtier lectured in Moral Theology. As a result of the First World War Father Galtier had a piece of shrapnel lodged beneath his skull. We found out about this quite by chance one day during a lecture when he suddenly became pale and rigid and stopped talking. He completely lost his orientation and did not know that he was in a classroom with seminarians. He started to froth at the mouth and his eyes glazed over. The Poles in the class assumed he was having a heart attack and rushed to help him but our Lebanese colleagues indicated to us not to intervene. They told us to wait a while. A deep silence descended on the class. They did not explain to us what was going on in order not to make the professor worse. After about twenty minutes he regained consciousness and continued to conduct the lesson. Apparently an operation was considered too risky. Some of the lecturers also served in the French army. When the aforementioned rector of the seminary Father Bonnet-Eymard was serving as an officer in the artillery, he reputedly shot down a German zeppelin. Father Paul Mouterde lectured in Holy Scriptures and Ignatius Ziade, a Maronite, in Church History. All the professors were extremely approachable and prepared to help us even after lectures. My spiritual director and superb retreat master was Father Valensin, a Jew by birth. He patiently put up with our unconventional life-style – relics from our Gulag days and military mannerisms.

We really loved our professors. The more educated they were the more humble and unassuming they were in their behaviour. No doubt all true scholars are like that. They had superb teaching methods. They did not make our lives miserable with endless exams, trusting us to get down conscientiously to solid work; those who did not study dropped out. Neither were they great advocates of learning by heart. They would say, "Don't rely solely on the professor's notes to act as a reminder as they will suffice only for the exam. Go to the best textbooks – there isn't time to indulge in mediocrity. Read the books of the best authors – every one of them has his own take on a problem and explains it in his own way. When you have read several different authors you will understand the issues and will be more likely to remember them. There is no need to memorise – as you should be able to present in your own words a well-understood problem."

Lectures in Dogmatics were conducted in Latin, others like Holy Scriptures, Church History, Canon Law and Liturgy were in French. For several weeks the lectures sounded like double-Dutch to me. The professors and students would smile at us but no one asked us if we actually understood anything. The implication was that learning French was to be our personal responsibility.

Mixing with the Polish students was a Lebanese, a student of Law, who went by the perfect Polish name of Miklasiewicz, who apart from his Polish ancestry and Slavic name of Włodimierz (Włodek for short), did not know much about his forefathers and did not speak the Polish language. He had very respectable parents; his mother Anna was Armenian and was exceptionally socially active among the Polish community of Beirut. Włodek's uncle – Józef Miklasiewicz – had been the Austro-Hungarian vice-consul in Beirut before the First World War. During our studies his parents would often invite us – the Polish seminarians – to their home.

Maronites and other friends

In time, because some priests had been ordained ahead of their normal schedule due to the war, they were also released from the army to conclude their unfinished studies. Thanks to this, our group of students numbered about twenty-three. The Reverend Doctor Kamil Kantak, an historian and like us a survivor of the Siberian Gulags and the Lubyanka prison in Moscow, was our immediate superior and the contact person between the university and ourselves. He lectured to us in the Polish language on Pastoral Theology and Homiletics and conducted exercises in the delivery of sermons.

The rest of our fellow seminarians came from the entire Near East region and belonged to various rites: Maronite, Greek-Melchite, Coptic, Syrian and Catholic of the Latin rite. The Maronites who formed the largest group used the old Antiochian liturgy. They looked much older than ourselves since in the southern climate they had aged faster and they had also grown beards as in the East this is a sign of masculinity and gravitas. One member of our group – an Egyptian Jesuit – was a widower, who was visited by his youngest son for tutorial help with his homework. His other sons were all adults and held important positions – I mention this as prior to his entering the congregation he was the editor of a widely read Egyptian newspaper. An interesting vocation.

Seven thousand Poles were accepted into Lebanon on the condition that they would not become a burden on the country. Therefore the responsibility for the people fell onto the Polish government in London. In spite of this we found out that the Jesuits were supporting our studies free of charge, repaying in this way a debt to Poland. This was because in 1836 a Polish Jesuit Maksymilian Ryłło was the initiator and founder of the so-called Asian College in Beirut from which the French Catholic University of St Joseph was later formed. Father Ryłło was known all over the Near East as a good shepherd. Apparently he travelled around in Arab dress with a turban on his head and a sabre under his cloak, in order to be able to protect himself against thugs. The Arabs gave him the nickname *Abuna Mansur* – the victorious priest. For the French he was *l'homme incroyable* – the incredible man.

The gratitude of the French towards the Poles was also manifested in a beautiful gesture. They invited the last five Polish seminarians - two Jesuits, two Franciscans and one diocesan student who later became Cardinal Władysław Rubin - to stay with them after their ordination and undertake doctoral studies. The Jesuits hoped to be able to offer to Poland, exhausted as it was with the war and the occupation, five priests with academic qualifications to replace – if only partially – the priests who had been murdered by the Germans and the Bolsheviks. Unfortunately, acceptance of this generous offer proved impossible.

The Polish dragoon regiment

There was also another curious reason why the Lebanese were grateful to the Poles. This time it was not something specific to the Jesuits but relevant to the whole Lebanese nation. The people showed great affection towards us, and the reason for this was the activities of a Polish dragoon regiment which had earned their respect while stationed in Lebanon. In the years 1860-61 all over Lebanon, Syria and in the countries under Turkish Islamic rule, terrible massacres of Christians took place. French Jesuits were also murdered. Two countries – England and France – supported the plight of these Christians and demanded from the Turkish government the appointment of a Christian as governor of Lebanon. Likewise, in order to put a halt to the massacres and to stop the recurrence of similar excesses they demanded that the armies in the garrisons should be manned by soldiers among whom there would be a proportion of Christians and that they should be under the command of Christian officers.

In Turkey at that time there was a significant number of Poles, mostly former participants in the insurrections of November 1830 and January 1863, who were now fighting for the freedom of Poland under the Turkish flag against the Russians. Since the Crimean War had finished a few years before, these Poles were now free to be redeployed elsewhere. Turkey, acquiescing to the requests of England and France, sent to Lebanon the Polish Ottoman dragoon regiment under the command of Catholic Colonel Stefan Gościminski (known as *Tufan Bej).* The regiment had about three thousand soldiers; two squadrons were deployed to Beirut, two to Tripoli and one to Beit el Din, the Governor's residence. All the officers were Polish and the regiment was not only under Polish command but also had its own red and white banner with a cross on it, and resounded to the sound of Polish speech, Polish songs and Polish prayers. The dragoons wore a uniform similar in style and colour to those of Polish cavalry soldiers from around 1831. The last commander of the regiment was Colonel Monasterski *(Lufti Bej),* whose descendants we would meet during All Souls' Day services at the cemetery.

Gratitude of the Lebanese people

The regiment brought law and order to the country. It was admired and respected and the people of Lebanon, both Christians and Muslims alike, were grateful to them. Later, Władysław Aleksander Czaykowski *(Muzaffer Pasha)* – a Polish Catholic who was the son of Michał Czaykowski *(Sadik Pasha)* – was nominated as the Governor of Lebanon. After the January 1863 uprising, the regiment became the last active Polish military unit operating outside Poland till the First World War.

During our stay in Lebanon the country was half-Christian half-Muslim. Arab nations which profess Islam put pressure on their co-believers to introduce Sharia (Muslim) Law. This law automatically reduces all non-believers to that of second class citizens, imposing unbearable taxes on them and in effect forcing people to become Muslim. Using these draconian methods, Muslims in a short space of time conquered lands hitherto responsive to the Christian faith, such as Asia Minor, the whole of North Africa (where they destroyed over three hundred dioceses) and the lion's share of the Balkans. In Lebanon the slaughter of Christians was also intended to serve the cause of Islamisation of the country. The Polish dragoons contributed a great service to the country by introducing peace and calming relationships between the two religions.

During the slaughter of the Christians the Muslims also murdered several Jesuits. One of my Maronite seminarian colleagues was born in a church during a fire when Catholics hid there from the Muslims during one of the massacres. By way of compensation the Turks gave the Jesuits a property by the name of Tanail in the hilly Bekaa Valley, between the mountain ranges of Lebanon and Anti-Lebanon. The Jesuit fathers established a retreat centre and vineyard there where we spent a few of our holidays. The wine produced on that estate is called Ksara and is well known in the Near East to this day.

A public theological debate

Every year on the feast of Saint Thomas Aquinas the theology department at the University of St Joseph organised a public theological debate. On one occasion the subject was the incarnation of Jesus Christ and within this topic the question of whether Christ would have come to us on earth if people had not committed original sin. Blessed Duns Scotus, the Franciscan philosopher, was of the opinion that Christ would have visited the earth out of His great love for His people. To defend this position they chose me, as I was a Franciscan, and for my opponent there was a Jesuit who upheld the traditional view of Thomas Aquinas that the sole motivating factor in the incarnation was our original sin.

Helping me to prepare for the debate was the previously mentioned Father Valensin, a mystic of Jewish parentage. Distinguished representatives of the various Eastern rites who were interested in the subject came to hear the debate, including the Assistant Provincial of the Jesuits Father De Bonneville, the representative of the Polish government Dr Zygmunt Zawadowski and also the diplomats Czosnowski and Tyszkiewicz. But the majority of the auditorium consisted of course of our own professors and students. Clashes with my opponent did not last long however, because the hierarchies from the Eastern churches joined in the dispute and they continued on with the arguments among themselves.

Feast of the Broken Shin

After the debate all the scholastics and seminarians together with their professors went for a picnic. This tradition goes right back to the founder of the Jesuits – Ignatius Loyola – who lost his leg during the siege of Pamplona and wore a prosthesis. One of the novices started to mimic the Master limping on one leg, to the delight of the rest. Father Loyola turned round and scolded the boys for making fun of a handicap. However, so that they did not think he forbade them to have any fun or make jokes he established the feast of the broken shin-bone – *festum cruris fracti*. The weather was perfect and the younger lecturers served the seminarians, teasing them in order to show their warmth and friendship.

In the seminary in Lebanon, standing 4th from R; 1944

Getting to know Lebanon

In order to maintain a balance in our lives we organised sight-seeing tours. An understanding of the French language had opened up for us the doors to French culture and through this to Arab culture. It was as if by the help of a magic wand in our imaginations, the history of this small country became animated and was made familiar to us. We became aware of so many significant people; so much had happened in this country over thousands of years even before the birth of Christ.

Firstly, history spoke to us through the tall spreading cedars, some of which would have been able to remember Biblical times. According to the psalmist, *God planted the cedars of Lebanon* (Psalms 80,11), which is why the Lebanese refer to them as God's cedars. Throughout antiquity, the mountains of Lebanon were covered in cedars, and the tree has earned such respect that its silhouette features on the flag of the Lebanese Republic. Today unfortunately there are not many of these trees left. Apparently the Turks deforested whole areas in pursuit of Lebanese partisans, who like the Poles often had to fight for their freedom. As a souvenir of our stay in Lebanon we planted in the garden in Al-Ashrafia a small cedar sapling. Unfortunately, when we left Lebanon after our four years there we could barely tell if it had grown at all.

We were also attracted to Roman and Greek antiquities; the most important of these ruins being in the Baalbek valley, between the two Lebanese mountain ranges. Even before Greek rule and later Roman, the local pagans would offer children there in sacrifice to the sun god Baal. The Romans built several temples on the site, among others to Jupiter and in honour of Venus. Columns from these temples are still standing today, testament to the greatness of the town which bore the Greek name of Heliopolis – City of the Sun.

Historic rock

Over thousands of years, various armies marched through the narrow Lebanese corridor of land between the Mediterranean Sea and the mountains, in order to conquer lands to the north and the south. To the north of Beirut, on a huge chalky outcrop, leaders of these Egyptian, Assyrian, Babylonian, Greek, Roman, Crusader and later Arab, French and English armies chiselled their names and military exploits, starting with cuneiform script. The oldest of these is a mark from the time of Ramses II who passed that way with his army against the Hittites in the thirteenth century BC. To this rocky autograph-book names of famous kings and rulers have been added. During our time in Lebanon there appeared for the first time on a stone pillar an Arabic inscription: *On this day 31 December 1946 the evacuation of all foreign armies from Lebanon was completed during the office of His Excellency Sheik Bechara El Khoury, President of the Republic.* For the Lebanese this was of great significance. Having thrown off the French Protectorate Lebanon gained its freedom and independence.

The oldest and historically most famous inhabitants of Lebanon were the Canaanites, who lived there three thousand years before the birth of Christ. They founded city-states, the richest and most important of which were Tyre, Sidon, Roman Berytus (modern Beirut) and Byblos. All the city-states conducted lively trade with the countries bordering the

Mediterranean and even with England. The closest trading partners were the Greeks, who were the first to use the term Phoenicians for the Lebanese Canaanites. The name became commonly accepted and later contemporary Lebanese liked to present themselves as descendants of the Phoenicians, even though over the centuries the population of the country became very inter-mixed. The most prized merchandise traded by the Phoenicians was *purpure* (a purple dyed material) used for centuries by monarchs.

Another Phoenician trading centre was the city of Byblos, where there were processing plants making paper from papyrus imported from Egypt. From the word *papyrus* we have the word for paper, and from *Byblos* the word Bible, *bibliotèque* (library in French) and the word bibliography. The Phoenicians also left behind for the benefit of the West twenty-two written symbols called an alphabet. Every sound corresponded to one symbol. The richest and most powerful city-state – which is also mentioned in the Bible – was Tyre, called the Queen-of-the-Seas.

A proud nation

Arabs came to Lebanon in the eighth century AD and over-ran the local population. Indigenous Lebanese are in the minority, but nonetheless the people readily refer to their ancient past of which they are proud. After all, the Phoenicians were considered to be famous corsairs of the seas; the best traders and merchants of antiquity, out-performing the Greeks, Jews and Armenians in their trade. This trading instinct has not abandoned the contemporary Lebanese, which is why small but rich Lebanon is a great temptation for barren Syria.

Notre Dame du Liban

Just as Catholic Poles go on pilgrimage to Częstochowa, so Lebanese Christians go to *Notre Dame du Liban*. Her statue, situated on the slope of a mountain overlooking the sea, sits high on a plinth and is visible from afar. With childish faith pilgrims insert letters to the Blessed Virgin into the cracks of the pedestal. Other venerated destinations for pilgrims are the painting of Our Lady of Lebanon in Harissa and the painting of Our Lady of Redemption known as *Notre Dame de la Délivrance* in Bikfaya (El-Metn). The Lebanese owe this latter picture to Father Maksymilian Ryłło. There is also a significant amount of interest in the relics of the Maronite monk Saint Charbel in Annaya.

Biblical connections

Lebanon is particularly close and endearing to those of us who are Christians. According to God's promise Lebanon was to form part of the territories of the Holy Land. In Genesis 15,18 it states: *To your descendents I give this land, from the river of Egypt to the great river Euphrates...* The Bible then goes on to list several peoples who will co-exist with the Hebrews, among others the Canaanites (Phoenicians) (Genesis 15,19). The Bible mentions Lebanon sixty-six times and always sympathetically. The psalms of David extol its beauty, especially that of the cedars which symbolise majesty, grace and strength. King Solomon imported cedar wood from Lebanon to build the Temple in Jerusalem and his palaces. He made an alliance with King Hiram of Tyre who supplied him with architects, builders, artists and stone-masons.
Luke the evangelist quotes the Lord Jesus saying that the great prophet Elijah went to Zar´ephath in Sidon, that is to Lebanon, to the poor widow (Luke 4,24-33). Moreover Christ himself was in Lebanon for a short while, in the vicinity of Tyre and Sidon where he miraculously cured the Canaanite woman's daughter who was possessed by the devil (Matthew 15,21-29). To this day Lebanese inhabitants of some of the villages speak Aramaic, the same language as Jesus Christ.

Next to the Holy Land, Lebanon is considered to be the cradle of Christianity. The apostles on their way northwards to Antioch (where the believers in Christ were first called Christians) took this route for their message about the Good News of salvation. From Antioch the Christian faith spread to Chaldea – today's Iraq. In the year 57AD Saint Paul visited the faithful in Tyre.

For Poles in Lebanon a particular attraction was the small mountain village and Maronite Catholic monastery of Saint Anthony (Mar Antonios-Khisbaou) near Ghazir, about 30 kilometres from the capital, where the great Polish poet Juliusz Słowacki stayed. He spent forty-five days there during a wonderful Lebanese spring, writing his epic poem *Anhelli.* Słowacki would often go on walks in the area, feasting his eyes on the beautiful sight of the capital, port and bay, all visible from the mountain and laid out as if on the palm of his hand. I think that he would have been sad to leave that sanctuary. As far as I can remember, based on the letters which he wrote to his mother, the monks equipped him with a donkey for the road and attached to its back a small barrel of wine. Amongst rocks, along tortuous and bumpy paths, and with a heavy heart the poet descended from the mountain to Beirut; where whilst waiting forty days for a ship, he wrote letters to his mother. This was in 1837. Due to the initiative of the inhabitants of Ghazir, the Polish refugee community in Lebanon placed a plaque on the walls of the Saint Anthony Monastery in three languages – French, Arabic and Polish – commemorating Słowacki's stay there.

Apart from *Anhelli* another epic poem was crystallising in the mind of the poet – *Father of the Plague-Ridden at El-Arish.* The subject matter was about a wealthy Lebanese Arab who in the El-Arish oasis (located on the borders of Egypt and the Holy Land) lost his wife and seven children to the plague within the space of three months. Only his brother survived. Słowacki heard this story from an Arab, Dr Steeble, during his own twelve-day quarantine at the El-Arish oasis. During my high-school days when I was studying Polish literature I was deeply moved by the fate of this man. This was my first contact with the Arab world.

Not far from the Monastery of Saint Anthony lies the little town of Ghazir, whose position amidst market gardens, orchards and small irrigation canals was the source of much delight a hundred years ago for the French historian Ernest Renan. Ghazir was the site of the largest and most important Polish refugee settlement, a miniature Poland, where there was a school, a cultural and educational centre, a Polish parish and a liturgical vestments workshop. In the Latin-rite church of the Jesuit Fathers I delivered my first-ever sermon, when I was standing in for a sick colleague – the parish priest Father Franciszek Zaorski. I had many friends in Ghazir. The second largest Polish settlement was in Zuk, where there was a secondary school attended by the majority of Polish children in Lebanon.

A trip to Egypt

Towards the end of our studies we decided to organise a trip to Egypt. First we went to Giza on the edge of the Sahara desert where the complex of pyramids is located and the Sphinx is hewn out of massive rock. Almost all of us attempted to ride a camel which due to the animal's hump and constant rocking was no easy feat. We were more impressed by the ancient towns situated in Upper Egypt – Luxor, Karnak and the Valley of the Kings – the City of the Dead – lying on the opposite banks of the Nile. The graves made a greater impression upon me than the columns of the Temple of Amen-Ra, the avenue of sphinxes, obelisks and the Holy Lake in which mummies were apparently prepared. Cut deep into the rocks, the twisting corridors leading to the tombs were booby-trapped in order to disorientate would-be plunderers. In spite of this, almost all the chambers which were covered in colourful hieroglyphs were empty. Mummies, sarcophagi, furniture and ornaments which the looters did not manage to steal, fell to the plunder of the Napoleonic armies and were taken to the museums of Cairo, Paris and London. The only mummy which has been left in situ is that of the young Pharaoh Tutankhamun, in order that contact with outside air should not speed up the process of decay of his desiccated body. We looked at the virtually untouched richly endowed tomb of the ruler in its gilded sarcophagus.

An idea that didn't come off

We conceived an idea to get ourselves from Cairo to Alexandria by plane. We were enticed by the historical nature of the town which lies on the edge of the Nile delta. In ancient Alexandria there used to be the largest library in antiquity. We also knew that in the early Christian era the large scale eremitic movement originated by the desert fathers developed in this area. It was here that Saint Anthony the Abbot lived and where his disciples would come to him asking for spiritual guidance.

With our airplane tickets already in our pockets, we decided to pay a visit to our friends from the Second Corps who were teaching Polish youngsters in the aircraft workshops of Heliopolis not far from Cairo. They poured scorn on our idea of taking a civilian aircraft to fly to Egypt. "They are old re-painted pieces of junk from the First World War," they said. "In the event of an accident on land, an Arab taxi will stop to help, but you could possibly crash in the middle of the desert. Before any appropriate help could arrive at the scene of the catastrophe, jackals and vultures would have plucked away at your flesh, so that even your own mothers would not be able to recognise whose bones belonged to whom." A Polish prelate who was living near Cairo and whose name I cannot now remember, put us to shame. "Have you even thought that in the event of an accident the entire Polish seminary would be lost? Have you any sense left at all?" And so it was that with some regret we returned our airline tickets and bought ourselves train tickets.

Contact with Muslims

Our contact with Muslims tended to be by chance and most often during our expeditions into the mountains. During one such trip we settled ourselves down to eat a meal under a shady tree. Nearby gushed a refreshing stream and in the distance shone the snow-covered summit of Mount Şannįn. Suddenly, out of nowhere, from behind some standing wheat an Arab appeared with his four wives, who upon seeing us covered their faces with their veils. The Arab told them to stop while making signs to us asking if we could move aside to allow the women access to the water. With friendly gestures we tried to make it known to them that we wished to invite them to our group. This was an occasion when we thought we could to find out from them about their way of life – their customs, their hopes and their concerns. The Arab stood silently for a while and then turned around taking the women with him.

On one occasion we decided to go up the mountain on the cog railway. This was no small adventure. While the train was climbing up the hillside we hopped off the wagon and continued alongside on foot, that is, for as long as the steam engine was still labouring and still engaging with the cogs. We took the chance that if we failed to get back on the train on time we could just as well say goodbye to the ride. Once we successfully reached our destination we decided to start on our meal. We had taken a lot of provisions with us for the trip, but an Arab saw us coming and spread out a tablecloth laid with sheep's cheese, little pies and some bitter herbs which were unfamiliar to us. He saw that we had our own food with us but anticipating our needs he demonstrated his own hospitality first. It was not considered polite to refuse traditional Arab hospitality and although our own food would have been more to our liking, we had to eat the food that was offered to us.

The Polish population while not exactly starving was still grateful for any additional help. Rysiek and I would purchase cakes and canned goods in the NAAFI store which we would then offer to an elderly Polish woman and her daughter who were boarding in the home of a wealthy Arab. On each visit to her we had to wait for a few minutes in front of the house while the young women of the Arab's harem whetted their appetite at the vision of young men through the key-hole; a secret confided to us by the Polish women. Passing through the house to their quarters we would admire the wealth of the Arab. Carpets covered the floors of the chambers and the furniture was encrusted with mother-of-pearl, there were gilded boxes, alabaster vases and porcelain, while on the walls hung curved sabres. On the couches lay masses of embroidered pillows. There was never anyone in the rooms as the young ladies of the harem were hiding while we passed through on our way to the Polish women's quarters. The facades of Arab houses were usually grey, and without ornamentation, in order not to provoke the jealousy of neighbours.

We were told a story about the German Kaiser Wilhelm who when he was visiting the Near East was taken to a very splendid house. The cultural protocol demanded that the host should say to the guest, "Everything that you see is yours!" To the utter amazement and disgust of the Arab the Kaiser later sent over transport in order to convey the objects back to Germany. I think, however, that this was just an anecdote told to amuse the visitors.

We used to attend a Polish dentist who was married to an Arab. She did not talk much but when we were leaving Lebanon she appeared to be sad that she would not see her compatriots any more. Perhaps there were other reasons for her sadness, in that as a Catholic she would not be able to attend the Holy Sacraments after we had gone or that in the internal rivalry amongst wives of other Arabs she belonged to a lower category.

The Boar and The Falcon

For the duration of the war the port of Beirut was the base for two Polish submarines – The Boar and The Falcon. They took part in patrolling the Mediterranean together with other ships of the allied forces. I cannot remember now exactly which sector they were responsible for, but most likely it was the Adriatic between the Apennine peninsula and the Balkans. Our sailors were searching for German and Italian tankers transporting soldiers, equipment and food. Once, after a ship had been torpedoed they were astonished to see through their periscope the sea strewn with oranges and tangerines, and amongst them Germans swimming for their lives. After a week of patrolling the vessels would return to their base. The sailors would take leave consisting of several days which they would use to meet up with the Lebanese Polish refugees. On Sundays they attended Mass at the university church where from the main altar they were welcomed by a painting of Saint Stanisław Kostka. They also visited us in the seminary and we offered them Ksara wine. We tried to persuade them to allow us to visit one of the vessels but they adamantly refused to do so. They withheld permission to visit because of a silly old wives' tale which claimed that the presence of a clerical figure on board would bring misfortune upon them and the vessel itself would turn into a coffin. We scoffed at that superstition so that in the end, ashamed of themselves, they let us on board.

The submarine that we had visited came back damaged from one of its patrols. The kitchen and radio station were badly damaged. What had happened was that they had gained entrance to a port where there were several German tankers. They found a passage through an iron net, hung below the water, and stealthily slipped into the port where they managed to torpedo two or three enemy ships. The reaction of the Germans raised a real hornet's nest. They started to set off depth charges, and the discharge tossed the submarine about forcing it to surface from the sea bed where it had been lying since the motors had been turned off. The entire crew including the officers fell on their knees and started to pray. Most probably they were saved from drowning and death by some spilt cooking oil from a leaking container which floated to the surface. The Germans assumed that the vessel had been sunk and stopped the bombardment. Meanwhile our sailors waited a while and then turning the engines onto the lowest revs possible laboriously sought out the passage in the underwater barrage and returned to their port. Because their own radio was destroyed they could not warn the exchange about their return to their base in Beirut, thus endangering their own vessel to attack from the allied forces. From the look in the eyes of the sailors we could tell that they wanted to say to us, "Didn't we tell you that you would bring us misfortune?" But they didn't dare. They were too ashamed to blame the damage to their vessel to our visit.

Angels in human form

There were some interesting people among the Polish exiles in Lebanon. Some were only passing through Beirut, while there were others with whom we didn't establish contact on account of our studies. Nor am I able to recall everyone I met, which I acknowledge may be a disappointment to those looking for a mention of their relatives in my memoirs. However I do have to mention one person, because I often met him at the university. This was Professor Stanisław Kościałkowski, an historian from Stefan Batory University in Wilno, who like myself had spent some time in a Siberian Gulag, but who by then was completely grey, like a dove. As a result of living a life based on the gospels, he emanated an aura of dignity and goodness. He delivered a course in Polish Literature at the American University and also gave lectures to the Polish community. He would often come over to the Jesuit library to ferret out information on Polish matters, for example, the lives of Poles in Lebanon. I did not know him personally, but no doubt he was aware that his life was drawing to a close and he was therefore always in a hurry. He was held in high regard by everyone. With his charming politeness, humility and Christian witness, he was the embodiment of the Light which Christ referred to in the gospels. How little is needed in order to spread goodness. Eventually, Professor Kościałkowski and his wife made their way to England and he lived there in exile, in the Polish boarding school for émigré girls run by the Polish Sisters of the Holy Family of Nazareth, in Pitsford near Northampton, till his death in 1959.

Beirut was the hub of Polish social and cultural life. The Polish Consulate organised lectures, celebrations, national holidays and anniversaries. Dr Wiktor Szyrynski, whom I have already mentioned, delivered public lectures in psychology. We had the opportunity to listen to some of the most notable people among the Polish community. Hanka Ordonówna-Tyszkiewicz, a famous pre-war singer, dancer and actress, came over to entertain us from Jerusalem. She is the author of the memoirs *Tułacze Dzieci* – Wandering Children. When tuberculosis prevented her from continuing with her performances she reinvented herself in painting and literature. Some years later she died in Beirut.

A national tragedy

In June 1943, the Polish Prime Minister and Supreme Head of the Polish Armed Forces General Władysław Sikorski came to Beirut from London. He stayed in Broumana, about 18 kilometres from Beirut in a hilly summer resort together with his daughter and closest entourage. We heard his speech over the radio. He sounded despondent since just a few weeks prior to his arrival in Lebanon, Stalin had severed relationship with the Polish government in London as a retaliation for their accusations against the Soviet Union of murdering Polish officers. This allegation followed the discovery of their graves in Katyn. A few days after making this speech he perished in a flight over Gibraltar. The majority of Siberian deportees and exiles considered the catastrophe to be the result of an assassination attack. If the cause of death was not an accident then the only chance to discover the truth about the tragedy will be when the British and Russian archives are made available publicly. In November 2010 the Russian government finally acknowledged Stalin's participation in these crimes against humanity.

This national tragedy affected all Poles. We predicted that from that day onwards our situation would radically alter and that after the conclusion of military activities, in which the Soviet Union was playing a major part, the return to our country would be made impossible. We also realised that the Red Army in pursuing the Germans over Polish territory, would stay on our land, with the tacit permission of the allied commanders, and would impose on us a Communist puppet government. Moreover, collaborators would attempt to return us forcibly to Poland in order to eliminate us, because we were witnesses to the Gulag Archipelago.

In the winter of 1943 the new Chief of the Armed Forces – General Kazimierz Sosnowski – was welcomed to Beirut. When I greeted him I mentioned to him that I was also an Artillery officer-cadet. He smiled wryly and, alluding to Father Robak from *Pan Tadeusz,* asked me whether I too carried arms under my cassock.

Return to the Franciscan order

Meanwhile our studies were coming to an end, and after the final exams and a retreat we would be ordained. A few Poles from the more senior grades of the seminary had already been ordained and were sent out to do pastoral work in Palestine in the high schools and the school for young women army volunteers in Nazareth and in Ein Karem and in the Engineering School in Heliopolis in Egypt. Father Zygmunt Dzierżek was ordained back in the USSR, but completed his studies with us in Beirut. In 1945 five of us still remained – Mieczysław Bednarz and Ludwik Paluch who were both Jesuits, Rysiek Gruza and me who were Conventual Franciscans and one diocesan seminarian Władysław Rubin. The youngest seminarian Zygmunt Rydz left us for the Polish seminary in Orchard Lake, Michigan in the USA to finish his studies and to be ordained there.

For Rysiek and me the approaching ordination prompted an issue of jurisdiction. Formally we were no longer Franciscans because as I have already explained our three-year vows which we had taken in Niepokalanów expired while we were in Siberia. In Lebanon we wore the cassocks of diocesan seminarians, but the time had come to decide whether to return to the Franciscan order or to place ourselves under the jurisdiction of the bishop. A few colleagues suggested we should enter the Jesuit order of Saint Ignatius Loyola. But our inclinations were in the spirit of the sons of Saint Francis of Assisi and Father Maksymilian Kolbe. At the time we knew nothing about his arrest by the Gestapo and his imprisonment in the concentration camp at Auschwitz. When the news finally reached us about how he offered himself in the place of another prisoner and how he died a martyr's death in the hunger-cell, it only confirmed our conviction to return to the Franciscan order. Both Rysiek and I had already "canonised" Father Maksymilian anyway, during our stay in Niepokalanów. Father Valensin, the French Jesuit who was a Jewish convert and who was our spiritual director in Beirut, was delighted with our decision to return to the Franciscans. A short while later he died suddenly while giving a retreat to members of the Lebanese government. In his diary there were numerous entries where he entreated God to take him away to heaven while still on active pastoral duties.

We sent a letter to Father Bede Hess, the General of our order in Rome, asking him to accept us into the order once again. We also asked him whether we should have to undertake the novitiate again. We received a letter back from him full of gratitude to God for preserving us since the friars had presumed that we were either lost in action, or possibly even dead. The second reason for his gratitude was in response to the generosity of the Jesuits in educating us. He dismissed any thoughts about us doing the novitiate again, stating that we had undergone our novitiate by living in Siberia.

We also asked him who should witness our vows as members of the Franciscan order, since there were no Conventual Franciscans based in Lebanon. We suggested to him two possibilities: Archbishop Rémy Leprêtre, the Apostolic Delegate or Father Jacques Bonnet-Eymard, the Dean of St Joseph's University. Father General left it to us to make the decision. Because the Dean was closer to us and had always shown a fatherly concern, we chose him, and into his hands we committed our perpetual vows. I have never heard of another such case where a member of an order had his solemn vows witnessed and accepted by a delegate from another congregation.

By means of this gesture, the Dean of the University demonstrated much goodwill and a great capacity for Christian charity. It has to be acknowledged that Pope Clement XIV who came from our branch of the Franciscans carried out the abolition of the Jesuit order. I remember an incident connected to Clement XIV which gave me much to think about. One of my seminarian class-mates, a Jesuit whom we all liked and greatly respected, playfully slapped me on the shoulder one day, exclaiming, "Oh, you Ganganelli!" He knew exactly who Ganganelli was but at that point I had no idea, so I did not fully appreciate the joke. The joke was about Pope Clement XIV, who before he was elected to the seat of Saint Peter, carried the family name of Ganganelli. I had to look up the history books. Cardinal Lorenzo Ganganelli was elected to the throne of Saint Peter during the eighteenth century, the Age of Enlightenment and the beginnings of liberalism, a movement which is still felt today in the Western Church; while the young Jesuit order was distinguishing itself by its intelligence and activities. Moreover, Jesuit education had spread all over Europe and was renowned for its high standards. The "enlightened" enemies of the church were overcome with jealousy as the order was preventing them from carrying out their godless plans. The greatest thorn in their side was the fourth vow which Jesuits take, that of obedience to the Pope. In this situation the Western European governments which exercised powerful influences over the life of the church agreed amongst themselves that after the death of Benedict XIV, his successor could only be someone who would not regard the Jesuits as friends. Cardinal Lorenzo Ganganelli took part in these discussions declaring that in his opinion the Pope had the authority to abolish any congregation if there was a serious enough reason, including the Jesuits. This statement had the effect that Cardinal Ganganelli was unanimously elected as the next Pope. He took the name of Clement XIV. After his election, the rationalistic European governments, which were under the influence of Freemasonry and rationalism renewed their petition for the abolition of the Jesuit order. For three years the Pope tried to deal with the issue but he finally succumbed to their pressures. In 1773 the order was abolished. Only in 1814, due to Divine Providence (one cannot think about it in any other terms) Pope Pius VII re-activated the order.

Final examinations

The time came to take the final examinations in front of the professorial board. The Jesuit advice about studying proved to be correct: don't spend time learning by heart. The crucial thing is to understand the problems and to read the best textbooks by the best authors. A consequence of being well-read will be a better understanding of the issues and therefore greater ease in remembering the facts. You should never neglect your studies and you should never put off studying till later. If a student neglected the required rigour for studying the board of professors would not allow him to be ordained. I was no great student, but I applied myself to the work and studied hard, to the extent that I sometimes even passed up an opportunity to go on an outing in order to spend more time over my books.

It was 1946. The last group of five Polish seminarians were undergoing a retreat in Tanail, in the Bekaa Valley. It was led by a Jesuit – Father Kozłowski – who was brought in from the army. Meanwhile about twenty of our Maronite seminarian colleagues were undergoing their own spiritual exercises in Beirut at the same time.

Doubts about my vocation which I had experienced in Niepokalanów returned again. I started to question if I had correctly read the will of God and whether I had a calling to the priesthood. Was I suitable for such a vocation? I didn't think I had any special talents. Compared to other bright students I was definitely of average ability. Take for example Józek Janus, a Jesuit seminarian, who even before the war in Poland obtained a doctorate in Philosophy and brought over to Poland the body of Saint Andrew Bobola from Rome. During his final examination in Beirut, the board of examining professors went no further than to listen to his first reply. Amazed by the sharpness of his intellect and his wide range of knowledge they listened to him with interest and satisfaction. After his ordination his superiors wanted to send him back to Poland so that his talents could be best utilised, but Józek had a yearning for the displaced Polish people and he decided to share their sad fate to the end. After his ordination he was sent to the Masindi re-settlement camp in Uganda, East Africa – later ending up in Australia, where he proceeded to build a huge church, parish hall and library.

But I did believe that God was directing my life and would lead me to the altar. After all, the apostles who were chosen by Christ did not stand out as particularly unusual people. They were simple fishermen with weaknesses and faults like everyone else. The point is to put one's trust in God and to surrender oneself to Him totally. When Christ calls us to a particular way of life, He also makes good our imperfections, if we only ask Him for help. Saint Paul wrote: *I can do everything in Him who gives me strength.* I reached the conclusion that in every vocation, especially in the vocation to the priesthood, love has primacy of place. This is quite natural, since God himself is Love (see I John, 4:8). Love can accomplish miracles and is mightier than death. That same Paul, in his Hymn to Love declares: *If I speak in the tongues of men and of angels, but have not love, I am a noisy gong or a clanging cymbal. And if I have prophetic powers, and understand all mysteries and all knowledge, and if I have all faith, so as to move mountains, but have not love, I am nothing* (I Corinthians 13,1-3). Everyone can repeat after Saint Thérèse of the Child Jesus that "*my vocation is love*". I am deeply moved when I recall the meeting of Saint Peter with the resurrected Saviour on the shores of Lake Gennesaret. What abundance of Grace. That same cowardly disciple who had been returned to a state of Grace deserted the Lord when He was arrested in the Garden of Olives. Three times in the courtyard of Caiaphas he denied any knowledge of Him. Jesus knew the spiritual potential of Peter and the change which had taken place in him after His resurrection. In entrusting His sheep to him, He did not ask him about his intellectual competencies but about his love. *"Do you love me more than others?"* (John 21,15). Three times He asked him about this, to prove to the disciple that his triple denial had been completely erased. Analysing myself I saw that as far as I was concerned love of God and love of people were always centre-stage for me, especially in regard to the "little folk" – to use an expression of Jakub Wujek, who translated the Vulgate Bible into Polish.

Ordination to the priesthood

The ordination ceremony took place in Beirut in the large university church dedicated to Saint Stanisław Kostka. The ceremony was attended by the patriarchs of various Eastern Rites, the Dean of the university and the professors, the Polish consul Dr Zygmunt Zawadowski and his staff, representatives of the Lebanese government, the families of the newly-ordained Maronite priests, Polish students from both universities and a huge number of Polish civilians from the settlements around the area, among whom were a large number of children and youngsters.

Ordination to the priesthood, 3rd from L; Beirut, 1946

But our hearts were sad. Although the war had ended we still could not make contact with Poland. The country was in ruins, having survived a debilitating war and occupation. Moreover, Stalin imposed a regime on Poland which was put into effect by Polish Communists who had been trained in Moscow. From the time of our deportation to Siberia we knew nothing about the fate of our families. Likewise our families did not know whether we were alive or still in the USSR. No one would even dare to presume that we were free, and that we had already finished our studies and were about to approach the altars of God in the service of Christ and the church. That was a cross that Divine Providence laid upon us. In the event the consecration to the priesthood was performed by the Apostolic Delegate, Archbishop Rémy Leprêtre.

Priesthood

My priesthood reminded me of the words of Our Saviour which Saint John records in his gospel. They are the words of the prayer of Christ the Arch-priest, which read as His last testament: *That they may all be one; even as thou, Father, art in me, and I in thee, that they also may be in us* (John, 17,21). The sacred priesthood is above all else a conduit leading to unity with God in the Divine Trinity. While everyone is called to that unity, it is the priests who should be leading the way along the conduit.

The road to unity with God leads through the faithful love of Christ. To help visualise this mystery Jesus used the parable of the vine. *Abide in me, and I in you. As the branch cannot bear fruit by itself, unless it abides in the vine, neither can you, unless you abide in me. I am the vine, you are the branches. He who abides in me, and I in him, he it is that bears much fruit, for apart from me you can do nothing* (John 15,4-5). These words about abiding within Him, Christ was to repeat in the cenacle on the eve of his death on the Cross.

Meanwhile I prayed in silence: May these words become the motto for my priesthood. I know that we will only achieve the fullness of unity with the Holy Trinity in eternity; however, I will start striving toward it now, in my own soul and in the souls of those people You have entrusted to my pastoral care, mainly through the sacrifice of the Holy Mass celebrated *attente et devote* – with attention and devotion – remembering that Jesus Christ is the High Priest. It is He who celebrates the Holy Sacrifice, while my role is to be *in persona Christi*, handing over to Christ my humanity – the power over my soul, reasoning and will, and the use of my eyes, voice and hands. I wish to take part in Jesus' salvific work of redemption as expressed by the words: *and I, when I am lifted up from the earth, will draw all men to myself* (John, 12: 32). So help me Lord God Almighty.

I celebrated my first Mass among Polish students in Beirut, assisted by a longstanding missionary in Lebanon, Father Malinowski, a Capuchin friar who was well-known to Polish émigrés.

Celebrating our first Masses in the Holy Land

Later, our diminished band of newly ordained priests went to Palestine. We had already become acquainted with the Holy Land during our summer holidays, during the period when Great Britain was governing the territory on behalf of the League of Nations. Jewish immigration had already begun and Jewish partisan units, reinforced by soldiers of Jewish descent from the Second Corps of General Anders, were giving the British a hard time. During my stay in Jerusalem the Jews blew up the David Hotel, which was the headquarters of the British army.

126

Disguised as Arabs they pretended to deliver milk containers. But instead of milk the containers held dynamite. In 1947 the United Nations decided on the division of Palestine between Arabs and Jews. The following year the Israeli state was formed.

Outside the Damascus Gate, Jerusalem, 2nd from R; 1946

Celebrating Mass in the Holy Land

Whenever we visited Jerusalem we stayed at either the Old or the New Polish House, both run by the Polish order of Sisters of Saint Elisabeth – *Elżbietanki*. The New Home came into being due to the efforts of Polish soldiers. The mother superior – whose religious name was Innocenta – we jokingly referred to as Inopounda, as the small offerings made by the soldiers were never considered enough for her. The only thing that really counted was the English pound. During our stay in Jerusalem we visited all the most important holy places and we took part in the mysteries of the Holy Passion – the procession on Palm Sunday and the Way of the Cross. A cross was carried in turn by Polish soldiers, clergy, seminarians and civilians, among whom were also Arabs. We all celebrated Mass as neo-presbyters in the tomb of Christ, in the Basilica of The Dormition of the Blessed Virgin Mary, in the Basilica of Gethsemane on the Mount of Olives, in Bethlehem, in Ain-Karem, where the Blessed Mother visited her cousin Elisabeth, in Nazareth, in Cana in Galilee and in Capernaum. I believed that during these meetings with Christ, at each Holy Mass, the celestial family was also taking part – Our Lady, the angels and the saints. Our Lord Jesus was present in a mystical way as both High Priest and Sacrifice. How my parents would have rejoiced to see me in those holy places at the altar.

The chaplain of the Sisters of St Elisabeth in Jerusalem was Father Pietruszka who offered me a commemorative ebony cross with an alabaster figure of Christ. In the foot of the cross was enclosed a piece of rock from Calvary. Can one ask for a more beautiful experience as a neo-presbyter?

The New Polish House, Jerusalem, 3rd from R standing; 1946

The Holy Land is part of the Middle East – perhaps even its heart. Poles refer to this land as the Near East, but the English, French and many others call it the Middle East. They form a bridge between Asia and Europe. Many countries come together to form the Middle East and we passed through some of them, while living in others, such as in Iran, Iraq, Lebanon and Egypt. It was in these lands that historic events took place which were to become part of God's Divine plan, to bring together time and nature with eternity and the supernatural.

It is an amazing fact that God chose this specific place for His incarnate son Jesus Christ to bring about the salvation of mankind. Here, where it is said that paradise once stood and here where God punished His people with the Flood, He undertook another covenant with them. The coming of God to our earth in a human form, and the act of redemption on Calvary, have meant that the Holy Land has become the centre of our world. The symbol of our redemption has become the Cross. *Stabat Crux dum volvitur orbis* – the cross stands where the world rotates. And it will be like that until Judgement Day.

Closure of the Polish Seminary in Beirut

When we returned to Beirut from the Holy Land, Father Kantak summoned Rysiek Gruza and me, and explained to us that Father Reginek, the Vicar General for the Army Bishop, wished to send two Polish priests to equatorial Africa to work in the Polish camps there. Apparently, this had already been discussed with two elderly priests who were afraid of tropical diseases and the climate, and declined to accept the proposition. Turning to us Father Kantak said, "But Franciscans have never refused me anything so far." This meant that the French Jesuits' plan for the five of us to remain in Beirut for further studies, burst like soap bubbles. We agreed on the spot to the proposition of our most immediate superior. We were young and hardened; in fact the dangers of the Dark Continent only acted as a challenge for us. There was also the awareness that in the camps there were Polish civilians, for the most part women, children and youngsters, who had been rescued from the

Soviet Union; this also acted as an incentive. Although the Italian Campaign had finished, the men folk were still in the army. We felt a spiritual bond with the Siberian deportees and we wished to give them our support and love, believing wholeheartedly we were doing this for Poland.

Two of our senior colleagues – the Jesuit Józek Janus and Wojtek Szkalny – had left earlier for Africa to go to Masindi in Uganda. Czesław Pawlak was sent to France to work among the Polish community there. Ludwik Paluch and Mieczysław Bednarz, two of our Jesuit friends, were called back to Poland by their Father Provincial. Władysław Rubin who was universally liked for his combination of friendliness, good cheer and humility, stayed on for a further period in Lebanon, first as parish priest in the hill settlement of Roumy, and then later as moderator of the Sodality of Mary and as university chaplain in Beirut. When the number of Poles in Lebanon started to decrease due to the policy of re-settlement in other countries, Father Rubin left to study in Rome under orders from his superior Archbishop Baziak. Walerian Gajecki was sent to work in the mountainous settlement of Adzaltun, where he earned a reputation as a zealous pastor, eventually ending up working with Polish émigrés in London, England. My youngest friend Zygmunt Rydz left for the USA to study at the Polish seminary in Orchard Lake, Michigan. And so it was that in the summer of 1946 the Polish Seminary in Beirut ceased to exist.

Taking leave of Beirut and Lebanon, 1st from R; 1946

The Polish General Military Hospital No 8 in Egypt

Before we left for equatorial Africa, Rysiek and I were assigned to do some pastoral chaplaincy work at the No 8 General Military Hospital at Al Qantarah on the Suez Canal, not far from Port Said. We were glad to be able to acquire new experience. We were to act in the capacity of army captains, but without a captain's pay, as a result of financial savings brought in by the Polish Government-in-exile. In ancient times, Al Qantarah formed the boundary between Egypt and the Arab peninsula on the caravan trail. Perhaps the Biblical Joseph who was sold into slavery and later became famous for saving people from starvation, passed this way. Perhaps the Holy Family seeking shelter from the cruelties of Herod were familiar with this place. The No 8 Military Hospital had the appearance of a small tent city. The wounded soldiers of the Second Corps were brought there during the Italian Campaign. The hospital comprised a multitude of departments and had around a thousand beds. There was an unusually high proportion of doctors and nurses working at the hospital. Just before our arrival, Dr Wiktor Szyrynski, the psychiatrist who examined me for first aid for my scouting badge of *Samaritan* in Nowogródek, had worked there. For the most part German prisoners-of-war were working as orderlies and they were quite satisfied with their relative freedom and grateful for the occasional cigarette and chocolate offered by the soldiers. The two senior chaplains who were handing over their duties carried on for a while longer at the hospital. One of them impressed me with his religious views which he would proclaim from a radio broadcasting-centre to the inhabitants of the tent city. Observing how much benefit these messages conveyed to the sick and wounded soldiers – survivors of the Siberian Gulags and missing their families – I made a decision to dedicate myself to the careful preparation of my sermons and homilies. We visited the sick in the morning and in the afternoon. We were also called to the dying in the middle of the night. It is evident that I had a rather atypical beginning to my priestly service – not a single wedding or baptism, but an awful lot of funerals.

Convalescing in the hospital at that time was Professor Czarnecki, who used to deliver extremely informative lectures to physicians and nurses. Before the war he used to teach at various foreign universities. He chose me – a mere youngster – to be his spiritual director, which embarrassed me somewhat. He had a great devotion to Saint Thérèse of the Child Jesus, and she was the main topic of our discussions. In spite of his profound knowledge he had the soul of a child and we learnt from his example of humility. I was most edified by him during the celebration of Holy Mass for the garrison. At Mass, during the Elevation of the Host, he would go down and kneel on both knees, while other officers would merely bend one knee and lower their heads.

In the field Hospital in Egypt, 2nd from L Fr Gruza, 1st from R Fr Królikowski; 1947

Humour on the psychiatric ward

One of the physicians working on the psychiatric ward was someone I knew from Beirut. He had managed to get some psychiatric practice in the Kulparkowa Hospital in Lwów, but he actually finished his studies in Beirut. He liked to go down to the port in Beirut for a beer, where the sailors from the submarines would congregate. Brawls would sometimes break out in the port bars, and in the fashion of Podbipięta (from Sienkiewicz's famous trilogy *By Fire and Sword*) he would restore order by up-ending the tables! He was also warm and very kind-hearted; and we managed to marry him off to a Polish student! In Al Qantarah they would invite Rysiek and me for Sunday tea, when the doctor would regale us with humorous stories about some of the patients.
In one enclosed sector there were patients who were referred to as "crazy", because during the *khamsin* season when there were hot and suffocating winds blowing from the Sahara Desert they would behave in an odd way. The wind would carry clouds of sand-dust as fine as flour which would force its way into our eyes and ears. Wearing an Arab turban was the best protection against it. The doctors protected the patients from the effects of atmospheric high pressure by administering injections to them, but the patients were afraid of them because they were very painful. A doctor would walk around the area – syringe in

hand – administering the injection according to a list. He was helped in this by two stout orderlies who would hold down the resisting patient. On one occasion all the injections were administered save one. The patient had disappeared. "Where could he have hidden?" the doctor mumbled under his breath. "The place is enclosed with three barbed wire fences and beyond that there is the desert." While he was grumbling like this a patient drew his attention to a tall and slender eucalyptus tree which the sought-after patient had climbed up and was making fun of the "quack". The physician called up to him, "Are you coming down or not?" "I won't come down," shouted back the "crazy" man shaking his head. Whereupon another "crazy" patient came up to the physician and said, "You trained at a university and you don't know how to get him to come down? I haven't even finished grade school but I will show you that he will come down faster than you can count to three." Whereupon he went up to the tree and with a stick in his hand leaning against the tree-trunk pretended to be cutting it down. The patient at the top of the tree fell into a panic and within seconds was in the arms of the orderlies.

Re-discovering my family

In Egypt I cashed in my allowance for an army overcoat. Trying it on I put my hands into the pockets and to my great surprise I found a note in it, written in Polish as follows: "Dear soldier! I am an American of Polish descent and I come from Buffalo, NY, USA. My name is Luna Misiewicz. I made this coat for you. If you need anything, and I can possibly help, please write to me and let me know. This is my address..."

I wrote back to her immediately, "Please help me to find my family, who up to the outbreak of war lived in Poznan, at such and such an address. I have had no contact with them, I don't even know if they are alive, and they don't know about my fate." I had written earlier to the International Red Cross with a request to help me find my closest family, but I received no reply. Perhaps there were simply too many such requests for lost ones after the war, so I patiently waited. Miss Luna managed to find my family, and as a result I started to send her parcels with food and clothing. Later, for many years she kept in contact with me and my family.

In the spring of 1947 Rysiek and I completed our demobilisation formalities in the Polish army camp of Al Qassasin in Egypt. A new chapter in our lives was about to open up – in the very heart of the Dark Continent.

Part V

Africa

The little-known Dark Continent

For Rysiek and me, the very thought of going to equatorial Africa sent shivers of excitement down our spines. At that time Africa was still a slumbering and relatively unknown continent. However, there existed historic accounts to the effect that the Phoenicians – rulers of the seas – had circumnavigated the continent. Neither was there any lack of evidence that the Egyptian pharaohs made expeditions into the heart of Africa in search of papyri, ivory, gold and diamonds. We were also aware that in recent times the continent had been affected by European colonial expansion. They parcelled out Africa at the Berlin Congress of 1884 like cutting up a wedding cake – with the biggest pieces going to the English, French, Portuguese and Germans. Africa was also missionary territory; and missionaries of various faiths worked there, among them Catholic priests and sisters. An example of someone with this missionary spirit was Albert Schweitzer, theologian, philosopher, physician, musician and Noble laureate for peace – who founded a hospital for leprosy patients in West Africa.

On the way to Port Said, Al Qassasin, 1947

Sailing from Port Said

Finally the day of our departure for equatorial Africa arrived; it was June in the year of our Lord 1947. Rysiek and I boarded a British ship in the Egyptian port of Port Said, at the head of the Suez Canal. In spite of our demobilisation the British still treated us as military. We sailed south, and our hearts stirred when we passed Al Qantarah and the No 8 Polish Military Hospital, where we had just recently performed our pastoral duties. I recalled well the familiar night-time sight of passing ships lit up like Christmas trees. One had the impression that they were a scene from the tales of a-thousand-and-one-nights, sailing down the canal, cutting through the sands of the desert.

It was hot and humid on the Red Sea, and we stopped in the port town of Aden, known from antiquity and located on the trading routes between India and Europe. A dark wall of hills formed the backdrop to the town. The passengers amused themselves by throwing coins into the water which were then retrieved by local children diving and catching them in their mouths. The game however ended tragically. A shark tore off the leg of one of the boys and from our ship a small motor boat was sent to rescue him. The boy was hauled out of the water and a missionary baptised him; but unfortunately the boy died on the way to the hospital.

The Indian Ocean

We sailed into the Indian Ocean and the rest of the journey was very pleasant. We proceeded along the coast of Africa, caressed by a gentle breeze generated by the motion of the ship. We were attacked by voracious and screeching gulls and shiny dark-blue agile dolphins emerged from the waves – all waiting to feed on scraps from the ship's kitchen. Time and again flying fish would rise up in front of their noses only for the whole shoal to fall back into the water again several metres further away.

For most of the passengers the big attraction was crossing the equator. The sailors organised the nuptial ceremony with the sea for us. This was an unusual spectacle. Everybody was fascinated especially the children and youngsters. Onto the deck came Neptune, King of the Seas, with a beard reaching to his knees and draped in a fishing net. In his powerful flippers he held a trident surmounted with arrowheads to represent lightning. He was accompanied by a retinue of sailors dressed up as water-nymphs. The nymphs would select young victims for the nuptial ceremony; then they would place them on a table, pour salty water into their mouths, shake talcum powder into their hair and check for the resilience of their hearts – before throwing them into the swimming pool accompanied with much laughter. After the ceremony the captain handed everyone a certificate of marriage with the sea.

Mombasa

We called in at the port of Mombasa, which services the whole of East Africa. For a Pole the name *Kilindini* harbour has a pleasing sound. We were fascinated by the sight of lush tropical vegetation and Englishmen in white cork-hats. The two of us were directed to the army Transit Camp, where we waited for a train to Nairobi, the capital of Kenya. At the crack of dawn we were woken by an African waiter bringing us cups of traditional English tea. This practice reminded us that we were in colonial Africa.

In the footsteps of Henryk Sienkiewicz

Opposite Tanganyika (today's Tanzania) – not far from the mainland – is the island of Zanzibar, which for a long time was the property of the sultan. It was one of the points from which captured Africans from the mainland were shipped out as slaves. Those who accepted Islam were not sold on but were granted their freedom. I mention Zanzibar because it was here that Henryk Sienkiewicz stayed in the nineteenth century, gathering material for his novel *W pustyni i puszczy* (translated into English as, In Desert and Wilderness). He took part in a safari not far from the shore with the intention of going into the interior, but the Germans who administered the Tanganyikan protectorate at that time would not allow the writer passage through the territory. Sienkiewicz however managed to get the information he needed from stories recounted to him by the White Fathers, missionaries who were working along the coast. Shortly afterwards however, malaria and the absence of medical care forced him to return to Europe.

It was in the jungles and savannahs of Tanganyika that Sienkiewicz placed the fictitious characters of Staś Tarkowski, little Nel Rawlinson, the elephant Kinga and the dog Saba. It was the very same place where now there were Polish children, victims of Communism who had been rescued by the armies of General Anders. The delegate for Polish pastoral work in Africa, Monsignor Władysław Słapa was sending me to work with these children, their mothers and quite a few orphans. I was to go to a settlement camp called Tengeru, while my Franciscan companion – through the good and bad times of the last few years – Rysiek Gruza, was sent to the refugee settlement camp of Koja in Uganda, on the shores of Lake Victoria, the largest lake in Africa.

Tengeru and Koja were not the only Polish refugee settlement camps in Africa. In total there were twenty-two of them, with about 19,000 people, of which almost 10,000 were children and youngsters. Tengeru was the largest settlement camp and had about 4,000 inhabitants, half of whom were children and young people with their mothers and the remainder orphaned children. The second largest was Masindi in Uganda. Two settlements, Rongai in Kenya and Outdshoorn in the Republic of South Africa, were specifically for children. The distribution of the camps resembled a string of beads; starting with Uganda and Kenya to the north of the equator right down to the Cape of Good Hope in the south. Their names in alphabetical order were – Abercorn (Mbala, Zambia), Bwana Mkubwa and Digglefold (Uganda), Fort Jameson (Zambia), Ifunda (Tanzania), Kidugala (Tanzania), Kigoma (Tanzania), Koja (Uganda), Kondoa (Tanzania), Livingstone (Zambia), Lusaka (Zambia), Makindu (Kenya), Manira (Kenya), Marandellas (Uganda), Masindi (Uganda), Morogoro (Tanzania), Nairobi (Kenya), Nyali (Kenya), Outdshoorn (South Africa), Rongai (Kenya), Rusape (Zimbabwe) and Tengeru (Tanzania).

In English, these settlement camps were also called refugee camps, and both forms were used interchangeably, although to my mind neither term adequately reflected the true nature of the inhabitants. The inhabitants of the camps neither came to the camps nor left their country of origin voluntarily. The Soviet NKVD forcibly displaced them from Eastern Poland and sent them to Siberia. One should call those who managed to survive and escape that Bolshevik "paradise" – thereby regaining their freedom – banished wanderers.

Tengeru settlement

The Tengeru settlement to which I was sent was located a few kilometres from Arusha, the tourist capital of Tanganyika. From there safaris would depart in various directions. Tengeru, a few degrees south of the equator, was situated on a plateau at the foot of Mt Meru and every day the residents looked out on it and its twin peak, the snow-capped Kilimanjaro. Scattered about were a few enormous spreading trees that had been left standing after the jungle had been cleared. The settlement itself gave the impression of a huge botanical garden where nature reigned supreme, with lush tropical vegetation and flowers, from which emerged small, round, white houses, covered with palm and banana leaves, reminiscent of beehives. In the big clearing next to the church the residents had established a big sign on which they wrote the name of their beloved country – POLAND – and the year they arrived on the Dark Continent, 1942. The sign was actually made from a living, neatly-clipped hedge, about a metre high. The heart of the community was the little church with a roof that looked like the spread-out wings of a bird ready to fly away. The side walls of the building consisted of bamboo poles made into a lattice-work of grills which guaranteed good natural ventilation. From the main altar reigned Our Lady of Ostrobrama, patroness of Poland, especially of its eastern border-regions, where most of the wandering refugee-exiles had come from. On a hillock, among lush oleander bushes stood the presbytery, next to the church. On the opposite side to the church was a wooden bell-tower and papaya orchard. On the clearing which extended from the "Polish" hedge, meetings, games, parades and processions were held.

The previously mentioned small, white single-family houses and various community buildings were located on a hill. These houses were representative of the old African culture. The rays of the sun slid around the circular domestic buildings heating up only small surface areas at any one time. The roof made from banana-leaves was placed significantly higher than the walls allowing for a pleasant draught. The public buildings however – the school, orphanage, village hospital administration block, kitchen and storehouses – had perpendicular walls.

In the so-called monkey-grove stood a theatre encircled by the jungle. In the theatre we conducted film screenings, plays, concerts, rallies and residents' meetings. In the valley below, the self-contained farm of Mr Zakrzewski flourished. The neatly-kept cemetery had already received quite a number of exiles, who would there await their Resurrection day. Behind the settlement sparkled the waters of Lake Duluti, resembling the alpine lake of Morskie Oko in Zakopane in the Polish Tatra Mountains. It was a very deep lake, and the waters had mineral properties. African mountains and lakes are of volcanic origin, going back to the time of the break-up of the planet's shell called the Tectonic Rift, from which originate the river-bed of the Jordan, the Dead Sea, the Red Sea and the Great African lakes.

First impressions

The houses were aptly referred to as resembling beehives since after lessons they were encircled by children and adolescents milling around like bees. One talks about falling in love at first sight – and it was with just such strong emotions that I related to these wanderers of varying ages. The first three encounters with them made the strongest impression on me. The first memory is from the school playground when I went for the first time to give the children lessons in religion. I was struck by a moving scene. Still wrapped up in the morning mist, rows of girls and boys were about to start their lessons with prayers and a hymn. I remember well the hymn to Our Lady, which they would sing quite often:

Mother of Consolation, Lady of heaven and earth
To you we sinners bring our hearts as offerings
We give them to you for safe-keeping
As did our fathers before us.
We give you homage and adoration
Holy Mother of Consolation
Don't abandon us.

That hymn always moved me deeply, and in their childish voices I detected pain, longing and the many hopes of all those young hearts. I have a similar reaction to the patriotic hymn of Polish exiled soldiers, composed at the beginning of World War II, and previously referred to in this book – *O lord who art in heaven...*

The next encounter took place in the little chapel on an evening in June during services to the Sacred Heart of Jesus. I had the clear awareness that in front of me were children and youngsters who had been led away under cover of darkness from their native land and scattered all over the Soviet Union. I was kneeling in the sacristy while the service was being conducted by Canon Piotr Roginski. I was made aware, through the fervour of their prayers and singing, of the whole tragedy of these small wandering-exiles. I furtively wiped away my tears.

The third encounter took place a few days after I arrived in Tengeru. It was at a meeting I had with the whole population of the refugee settlement, when everyone had left their huts to take part in the Corpus Christi procession. Everything and everyone was new to me, so they assigned me the role of assistant for the procession. I looked after order and continuity. The colourful procession made a charming sight; the girls in navy-blue uniforms and white blouses with sailor collars, standard bearers, feretories, children in white strewing flowers before the Holy Sacrament, the golden canopy and behind them all the singing crowds. The procession would halt by altars set up underneath the spreading trees. One would have to have been a painter to recreate adequately the unique artistic colour of that picture, which was rendered even more unusual by the indigenous flora.

Canon Piotr Roginski

A characteristic of all the teachers and carers in Africa was their love for the children in their care and their love of their lost country. Above all they loved God – which is engendered both by reason and emotion as He is the source of all life and all human happiness. Although the teachers and carers of the children were not all professionals they were all extremely reliable and sacrificed themselves unsparingly to help the children.

Among the teachers there were many people worthy of mention, as testified in the letters and diaries of the youngsters. Father Śliwowski, who had won over the hearts of the people especially the youth with his kindness and organisational skills, was no longer there by the time I arrived in Tengeru. During my time there, another priest was universally respected, a great patriot, Canon Piotr Roginski, who came from around the Wilno region of pre-war Eastern Poland. He had set about building schools in Poland after the First World War. He was also an army chaplain during the invasion of Poland in 1920, when Lenin over-ran my country in an attempt to create a Bolshevik revolution in the whole of Europe over the corpse of Poland. During the Second World War, Father Roginski was captured by the NKVD, interrogated and tortured. They were trying to force him to divulge the names of participants of the 1920 campaign; but he didn't betray any of them. He left Russia with the army of General Anders and later found himself in Africa. After the cessation of hostilities, when Communist agents tried to encourage the people in the settlements to return to their enslaved country, Father Roginski reminded his compatriots of the events of 1940 – the night arrests, travel to the East in packed cattle-wagons, hunger and the cries of children for water and bread. He was greeted with criticism for this attitude by some of the people in the refugee settlement who wanted to believe the Communist agent's propaganda. But even they couldn't accuse him of lack of love for his country. The youngsters in high school and lycée classes adored him for his wisdom and warmth.

After my arrival at Tengeru, Canon Roginski, who was the parish priest at the refugee settlement, let me into the obvious and not-so-obvious secrets of camp life; he gave me sound counsel. Once he took me aside on the shores of Lake Duluti, which was covered in tall grasses. We were dressed in the white cassocks that were typically worn in the tropics. During our discussion the Canon suddenly started to jump up and down and scratch himself all over his body. He was attacked by red ants, excellent first-aiders of the jungle; who much like hyenas, vultures and bats preserve the environment from epidemics. However woe betide the person who stands in the way of marching ants in search of carrion.

Education in school

A casual observer may easily have made the erroneous assumption that the refugee settlement camp was a holiday camp. There would have been nothing strange in that. After the sufferings of the war, and in particular the forced exile in Siberia, the inhabitants of the camps needed to renew their physical, emotional and spiritual health. The expression *dolce far niente* typical for that part of Africa resulted in a slower pace of living. Especially in the evenings, one would see women sitting in front of their houses and in their gardens, just as they would have done back in their borderland homes in Poland. Here they lived exclusively for their children, who constituted over half the population, as many of their husbands were still in the army.

The refugee settlements were centres of education on account of the large numbers of inhabitants belonging to the younger generation. The three primary schools had a total of 1,332 pupils. There were also secondary schools, vocational sewing and trade schools, a general high school with a lycée and engineering and agricultural colleges. The school of music was also very popular with a goodly number of students, and even I enlisted for violin lessons in order to encourage students to practice difficult exercises. For the older girls they arranged supplementary vocational courses in first-aid, sewing, embroidery, basket-weaving and home economics. In spite of the tropical climate and five to six hours of lessons a day and frequent bouts of malaria, the youngsters studied diligently, and were brought up idealistically to a high moral standard. No doubt their experiences of war and their prematurely acquired wisdom played a role in this. These youngsters had lost something of the innocence of a normal childhood. Their faces would often cloud over with reflection and sadness. Their keenness to study stemmed from their hope that they would indeed return to their devastated Poland after the end of the war. They dreamed of being able to help in the rebuilding of their country. These hopes were dashed however when it became clear that the Allied governments had betrayed Poland by handing her over to the Communist regime imposed by the Soviets. Polish soldiers, victors of the battles in Tobruk, Narvik, Monte Cassino, Ancona and Bologna refused to be sent back to their enslaved country. Ironically, those who had from the very beginning opposed Hitler and had fought on all fronts on the side of the Allied Forces were not even invited to take part in the Victory parade in London in 1945. The young people were deeply affected by this betrayal. They still studied with great passion, convinced that education is always universally useful and that God would see to it that they would bring honour to Poland.

Occasionally some of the boys and girls would escape into the jungle where they would play truant, swinging from huge ropes, imitating what they had seen in Tarzan films. The headmaster would then have to call them to order. One boy in an essay entitled *Experiencing life in the jungle,* wrote: "What do you mean by *the jungle*? I have not yet seen an elephant, lion, leopard, or any other wild animal, except the headmaster."

The teachers and carers unremittingly devoted a lot of time to the youngsters, transmitting to them all their knowledge and values. One young teacher recalled, "I used to fall asleep standing up, and sometimes I would lose orientation as to which direction was up and which was down, losing my balance both in terms of body and spirit. The world was whirling in front of my eyes. For the last few years my work has been without a break from morning till eleven at night."

The teachers experienced the horrors of Bolshevism more consciously than the young, therefore they did not spare themselves in working with them. Many teachers would help the youngsters with their class-work after school and their homes were always open to them; moreover they would also meet them in the youth centre where in the evening there were lectures, talks, organised events and dances.

The violin

Talking about education I cannot omit to mention the music school run by Mrs Kopijczuk. She persisted in encouraging me to take up playing the violin. Playing a musical instrument was always one of my ambitions – as I have already mentioned. This encouragement by the teacher had a sound pedagogical reasoning. Learning to play the violin requires patience and regular practice; but the pupils were impatient. Effortlessly and immediately they wanted to play a waltz or polka or any other popular composition, so they tried to cut corners. Mrs Kopijczuk wanted me to be a good role model. I would practice scales for hours so that the neighbours would have to close their windows. After some improvement she suggested that I play a duet with her on the stage in the monkey-grove. But this never came off as I was afraid that due to my stage-fright the palms of my hands would start to sweat. But even more I was afraid of the hundreds of young people who threatened to come to this concert. When I left Africa I stopped taking lessons. I played one last sad impromptu melody, put the violin into its case and a distraught altar-server returned the instrument to the school.

The camp exuded youthfulness

The refugee settlement camp exuded all the joys of youth. I am not even going to mention sport as it's a natural inclination that young people are attracted to sport. But I was surprised at the large numbers of young people who enrolled in the Sodality of Mary. I was particularly fond of this organisation, as it evoked for me pleasant memories of my sister Władzia, who would fill our house with the Sodality hymn. In a way her Sodality hymn had also become my own hymn and my prayer:

...I have sworn allegiance to my Queen, and from now on I will serve only her. I have also taken her as my mother and placed all my trust in her...

Baden-Powell and the Polish Scouting Movement

In the Polish refugee settlement camps scouting was one of the most popular youth movements. Robert Baden-Powell, the creator of the world scouting movement, who had died in Kenya in 1941, would have been proud and happy to know that in his beloved Africa there were Polish scouting troops scattered about from the equator to the Cape of Good Hope. The scouting movement had its natural base in Africa. It was here on the Dark Continent that Baden-Powell came to the conclusion that *"nature should become the great master of the young, and that physical work should never only be for pleasure, as it also develops the ability to sacrifice, it ennobles, and forces one to co-*

operate and seek mutual help – facilitating a sense of unity and friendship. It makes people humble and strong, noble and courteous."

That great advocate of outdoor activities was also a true educator. This is what he has to say: "It is of the utmost importance that each day boys should do something good for someone else. The good deed may be small (giving-up your seat to someone, picking up a banana-skin from the pavement, or putting a coin in the poor box) but it is an efficacious method of eradicating egoism in boys."

Baden-Powell took the principles of education and combined them with a reverence for God. He wrote: "A true educational system demands the recognition of God. Not a God who has his weapons targeted at us as punishment, but a God who smiles at us and gives us the courage to become people full of respect towards His masterpiece – which is nature... Religion is very simple to understand: first you need to love God and to serve Him; and secondly you need to love your neighbour and also to serve him." Our youth incorporated these principles into their everyday lives.

In the desert and jungle

In the scouting movement in Africa, the girls were more energetic and more numerous than the boys. They also managed to organise themselves extremely well. I would monitor them while they were stalking, or attending scout gatherings by the lake, or when awarding scouting badges or climbing up ropes to the tops of trees. Thirty-five senior scouts took part in the African Jamboree by Lake Victoria, during which there was a race and seventeen-year-old Jurek Międzyrzecki from Tengeru suffered a heart attack and died. The Polish troop however won that race maintaining a big advantage over the African scouts.

Polish Girl Guides, Tengeru, 1948

We heard stories of how in the Polish refugee settlement camp in Lusaka, Northern Rhodesia (now Zambia), the parade of Polish scouts was attended by the daughter of General Baden-Powell. Our scouts from Oudtshoorn noted in their diaries that their refugee settlement was visited by the British royal family: King George VI with his wife Queen Elizabeth and two daughters, Elizabeth and Margaret. They were the same age as our girls. The Polish scouts took part in welcoming the guests, during which King George paused in front of the Polish standard and expressed interest in the epic quality of their lives. Meanwhile Queen Elizabeth conversed with the girls who invited favourable attention from onlookers because they were wearing their colourful regional folk costumes.

A return to nature

The wolf is called back to the forest by his nature – according to an old Polish saying. In spite of living in the jungle, the girl guides in Tengeru liked to establish their camps on the forested slopes of Mt Meru. During one such camp, I went with some older scouts and guides into the interior of the jungle where we assumed no human being had been before. We were confronted by nature unspoilt by human intervention; we marvelled at the splendour of flowers, trees and shrubs unique to the jungle. Only in the jungle can one find the delicate ecological balance of the sun's energy, humidity, shade and wind which ensure vitality for the dense tropical forest of the volcanic plateau. Charmed by the various bird-songs which combined to form a heavenly orchestra, we recklessly penetrated deeper into the forest, forgetting the passage of time. In the tropics the sun sets very quickly; one has the impression that someone is lowering a lamp on a rope.

Darkness intensified. We were overcome with fear, because at night in the thick forest it is easy to lose one's sense of direction and the jungle itself is more dangerous at night than by day. Some forest animals come out only under cover of dark. In the camp they had noticed our absence, so we waited a few minutes in silence listening for sounds coming from the direction of our camp. Someone managed to reach us with the sound of calling and so we ran in that direction. We were greeted in the camp with shouts of joy. Meanwhile, behind our backs an impenetrable blackness enveloped the jungle.

The German lady's farm

Both the scouts and the guides liked to pitch their camps on the farming lands of Mrs Trappe, a German lady who together with her husband had settled there before the First World War, when Tanganyika was under German rule. The son and daughter of Mr and Mrs Trappe were children of the jungle and loved it as if it were their own country. Mrs Trappe was a widow by the time we met her. Her daughter had a somewhat secretive nature but was an excellent rider, resembling the mythical horse-women of the Amazon forests. Previously she had been accompanied on her journeys by a panther which she had brought up from a kitten, but she had to return it to the wild when Hitler started his aggression in Europe and the British authorities started to intern expatriate Germans. Her son was more approachable and helpful.

Often at night, herds of elephant and rhinoceros would pass through their land playing havoc with the vegetable garden. In view of these dangers the girl guides would organise a double night-watch when bivouacking – burning the campfire all through the night. Some of the most idyllic scenes during camp occurred at dawn. Reveille was conducted in thick mist, so that the surrounding area looked like an enchanted fairyland. Before the mist lifted I would celebrate Holy Mass in the open air and as a result the altar-cloth, missal and host were all damp.

We asked Mrs Trappe's son to accompany us on a safari. As these were virgin lands, thousands of animals were grazing on the savannah – antelopes, zebras and buffalo, in addition to many different types of birds. On the shores of the lake hippopotami were basking. The risk of danger cautioned us to be careful. The German chose around eight older boys and girls. He took us into the interior of the savannah; two Africans went at the head of the column to prevent any accidents. They would shake the bushes, throwing stones into them to scare away any wild animals.

As the march proceeded the Africans stopped leading us and went alongside us, the machine-gun in the hands of the young Trappe giving them a sense of false security. The air was filled with the buzzing of insects. All of a sudden, about fifty metres in front of us, the enormous bulk of a rhinoceros rose up from the undergrowth. The animal has poor eye-sight and is dependent on its sense of smell. It was charging straight at us and could have easily trampled any one of us to death impaling the victim with the horn on its snout. I didn't see when the German lifted his gun and fired – it all happened so quickly. The animal, although shot, took a while to stop, as with a groan and embedding its hooves into earthen grooves, it slid to a halt not far from us. The bullet lodged above the animal's eye. Meanwhile the young Trappe was visibly shaking with fear, aware of his responsibilities; mostly he was afraid of the British. At the beginning of the war due to his nationality he had been interned together with his mother and sister. Now he was afraid of being deported to Germany. We returned hurriedly to camp, and the following day Trappe instructed the Africans to saw off the horn from the rhinoceros in order for the accident to look like the activity of poachers.

In the company of the African safari guides who were armed with spears and *panga* (machetes) the younger girl guides and I went on a trip to a nearby waterfall. At the base of the fall elephants could often be seen drinking and cooling off. The Africans did not allow children to approach too closely, especially if there was a baby elephant among the herd.

In the evening by the hearth Mrs Trappe would regale us with stories of her adventures. Once, when she had taken the car to the local town to do some shopping, her path was blocked by a family of elephants. The female elephant fearing for her young approached the car. Mrs Trappe had already got out of the car for fear that the elephants would descend in a fury and trample all over it. As the elephant approached she looked it straight in the eye; she maintained that the animals naturally felt the superiority of humans. After a while, waving its trunk about as if unsure what to do, the elephant returned to the herd and retired with them to the jungle.

"The night draws near..."

Both in the refugee settlement camp and during scout camps I would participate in the scouting camp-fire gatherings. At each gathering we would perform a rich repertoire of scouting songs, army songs, folk-songs and ballads from Lwów, plus a variety of skits and dances. The subject of the scout-master's yarn was often about Poland. The camp-fire gatherings always finished with the prayerful scouting hymn, *The day is done, gone the sun, from the lakes, from the hills, from the sky, all is well, safely rest, God is nigh.* The first time one sings the song loudly, the second time more quietly and the third time it is hummed. Then, embracing each other, we would unite ourselves spiritually with the thousands of Polish scouts under the Southern Cross from the equator to the Cape of Good Hope who at the same time were also singing that song around the camp-fire. Wishing each other good night we would entrust our wanderer's lot to Divine Providence.

Baden-Powell died in Africa, at the foot of Mt Kenya in January 1941. The appeal of Powell to his beloved scouts, delivered just before his eighty-fourth birthday, reads like his last testament, and is still relevant today: "*My life has been very happy which is why I wish that each one of you should have a happy life. Look for ways to leave the world a better place than you have found it; so that when the time comes for you to leave it, you will be able to depart in the reassuring knowledge that you have done the best that you could."* During the 1937 World Jamboree he appealed to scouts with words that resonated in the hearts of our Christian scouts – *"Spread the Kingdom of God's peace among peoples."*

Tengeru, East Africa 1949

Africans

Christianity engendered a positive effect on the relationships between the Poles and the Africans. This was most notable among the scouts who found it easy to make friendships with them, even though there were not too many opportunities to do so. The boys and to a lesser extent the girls picked up Swahili, a language used to communicate with all the different people of East Africa. Knowledge of this language was necessary for the youngsters when they went to market to buy fruit. The Africans were often working around the camp, digging trenches, repairing the banana-leaf roofs and often searching for the elusive queen termite. The termites, by digging underground labyrinths and building copious mounds on the surface of the soil were threatening to destroy the garden. But after the destruction of the queen, and thus the constant laying of thousands of eggs, the whole swarm of termites perish. The Africans would eat the termite queen in the following fashion: In the palm of one hand the finder would demonstrate his trophy, for which he would receive a pound, while with the fingers of his other hand he would put the fat mother termite into his open mouth, smacking his lips and tapping his stomach. The Africans always accompanied their work with singing, as this made the work "go better". One of them would stand next to the team and with rhythmical singing keep the beat. Africans sitting on the roofs (in order to repair them) would often sing the Latin songs which the missionaries had taught them, like *Ave Verum* or *Tantum Ergo* and the *Salve Regina*.

I can recount an African fable from the region around Kilimanjaro-Meru which resembles the story about original sin. According to African belief the closeness of God to His people – whom he created – is symbolised by the sky which hangs low over their heads like a canopy. Unfortunately, one day, after the women had finished their work in the fields they wiped their hands on the heavenly firmament instead of taking the trouble to wash them in the stream. God was angry about this and as a result moved the heavens further away from His people. A primitive tale, but it contains the elements of our Christian belief concerning original sin, especially the point that it was the woman who first fell to the temptation of Satan.

Mr Korzeniowski

In my previously published book *Stolen Childhood* I dedicated a whole chapter to Mr Korzeniowski because of his extremely interesting personality. However, I changed his name from Korzeniowski to Korzen in order to side-track the Communists who could have otherwise taken vengeance on his wife and children who still lived near Nowogródek. It could have meant severing relationships with his family and that he could not have endured. He lived for his family and he hoped that he would be reunited with them. In our settlement camp he performed the duties of sacristan. He was a man of great simplicity, honesty and goodness. He had plenty of innate intelligence and possessed exceptional resourcefulness, which meant that he was comfortable wherever he found himself and could always find a solution to life's many challenges. He could repair shoes, build a boat, construct an apiary for woodland bees and was a knowledgeable gardener. He made a suitcase from the skins of wild animals which he had hunted himself. In Poland he had been a farmer while in Africa before he became the sacristan he worked for an Englishman on a plantation. There he could really show his ability as he not only managed the local Africans but also hosted the guests who came from England and acted as their guide huntsman during their safaris. Apparently he once stopped a lion in its tracks just by looking at it.

One day in his early years in Tengeru he went to an African village to buy some eggs. The Africans did not bother much about the commercial value of their hens. He went from hut to hut but he was not satisfied with the produce. The hens' eggs were as small as pigeon eggs. He was about to leave when he heard behind him a grave voice saying, "Go on, buy some eggs from her; you can see she is old and toothless". Turning around he saw a group of African warriors with brightly painted faces leaning on their spears. Now Korzeniowski was not afraid of the Bolsheviks when they advanced on Warsaw in 1920; but then he was young and prepared to pay with his life for the freedom of his country. But here he was overcome with fear. He had no intention of risking his life over a couple of eggs. In the predicament of the moment he suddenly had a brainwave which he immediately put into practice – he removed his false teeth from his mouth and showing them to the warriors said, "I also am an old man and toothless." The Africans fled, presuming that he was a witchdoctor. Meanwhile, Korzeniowski took advantage of the ensuing confusion to return to camp quickly.

Safari to the crater of N'Goro N'Goro

The Polish young people longed to visit the interior of Africa. Most of all they wanted to see the largest African crater N'Goro N'Goro, which was considered to be one of the wonders of the natural world, and adjacent to it the Serengeti National Park, which stretches over one million four thousand hectares. It is covered in savannahs, acacia and sky-scraper forests and wetlands. It harbours the largest number of wild animals in the world, especially ungulates, such as rhinoceros, buffaloes, giraffes, ostriches and antelopes, which in turn are the fodder for lions, leopards, cheetahs and hyenas. There are so many species of birds that it is impossible to list them all. This whole strange arena – which is a geological basin and is home to so much flora and fauna – came about as the result of the creation of the Tectonic Rift, when two plates on the earth's crust drifted apart.

We left N'Goro N'Goro in three uncovered lorries carrying the older high school and college students and some of the teachers. The route of about 160 kilometres constantly climbed upwards, passing through picturesque Maasai villages abundant in water and surrounded by vegetation. The youngsters amused themselves by singing scouting, patriotic and folk songs. Towards the evening we arrived at the forested rim of the crater and settled into our chalets which reminded us of Polish mountain huts. The chalets were managed by the colonial government of Tanganyika with a permanent staff of local Africans. Every building had its own kitchen and fireplace because the nights there could be extremely cold. Just before nightfall we went over to the edge of the crater to see the site of our next day's expedition. Surrounded by hills, the mists were beginning to cast a veil over the crater, which was six hundred metres deep.

The next day as we stood on the edge of the caldera we were told that at its base it had a diameter of 22.5 kilometres, in which there were several large volcanic vents, the largest of which was now a volcanic salt-lake, twelve kilometres in diameter. Climbing down the steep sides of the crater was accomplished with shouts of joy and laughter. We had to grab hold of shrubs and lean on overhanging rocks in order not to roll down the sides and be injured. As we approached the base of the caldera containing the volcanic vents a forest loomed up in front of our eyes, which from above had looked just like dark green stains – or the shadows of clouds.

After we had encircled the forest, through which flowed a rushing stream, we came upon an amazing sight – herds of zebra and near to them animals called wildebeest, rather like restive bullocks, cavorting around. It seemed to us as if our presence had agitated them, but this was not the case, as was later explained to us. They simply like to clown about. The well-fed zebras lazily observed their activities; but the

155

jumping up and down of the wildebeest made us uneasy. What would happen if the herds, unsettled by our presence, automatically rushed forward in a blind panic? They could trample all over us. Few of us would survive underneath all those thousands of hooves. Some of the older girls, thinking that the wildebeests' dance was a preliminary activity to attacking us, wanted me to head back to the chalets as quickly as possible. Some of the others fainted from hyper-fibrillation of the heart, brought on by bouts of malaria. Their friends took them over to the stream to bring them round and one of the teachers even climbed a tree in panic. We really didn't know what to do. I was unfamiliar with the habits of these animals, but I observed the behaviour of our African guides, armed only with spears. They stood still, calmly leaning on their weapons. Instinct was telling them to remain still so as not to frighten the animals. According to the earlier advice of Mrs Trappe, we knew that animals sensed the superiority of humans. This was confirmed, as all of a sudden several of the wildebeest started to gallop into the open plain in the opposite direction to where we were standing. They were then followed by an avalanche of other four-footed beasts. Once the animals felt safe they stopped running and started to nibble the grass. Meanwhile, the crater-lake, covered in a film of salt unveiled itself in front of our eyes. The actual crater itself did not make much of an impression on us. The journey back up to the chalets was a lot harder than going down and what's more we had to carry the sick girls.

After spending the night in the chalets it was time to set out on the return journey to Tengeru. In spite of the difficulties the youngsters were always eager for new experiences and were not anxious to leave. As luck would have it, not too far from the chalets, the axle of one of the lorries broke. This accident was greeted with great applause as this meant that a third of the participants in the expedition would have to stay behind until the company from Arusha, from whom we hired the vehicles, could deliver a new axle; and this could take up to two or three days! Meanwhile the stories told by the youngsters who had already returned to camp, especially the episode about the dramatic confrontation with the animals, only made the mothers waiting for the late-comers even more anxious. They waited for them till late at night.

Although I was not working in Africa as a missionary I did manage to observe the activities of many in the mission field. I felt sorry for the Catholic bishops who were constantly called to attend futile meetings with the Governor of Tanganyika. The British in their attempt to keep the people of the colonies subservient only reluctantly gave permission to open schools for local children and youngsters. I witnessed the difficult work of these Catholic missionaries, whose efforts seemed to be undermined by the authorities. The pastoral duties of the missionaries often covered enormous areas and the very challenge of moving around them was extremely burdensome. Once, I was substituting for an absent American missionary when an African catechist came to our settlement with the request that one of us go with the Holy Sacraments to a dying woman. It was a Saturday. I had only just returned to my "beehive", relieved that I would soon have supper and be able to have some rest, when I was startled to hear salutations voiced in my direction – increasingly loudly. The British had taught the Africans to respect Europeans by announcing their presence when approaching them, and to do so in such a manner as not to startle anyone! But after having conducted six lessons in the school that day I was really tired. The catechist was adamant however that I should leave immediately as the life of the woman was in danger. He assured me that the village was not far away, just past the banana grove. I did not change my clothes but set out in my dog-collar and black suit. The sun was at its zenith and rivulets of perspiration poured down my body. We passed not one but several banana groves; meanwhile the African was racing ahead so fast that all I could see were the pink soles of his feet. Finally we reached our destination; a low chimneyless mud-hut, in the shape of a large lamp-shade, covered in banana leaves. I was initially prevented from entering by the stinging smoke from the hearth which was positioned in the centre of the hut. Every time I bent down to enter I was overwhelmed by the smoke which made my eyes water. When at last I got used to the smoke I managed to get inside. The catechist pointed to a pile of skins; the woman lay underneath them. On her young dark face I could not discern any signs of disease. I did not know Swahili so the catechist had to translate my introductory words as I administered the Sacrament of

Extreme Unction to the sick woman. During this ritual young goats were playfully jumping over her body and over my hands. I never did find out whether the woman recovered.

On another occasion I met an Italian Passionist missionary, Father Benedetto Barbaranelli. He invited me to give a retreat to the inhabitants of a Polish settlement camp in Kondoa, to the south of Arusha. There was no available Polish priest to serve in that settlement on a permanent basis, so he volunteered to go. From his very first meetings with the Polish refugees he fell in love with them and gained their affection. The children adored him and taught him the Polish language, which he quickly learnt, at least at a basic level. Meanwhile he continued deepening his knowledge of Polish culture and language by reading the novels of Henryk Sienkiewicz. He would sometimes mispronounce a Polish word, although this occurred very rarely and led to some comic situations. The children really liked Father Barbaranelli.

He once told me the story of a gang of twenty cannibals. They would dress up in lion-skins and kidnap girls and young women as they went to fetch water from a stream not far from the village. One of the women managed to escape and when she reported to the police that lions were walking on two legs, they were at first completely disbelieving, but then they soon realised what she was actually describing. For some time women had been disappearing without trace. The cannibals were eventually caught and sentenced to death. Father Barbaranelli was asked to prepare them spiritually following their sentencing.

A missionary "par excellence"

Of all the missionaries, the most interesting and most popular was a Polish sister from Silesia, Mother Matilda from the Missionary Congregation of the Most Precious Blood. When we visited her in the foothills of Mt Kilimanjaro she was the superior of the Kilema mission. She had arrived in Africa as an eighteen-year-old girl to complete her novitiate in South Africa. After taking her vows she was sent into the interior of the Dark Continent. From the shores of the Indian Ocean to the foothills of Kilimanjaro she travelled around on foot with a group of missionaries. They would spend the night in the bush, under the open skies, protecting their camp with guards and thorny bushes – whilst keeping a bonfire burning all night long. The missionaries would carry on their heads the bricks used to build their church. Eventually a beautiful mission station was constructed.

At each visit there was something new to see and inspect – classrooms full of school children or stables or barns. While still a young sister, Mother Matilda, armed only with a pitch-fork had once confronted a stupefied boa-constrictor, who had just finished digesting a captured bird in one of the barns. The children's orchestra would perform its latest pieces for us. When our girls asked her if she ever felt any prejudice towards people of darker skin she replied that African children were as lovely as European children and when one recalled that they too have been loved by God from all eternity, then the work among them became truly exciting.

Mother Matilda was a living story-book full of the most varied and interesting sayings and tales, so it was little surprise that the children from Tengeru loved to visit her. Perhaps she reminded them of their grannies from Poland or Siberia. Only the older children and youngsters were taken on the potentially dangerous far-flung trips; the little ones were left behind with Mother Matilda and the enchanting scenery around the mission – which had as its backdrop the tallest mountain in Africa Kilimanjaro, which an earlier visitor had described as the roof of Africa.

The roof of Africa

Every morning, the inhabitants of Tengeru would look up at Mt Kilimanjaro covered in perpetual snow and glaciers in silent admiration of its Creator. Depending on the time of day, the snowy cupola would take on different hues: rose-pink, white, grey-green or azure. The proximity of the mountain tempered our hot climate. One of the legends attributed to the local tribesmen, and which dated from a time before anyone had actually reached its summit, claimed that on the top of the mountain could be found a white magic medicine: *Kilima ja Njaro*. The mountain also has other names, such as the Crown of African Mountains and the Lion in the Valley. Mountains evoke in us a sense of mysticism, a feeling of the closeness of God. Monks throughout the ages have been aware of this connection as they have tended to build their abbeys on hilltops.

The height of Kilimanjaro at 5,895 metres is greater than the Alps. Its crown of eternal snow appears to be lopsided, because with amazing regularity, all year round, warm winds from the Indian Ocean blow on it, melting the snow on the eastern side. Our proximity to the mountain called out for adventure and so it was that in 1949 three Polish mountaineers – Jakub Hoffman, a teacher from Wołyn, Maria Sidor, the high school natural history teacher and myself, author of these memoirs – were tempted to climb it. We were accompanied by the children from the refugee settlement camp up to the foothills of the mountain where the Kilema mission was based.

Undertaking the expedition evoked many conflicting emotions. When we climbed to four thousand metres, the jagged stone lace-work of the volcanic summit of Mt Mawenzi made a huge impression upon us. However, the goal of our mountain expedition was another higher peak, also a crater, called Mt Kibo, from whose centre, which had a diameter of two kilometres, smoke constantly rose. The hardest challenge was to reach the top under the cover of darkness, since during the daytime the sun's rays were lethal to humans. We were protected from the frosts of minus 14 degrees centigrade by our winter clothing. We reacted oddly to the rarefied air at that height; it felt as if we were going crazy. Every word from a companion or from our guide Johann seemed to split our heads open. The eastern approach which has little snow was covered instead in volcanic ash, and in addition was so steep that we would take seven or eight steps forward only to slide backwards another three or four. An almost Sisyphean labour. I kept asking myself, "You fool, why did you come up here?" But with the dawn, when we stood at the summit and in front of us unfolded a hitherto unknown sight – the streak of the Indian Ocean, and land covered in the white fluffy bedding of clouds – we were stunned by the miracle of nature and started to devise plans for a further expedition to Mt Kilimanjaro.

I keep returning to Kilimanjaro in my thoughts, in my conversations and at scouting gatherings. It has become for me a symbol of the variety of human existence.

Kilimanjaro has a wide range of the world's climates and various ecological pockets for flora and fauna. At the foot of the mountain are the sprawling savannahs, and lower still agricultural fields, and plantations of coffee, bananas etc. There is also a belt of evergreen forest which is supplanted by bamboo and heather scrubland. At the height of four thousand metres there are expanses of alpine meadows covered with beautiful flowers, then higher still are the mosses and lichens; and finally between this plateau and the snowline and glaciers, Mt Kibo has a scattering of enormous boulders. Each of these varied biospheres is inhabited by different mammals, amphibians, reptiles and birds.

I associate the expedition to Mt Kilimanjaro with life, because it contains the periods of grateful childhood, exuberant youthfulness, maturity and old age. The gorgeous view from the top reminds me of God's promise of paradise – an eternal Kingdom of happiness, about which St Paul says: ...*no eye has seen, nor ear heard, nor heart of man conceived, what God has prepared for those who love him* (I Corinthians 2,9).

An expedition into the heart of Africa

While in Tengeru, I received an invitation to deliver a series of retreats for high school youngsters in the Polish refugee settlement camp of Koja, situated on the shores of Lake Victoria. The parish priest was my oft-mentioned companion of the Soviet Gehenna, Rysiek Gruza. The road to Koja ran parallel to the equator. The journey took place in accordance with colonial custom and the place for the white man was next to the driver, while behind our backs a net was stretched out separating us from the local Maasai tribesmen. They rolled around like chickens in a small cage with their bundles and birds destined for the markets. At every opportunity the British would emphasise that the Africans belonged to a lower order of people. Thank God the passengers didn't know anything about this. They simply accepted the status quo; they assumed that the white man was an untouchable demi-god, to whom they owed respect. Only when they were conscripted into the army and were sent to the front with machine guns in their hands and an order to shoot at white folk, did an understanding of God's truth start to break through to the minds of the Africans! We are all members of one human family; brothers and sisters. The Africans on the bus instinctively behaved as God commanded: *If you don't become like children, you will not enter the heavenly Kingdom.* That is exactly how the passengers behaved – like children; therefore there was no end to the laughter, jokes and shouts of joy.

We made a wide arc around Mt Meru and then went straight ahead towards Nairobi. The scenery kept changing. In one place I was intrigued by a hill covered in what looked like white flowers. Nowhere else had I seen such a concentration of white wild flowers, so I couldn't take my eyes off the sight. As we got closer, to my utter amazement I realised that they were not flowers but birds. First I made out their tall red legs and beaks of the same colour and later still the black flight-feathers on their wings. The storks finally emerged complete as if from a finished jig-saw puzzle. I was filled with immense joy. Perhaps some of them were from Poland and had flown south for the winter; in any event they would all fly back to Eastern and Central Europe, and some even to my own country, from which I had been banished eight years previously. They would make their nests in tall trees, on telegraph poles or on chimneys. They would walk behind the ploughs of my compatriots picking out reptiles, frogs and small snakes. The storks were preparing to depart and were trying out their wings for flight; perhaps they were choosing a leader for their long journey of several thousand kilometres.

Nairobi

Closer to the Kenyan border the bus started to empty out. I had already become acquainted with Nairobi two years previously when I was on my way from Mombasa to take up my appointment in Tengeru in Tanganyika. It was at that time that Rysiek Gruza was sent to the refugee camp in Koja, Uganda. In Nairobi I was the guest of the head of the pastoral services for Poles in Africa, Monsignor Władysław Słapa, who hailed from the Polish mountains. He shared his house with

Seweryn Szczepanski, the representative of the Polish Government-in-exile for the education of Poles in Africa.

Situated at a high altitude, the town has a very pleasant climate - just like Zakopane in the Polish Tatra Mountains. It was easy to forget that it was positioned on the equator. Beyond the town spread the National Park, which is an animal reserve, where hunting is forbidden so that it is possible for tourists to observe elephants, giraffes, buffaloes, lions, and gazelles – and all from the windows of their cars. We didn't visit it however, because it was possible to see animals everywhere in the wild. Before continuing the journey to Uganda I delivered a retreat for the Poles who were working professionally in the capital.

In Nairobi I experienced an interesting celebration in honour of Our Lady of Fatima, whose statue had been brought over from Portugal. The evening procession with lighted candles, torches and lanterns forms one of my most treasured memories. All present, without distinction of tribal allegiance or nationality, took part in this manifestation of faith. All night long the rosary was recited with the singing of hymns in the Irish church and the faithful, many of whom were handicapped, moved past in front of Our Lady's statue. Many Muslims, who also regard Our Lady with much reverence, came to the celebrations. According to the Qur'an, the mother of Jesus Christ is the Immaculate Conception - the Holy Virgin. She is mentioned several times by name in the Qur'an. It is a mystery known only to God why the Blessed Virgin Mary appeared in a tiny, forsaken Portuguese village by the name of Fatima. Fatima was the favourite daughter of Mahomet, and yet the Qur'an gives precedence to Our Lady. What significance can we draw from this? The American Archbishop Fulton J Sheen used to say that there are no such things as co-incidences with God; everything that occurs, including the wrath of God, fulfils a specific purpose. And so it must be in this case.

A country of contrasts

I left with Monsignor Słapa for Uganda in his car. Ahead of us lay a journey of a thousand kilometres along the equator. The road kept climbing upwards along the eastern escarpment to a height of three thousand metres above sea level. Between the eastern and western escarpment runs the Great Rift Valley, which in prehistoric times was covered with water; today only the great lakes remain as witnesses. Most of the lakes have salty water except Lake Naivasha and Lake Victoria, both of which are fresh water lakes.

The sight of myriads of flamingos on Lake Naivasha was a novel and pleasant surprise for me. From afar the lake looked as if it was covered in red flowers, but it was only the stately flamingos with their turned up beaks, standing on their long legs in shallow waters. At the sound of the car's engine the birds took flight but they soon returned to the lake. Apparently
hippopotami and pelicans also live in the lake, but I did not see any.

Baboons

One day our path was blocked by a family of baboons. They are the largest exemplar of the monkey species. It would appear that they prefer to walk along the ground rather than in the trees. They have characteristically long up-turned tails, which run in an arc along their backs. Baboons are exceptionally ugly animals; they have a dog-like snout adorned with violet spots and a large, hairless, crimson behind. We had the impression that they were constantly quarrelling with each other and always ready to fight. I was told once about some nasty people who shaved a baboon and having painted it blue all over returned it to the wild; but the herd would not accept it and with one accord drove it into the bush, where no doubt it fell prey to a leopard. I am reminded by this story that in our own human family we often discriminate against our neighbours on the basis of their race, nationality, faith or political persuasion. What a great source of goodness lies in our religion, which teaches us that we are all members of God's family, all brothers and sisters – and that God is our Father.

Kisumu

We reached the little town of Kisumu, situated on the shores of Lake Victoria, towards the evening. We took up our lodgings in a hotel, where the lower parts of the walls in the rooms were fitted only with netting to create a breeze. Meanwhile the British were gathering at this hotel from all the neighbouring plantations in order to spend the weekend with their fellow kinsmen. The stifling and humid air prevented us from falling asleep, even though we desperately needed sleep to restore our energies for the last leg of the journey to Koja, also located along the shores of Lake Victoria. But it was impossible to sleep, so we decided to go out into the town. The raucous shouts of the English reached us all the way from the hotel restaurant. The town was enveloped in darkness but the bright rays of the moon illuminated the path. We made our way towards the shore, but there was just as much humidity there as in the hotel. After a while we noticed that from the lake huge, shiny, grey-violet bodies were starting to emerge and were heading towards us. We presumed they must be hippopotami who had also found it too uncomfortable in the warm water. Perhaps they were coming onto the land out of sheer curiosity – who can know what an animal is thinking?

Not being sure what the result might have been from an encounter with hippopotami, we decided to return to the hotel, throwing ourselves back onto our beds. But sleep continued to elude us. To make matters worse singing, music, shouting and the stamping of feet were still to be heard emanating from the centre of the hotel. Monsignor Słapa wanted to find out when the night-time revelries were likely to finish, so he put on his dressing-gown and went on a reconnaissance. He returned two hours later! The merry-making English noticed him hiding behind the coal-bins and dragged him into the party. They had no idea who he was; it was enough for them to know that he was a European and spoke English. The desire to communicate with people of the same race and civilisation can act as a very strong magnet. None of us is an isolated island.

On the shores of Lake Victoria

The next day we went round the northern shores of Lake Victoria, the second largest lake in the world. After we passed the small town of Jinja we increasingly came across flood-waters and wetlands covered in lush grasses from which emerged clumps of papyri. We passed the bridge over the River Nile, which according to some scientists flows out of Lake Victoria, but according to others its source lies somewhere back in the

165

marshy hinterland. As far as its length is concerned the Nile can rival the Amazon River; the ancient scribes used to call it the Father of Rivers. It is of course due to the River Nile that the Sahara Desert owes its splendid civilisation and the culture of the Pharaohs.

The refugee settlement camp in Koja, situated on one of the bays of the lake, consisted of domestic barracks, warehouses and a covered open-air chapel with a picture of Our Lady of Ostrobrama, confirming that most of the inhabitants had come from Wilno (now Vilnius, capital of Lithuania). It was from this altar that I would later deliver the retreat. The area was spoilt however by the sheer number of tall termite hills. Termites turn fertile soil into sandy desert and their vast underground kingdoms petrify into stone. Father Rysiek Gruza took us around this lunar landscape.

The cemetery, as in every other camp, was silent witness to how many Siberian exiles had fallen by the wayside on the journey back to their homeland. Our eyes were drawn however to an aesthetically pleasing monument smothered in flowers, erected for the seventeen-year-old boy scout Jerzy Międzyrzecki. As I have already mentioned, Jerzy had a heart attack while participating in scouting activities during the International Jamboree.

In spite of the altitude (Lake Victoria is 1,134 metres above sea level), the terrain was malarious. In some places the tsetse flies put the population in danger of contracting sleeping sickness. Hippopotami and crocodiles also live in the lake and the water is polluted with the micro-organism *bilharzia*, which enters the blood circulation and upon reaching the heart can cause its destruction. Father Rysiek contracted the disease which weakened him towards the end of his life, in spite of the change of climate. The danger of acquiring this disease was so high that it was forbidden to swim in the lake. This ban was particularly hard on the youngsters. Two youths once decided to risk it and started to swim to the opposite shore of the bay. The women washing clothes by the shore became paralysed with fear when they saw a crocodile heading after them. They started to shout at the boys. The boys separated, but the crocodile caught hold of one of them, fifteen year old Roman Śliwa.

The crocodile momentarily dived back into the water, but only so that it could come up again, mouth wide-open, in order to cut the boy in half. He was never seen again. They tried to retrieve what they could of the body (if only to give it a decent Christian burial) but the men in the rescue boat quickly got out of the crocodile's way when the irritated reptile angrily swiped his tail in their direction. The women said that it must have been an old blind crocodile, which would come out of the water to hunt for geese or chickens. This time it ate a boy.

Immediately after the retreat we made the return journey to our bases in Kenya and Tanganyika. The rainy season was approaching and this could make our driving difficult. The rainfall is so heavy and so frequent at that time that dry riverbeds turn into raging torrents which cannot be crossed in a car.

Africa awakens from slumber

At the beginning of 1949 I began to notice signs that colonial Africa was awakening from its slavery-induced lethargy. The first unrest among the locals which attracted my attention occurred while I was taking a group of children from the Association of the Eucharistic Crusade for a trip to the jungle at the foothills of Mt Meru. I was responsible for this outing. About seventy children moved in crocodile formation through thick undergrowth, past banana groves and coffee plantations. They behaved as if they were in church, because nature has a way of bringing us closer to God and in return evokes a response of silent admiration, peace and an indescribable sense of nostalgia. All of a sudden there appeared from the banana grove a group of Africans with wild looks in their hazy eyes – probably as a result of drinking banana moonshine. Angrily, they looked at us with menace. Some of them were carrying machetes. They fixed their eyes on us as if looking for some sign of provocation. This hitherto unfamiliar behaviour on the part of the Africans intrigued some of the boys. They stopped in their tracks trying to scrutinise their faces, unaware of any danger. Seeing menace in the faces of the natives filled me with fear for the safety of the children. Calmly, so as not to raise any suspicions among the Africans, I ordered the children to keep moving and not to slacken their pace.

Later I had another experience. It was at a scouting camp in the woods. A young African asked me for some cigarettes. Since I didn't smoke I didn't have any. He reacted with anger, so I showed him my empty pockets. Then the accusations started to fly: "What are you doing here? This is not your land. Get out of our country. You don't do any work but you have everything you need". Maybe he would even have done me some harm but I had a German shepherd dog at my feet guarding me.

Yet another incident took place at the Polish refugee settlement of Koja. One evening, on the hill in front of the camp a crowd of Africans gathered – men, women and children. They were demanding that the warehouses be opened up. The camp guards informed the British – since Uganda at that time was under their protection. The British sent out a platoon of armed Africans belonging to another tribe antagonistic towards them. The officer ordered the crowd to disperse but nobody listened to him. He repeated the order three times. He then gave the command to send out a volley of shots. Several people were killed. The Africans took the bodies away closer to their village, where they made a bonfire. Right through the night, in a macabre parade, they carried the bodies of the victims of the incident high in the air, whilst dancing and singing.

Little by little, the attitude of the Africans started to change towards the Europeans. A major reason for this was the conscription of the Africans into the army. Apparently, Communist agents were also agitating amongst them. I don't know how much truth there is in it, but apparently in the Sudan or possibly in Abyssinia (now Ethiopia) Soviet Communists were said to have opened a hospital where they treated the local population free, while conducting indoctrination among them.

After the Second World War, one by one, the African nations gained their independence. But *o tempora, o mores* (alas for the times and the manners) at the same time as Black Africa was awakening from its lethargy, the nations who had brought shame on themselves through the slave trade (Great Britain and the United States of America) now gathered in Yalta and Potsdam to betray my homeland Poland, a country with a thousand-year Christian culture.

The settlement theatre was very popular. Various celebrations would take place there (like the annual harvest festival), anniversaries and commemorations such as 3 May (Constitution Day), 11 November (Independence Day) and 6 December (Saint Nicholas's Day), and concerts given by the pupils of the music school. The most popular events were plays organised by Mrs Grosicka, in which over eighty children would take part – most of them orphans. They put on *The Legend of the Flowering Fern*, *The Awakening of Spring*, *Krakowians and Mountaineers*, *Mid-summer Night*, *King of the Baltic* and *Cinderella*. American films were also shown in the theatre.

Tenguru settlement theatre, 1947

The orphanage

It only remains now to mention the orphanage, which was the creation of Mrs Eugenia Grosicka, who had had experience in directing children's homes from pre-war Poland. The orphanage, which was referred to as The Institution, was not separated from the rest of the settlement camp and the children could meet with their friends whose mothers were present. They would go to school with their friends, to scouting meetings and to church. Even though they spent most of their time outdoors, they enjoyed short breaks for a change in scenery at the farm of Mr Albowicz not far from Arusha. Approximately three hundred orphans had no surviving relatives in Poland or in England, and of these, two hundred children were below the age of seventeen. They came from various social spheres; they were the children of farmers, artisans, civil servants, officers and landed gentry. They were brought up as Catholics in a spirit of patriotism. They were trained in various professional skills, such as tailoring, hand-crafts, decorating, knitting, book-binding, agriculture, home economics, cooking and baking.

The Institution had an orchestra and a choir. On their own initiative they built a theatre, a playing field, a community centre and much else. The greatest treasures of the establishment were the sewing machines, musical instruments and regional costumes from all the provinces of Poland. They had one hundred and sixty complete sets of costumes, not to mention about sixty complete fancy-dress outfits.

Children from the orphanage, Tengeru 1947

The Institution was the apple of the eye of the whole settlement community. These were special orphans. The inhabitants of Tengeru, all of whom were survivors of Siberian exile, perceived the orphans as children of national heroes who had suffered for Poland. These children were touched by the cruelty of war and became victims of what today is referred to as ethnic cleansing. After all they were persecuted solely because they were Polish. Even today when I talk with the orphans they are quick to emphasise that despite the beauty of Africa and the attempt to give them back some semblance of a lost childhood, the absence of their parents was then – and still is today – the source of their greatest sorrow.

With time, as some of the orphans grew up and left the orphanage in Tengeru, orphans from other settlements were brought over, among them children from the camp in Rongai, Kenya where the Polish sisters of the Holy Family of Nazareth ran a children's home. Some of these sisters later ran a boarding school in the little village of Pitsford, Northamptonshire in England, for daughters of demobilised Polish soldiers from the army of General Anders. Children from Jamnagar and Valivade in India also joined the orphanage, as a result of the policy to remove all foreigners after the assassination of Mahatma Ghandi.

On the steps of the Sanatorium, Tengeru, 1948

I liked to drop in on the orphanage. I knew many of the children from religious education classes. Most often I would visit them on a Sunday afternoon, spending time talking to them, playing volley-ball or draughts and singing with them. I also went on trips with them. It was with these orphans that I was to be so intensely united by Divine Providence in the near future.

Part VI

Europe

Dismantling the refugee camps

By 1949 a considerable amount of time had passed since the end of the Second World War. Moreover the IRO (International Refugee Organisation) had been intending to wind up the Polish refugee settlement camps in Africa for a long time after the turmoil of war had ceased. This plan was also acceptable to the British colonial authorities; but the wandering-refugee inhabitants of the camps were filled with apprehension at this prospect. Return to their country had been barred; Poland was now under the influence of her centuries-old enemy Russia, this time under the guise of Communism. It was that same enemy who had thrown them out of their country, sent them to Siberia, condemned them to adversities and finally confirmed their fate with the betrayal of the allies in Teheran and Yalta. The hope of returning home after many years of wandering burst like soap bubbles. They felt as if someone had pulled the rug from under their feet. What were they to do? Where were they to go? Which country would accept them?

The regime that had been imposed by Stalin kept appealing for people to return. It boasted about its initiative to rebuild Warsaw. But the exiles knew that the capital and other towns and villages would be rebuilt at great cost and sacrifice to ordinary people. They remembered that when Warsaw was in its death throes during the 1944 Uprising the Red Army had halted its progress westward at the orders of Stalin. Even the Polish soldiers from the Kościuszko Division, which consisted of ex-Siberian refugees, were not allowed to help their fighting compatriots and give them some effective aid. The blood-thirsty tyrant looked on with pleasure from the Kremlin as the Germans burnt and bombed Warsaw; this is why now in 1949 none of the wandering-exiles believed the Communist propaganda.

But nonetheless we had to leave Africa. At first the British authorities and the IRO planned to leave the orphans in Tengeru, but their education and upkeep would have been too expensive. Then there was the idea of transferring the orphanage to Europe, where apparently there were well-equipped camps already set up and which could accept the children. Finally, it was decided to start the liquidation of the Tengeru settlement camp by moving the orphanage, that is, by separating the children from their only social support network which was the community of the camp. Additionally, it was considered to be a deliberate policy to remove the children from the supervision and care of the Welfare Committee which had formed in Tengeru in 1945, when the legal rights of the Polish Government-in-exile had been withdrawn by the American and British Governments.

Meanwhile the Welfare Committee in Tengeru, aware that the primary aim of the IRO was to repatriate war victims to the countries of their origin or to resettle them in other countries, was trying to find a solution for the children. It started preparations for a group exit to Great Britain or Argentina, at the same time protesting at the idea of sending the children back to continental Europe. This position of the IRO was upheld by a meeting of all the inhabitants of the refugee settlement. The ex-Siberian exiles feared a Communist trap. They were well aware that Communists had infiltrated the IRO and later UNHRA (United Nations Humanitarian Relief Agency). It was possible that these agents could then direct the children to countries under Communist rule in Eastern and Central Europe. Psychologically the Polish orphans would have found it disastrous for their survival to fall in with the Soviet attempts at making them happy by force. Their experiences of Soviet "paradise" were permanently etched into their psyche. Forceful return to a Red Poland could have resulted in their experiencing the same fate as that of Greek orphans taken to the Soviet Union. After the war, as adults, they were accustomed to seeing Soviet citizens who were hiding in countries of Western Europe trying to evade forceful repatriation. The governments of Western Europe were not over-concerned with the tragic fate of these people who were hunted down, or with their protests which in some extreme cases took the form of suicide. In the particular case of the Polish orphans the Kremlin was afraid that should they remain outside Poland they could act as a permanent reminder to the free world of the true nature of Communism.

The Welfare Committee of the orphanage in Tengeru was working on a plan to send the children to a free country in the West that would secure political asylum for them. There was talk of the USA, Canada, Great Britain and Ireland. But the governments of these countries refused admission to the orphans, some because they feared that the financial burden would be too great and others who were afraid of provoking the disapproval of Stalin, their great war-time ally. How quickly the politicians forgot that Stalin had previously been the friendly ally of Hitler. The USA had indicated to another orphanage that rather than come to its territory it should go to Santa Rosa in Mexico; but at least they helped the children to live there until they eventually settled in the USA.

Even though the Polish Embassy in Rome, which was accredited to the Holy See, was no longer officially recognised, it still had some possibilities of manoeuvre. The ambassador Dr Kazimierz Papée turned for help for the children to Pope Pius XII. As far back as 31 March 1947 he had sent a memorandum to the Vatican informing the Holy Father about the fate of the children, bringing to his attention the possibility of real danger should they be repatriated. The highest authorities in the Vatican took a concerned interest in the affair and started to undertake measures to include the Polish children with a group of European orphans who were under the protection of the Canadian Episcopate and were due to settle in Canada. The *spiritus movens* of this activity was the then Secretary of State, Giovanni Battista Montini, later Pope Paul VI. While the fate of the Tengeru orphans was being decided, Monsignor Montini requested the Canadian Bishops who were in Rome for their *ad limina* visit to accept the Polish children.

Agreement to accept the children came from a man with a huge heart – the Archbishop of Montreal, His Excellency Joseph Charbonneau. The inhabitants of the settlement camp saw in this gesture the hand of God, and even more vigorously protested against sending the children back to Europe, that is, to Communist Poland.

But the IRO doggedly stuck to its plan (perhaps under the influence of Soviet agents) to send the children back to Europe, where they said they had special people ready to deal with the case. The first point of refuge was to be Italy. The authorities of the IRO probably wanted to free themselves from the Tengeru Welfare Committee and pressures from the refugee settlement camp community. The Central authorities of the IRO in Geneva threatened to cut off all financial aid to the camp if the Poles continued with their refusal to send the children to Italy and to the care of the Polish Communist officials.

Japanese mission

In the face of the imminent winding up of the African refugee settlement camps a calling arose in me to undertake missionary work. When Saint Maksymilian Kolbe opened his Junior Missionary Seminary in Niepokalanów, he set himself the goal of preparing missionaries, setting an example himself by leaving for Nagasaki in Japan. I was an alumni of that Junior Missionary Seminary. I therefore arranged with the Father General of the Conventual Franciscans, Bede Hess, that he should send me an *obediencia* from Rome, to enable me to leave for the missions in Japan. It was my dream to be sent to the missions; but it transpired that my dreams were never to be fulfilled.

Each day brought us new information. The most promising was the advice from the Vatican that the Canadian Episcopate was trying to get permission from the Canadian government for all medical checks and signing of visas to be conducted in Tengeru itself through the Canadian consul. This proposition seemed to us to be the simplest and most rational. A direct journey from Africa to Canada would entail less cost and avoid any possibility of a Communist trap should the children be in Europe; so overall it was an ideal solution. But the negotiations dragged on, delaying their finalisation. The IRO meanwhile maintained pressure for their project: that the children be returned to Europe.

Departure for Italy

Mr Milker, the director of The Welfare Committee in Tengeru wrote: "After seven years of living together we are parting company with the children. The children grew up and developed in front of our eyes. It is understandable therefore that the whole of the Polish community here is full of anxiety and worry concerning their future." Meanwhile the camp in Tengeru was in turmoil and tensions were growing from day to day, from hour to hour. It became so bad that two of the older boys – half-orphans

– ran away to the jungle to avoid deportation, because their families had demanded their return to Poland. The youths took with them blankets, matches, a lamp and food. The camp community was gripped by hysteria. How would they cope without fire-arms? Where would they sleep? Who would be responsible if wild animals tore them apart? These and other thoughts dominated the minds of the settlers. The Welfare Committee interceded for the boys with Mr Lorriman from the IRO, to whom they voiced their grievances. The frightened administrator revoked his deportation order and the boys returned safely from the jungle. A semblance of peace returned to the camp. News also reached the camp that a Welfare Committee was being set up in Rome with responsibilities for children in Italy. The committee consisted of Count Emeryk Hutten-Czapski, Editor Witold Korab-Laskowski and Monsignor Walerian Meysztowicz.

A new problem now arose for the Welfare Committee in Tengeru; who would accompany Mrs Eugenia Grosicka on her journey to Europe? After all, she could not manage completely on her own. Several senior people were approached but each one declined, either fearing trouble from the Communists or considering that the fight with them was all but over.

Meanwhile in spite of the dark clouds hovering over them the wandering refugee children managed to distance themselves from these nagging questions, trusting in the loving concern of their adult carers. In their own childlike way they prepared to say goodbye to the Dark Continent which had penetrated so deeply into their memories and hearts. Their image of Africa consisted not only of the jungle, dense foliage, the forest animals, the clear skies above their heads, the two twin mountains of Kilimanjaro and Meru, and the crystal clear waters of Lake Duluti; but also of school desks and classrooms covered in banana-leaf thatch where they learned by heart the historic facts needed by them for their return to Poland. They also remembered the little church with the picture of Our Lady of Ostrobrama – Protector of Eastern Poland – by then already incorporated into Communist Lithuania. The shrine of Our Lady of Ostrobrama in Wilno existed without a break throughout the Communist era and is now the national Marian shrine of the free and independent Lithuanian State. The hardest was to part from one's peers –

confidantes of youthful highs and lows. They also needed to visit the cemetery, where many an exile was buried – one's mother, or the mother of a friend. Photographs were taken with the little round beehive huts in the background, of exotic flowers, with one's peers and pet cats and dogs. Although the faces were smiling the hearts were breaking and eyes were misting over.

The fate of the children weighed heavily on my heart. I was their companion for recreation and for conversation; I taught them in school and took them on trips. My heart was torn apart with compassion. Of all the children these had been the most hurt by fate. They had lost everything: their country, family home, parents, school, parish church... Their future was bleak. And so it was that the last night before the children were due to leave I could not sleep. I tossed around all night in my indecision. In the morning, even though I did not feel I had the energy to confront an uncertain future, and in spite of all common sense, I decided to go with the children and to trust Divine Providence.

On the Indian Ocean

On 4 June 1949 we left the Kenyan port of Mombasa on an Italian ship *Gerusalemme*. We sailed north through the Indian Ocean. As I have previously mentioned, one of the traditions of the sea is the ceremony of "baptism" with the god Neptune and his nymphs when crossing the equator. The crew of the ship organised a hunt for pretty maidens who were to become victims of the colourful ritual. Mrs Grosicka organised the children in the performance of regional dances for our entertainment to the accompaniment of the ship's orchestra. Sailing along the Red Sea and passing down the Suez Canal was a pleasant experience for the children while I was reminded of Al Qantarah and my service in the General Military Hospital there. Our orphan-family was still fast asleep when we left Port Said and passed the huge statue of de Lesseps, the engineer-creator of the Suez Canal. We sailed on, sheltered from bracing winds by the mountains of Crete. The boys and girls visited the captain's bridge and looked at the navigational instruments and maps with keen interest.

On boat the *SS Gerusalemme* on the way to Bari, Italy 1949

While still in Tengeru, the camp authorities decided to send some of the less well behaved older boys and girls along with the orphans. It was the intention of the authorities that these adolescents, who had almost reached adulthood, should take advantage of the transport and settle in Canada. Apparently two other people unfamiliar to us – Mr Walczak and Mrs Szyszko – also had similar intentions, and sailed with us. The Welfare Committee suggested that they might even be of help to us. It was to prove the opposite. As we approached Italy they started to spread misinformation among our charges – stories that when we reached land they would take control of the orphanage as Mrs Grosicka was leaving for England and I was bound for Japan. We suspected that they were Communist agents and their presence among us alerted us to be especially vigilant.

On Sunday 19 June we made landfall in Italy. No sooner had the ship docked at Brindisi than guests came on board to welcome the children – the local Bishop the Reverend De Philippis, several priests including Father Tadeusz Milik from Rome, discoverer of and researcher on the

Qumran Dead Sea Scrolls, some religious sisters and ladies from Catholic Action. The Vatican had alerted the local bishop about our arrival. Father Milik, who was the same age as I was, wished to accompany us to Salerno. Members of the IRO also came to greet us. That same afternoon the *Gerusalemme* arrived at Bari. Dark rain clouds enveloped the town, creating in us a sombre mood. We transferred from the ship with all our baggage onto a shabby, slow-moving train. They squeezed all of us into three railway carriages. IRO officials – there were about fifteen of them – served us supper. The train tore across the Apennine Peninsula towards Salerno, which is situated twenty-five miles to the south-east of Naples. I managed to find some space for myself on the floor by the toilets; and I lay down on my coat. I did not sleep a wink during the whole journey. The night-time travel, the cramped space, the filth, the smoke, the clatter of wheels, the rushing in and out of tunnels and the pervasive darkness all conspired to create a feeling of unease. The youngest children were quietly snivelling.

The children's camp in Salerno

We arrived in the region of Salerno before noon on 20 June 1949. After the depressing night journey our mood started to lift at the sight of the pines, palm-trees, olive groves and vineyards running down the hillsides. Meanwhile the magical panorama of the Bay of Salerno with its picturesque small towns of Amalfi and Ravello, situated on the mountain-side, completely restored our good spirits. It is not surprising that the Etruscans, Greeks, Romans, Goths, Byzantines, Lombards and Normans all fought over it. Over the centuries its beauty has attracted troubadours, poets and artists; but in spite of this there was a feeling of sadness in our hearts for Africa.

We were quartered at the International Children's Camp, set up on the beaches, where during the Second World War the American Fifth Army led by General Mark W Clark landed under violent German shelling. One could still see, scattered around the mountain-sides, the sunken eye-sockets of abandoned German bunkers remaining from those days. From the Americans who had made a beachhead for themselves there remained barracks which the Poles referred to as barrels-of-fun. Indeed they had the shape of a barrel cut in half long-ways, constructed from thick corrugated steel sheeting. They were arranged in rows along the beach, the lapping waves of the Tyrrhenian Sea all around them.

The director of the camp – a Yugoslav, Mr Martynowicz – was very sympathetic towards us. We had no idea how long we would be in Salerno. As an introduction to continental Europe the first thing that was done was to enliven our appearance, especially that of the boys, and so their long trousers were exchanged for blue shorts and white shirts with a measure of elegance. We were issued with sporting and games equipment: bowling-pins, balls, bats for playing rounders and ping-pong rackets. We introduced some discipline and a timetable based on our experience of running scouting camps. Wake-up call was at 6am after which they had prayers and gymnastics. The children had lessons from 8am to 11am every day. The older high-school girls acted as teachers, taking lessons in geography, natural sciences, history, Polish and English language. I took on the function as the director of the "school". I celebrated Holy Mass every day, also teaching religious instruction, while Mrs Gosicka kept everything in order. The adolescents attended courses run by the camp: the boys took carpentry classes while the girls attended horticultural, agricultural, sewing and knitting classes. The teachers were people hired by the IRO.

There was time set aside for swimming, sun-bathing, games and sport, a rest period after lunch and home-work. Two women, Mrs Łukasiewicz and Mrs Czarniacka helped Mrs Grosicka to keep order and discipline among the children.

In front of every barracks the children had planted flower borders, while the older children helped in the running of the camp in the canteen, kitchen, store-house and in the guard-room. They were paid token wages from which they could buy fruit for themselves. The close proximity of the beach and the sound of the sea made it difficult to maintain discipline and conduct lessons. The possibility of daily swimming sent the children into a state of euphoria. The azure skies, the wind from the sea and the sun were all alluring. It would have been wrong not to have taken advantage of these exceptional holidays, so games, sport and swimming took up a large part of the day.

After some time a commission came to us from Geneva, the headquarters of the IRO. At the head of the commission was a Belgian Catholic lady Yvonne De Young. The main purpose of the visit was to determine if there were among the orphans any children who still had parents or relatives in Poland and who wanted to return to them. The delegates were preparing defensive arguments against the anticipated eventual attacks from the Warsaw regime. The visitors put no pressure on the children, they simply wanted to find out for themselves the reason why they were refusing to return to their own country. The most commonly given reason was that the parts of Eastern Poland where they were born were no longer within Polish borders; those lands had been incorporated into the Soviet Union. They did not have a home to go back to. The delegates accepted this rationale. One felt that they themselves were not that impressed with the Communist regime and what was happening at the time in Poland.

The other occupants of the camp considered our group to be more privileged. Each one of them had to queue in line at the various offices not knowing which country would grant them asylum. The officials took note of us; besides they wanted to save themselves extra trouble. With our arrival new parasols appeared on the beach, in addition to a rowing boat and other facilities. Our presence in the camp generally changed the atmosphere for the better – the place became more cheerful. We were also constantly being photographed at every opportunity – in chapel, in the school, in work-shops and so on.

Not far from Salerno I visited a camp for adults who had also applied to go to other countries and among them there were 20,000 Poles. There was a depressing atmosphere of monotonous inertia. When time allowed we would go on sight-seeing trips. First we went to Salerno which was close by and later to Paestum, which in antiquity had been a Greek colony. The Greek settlers built a temple there to the sea god Poseidon and a temple to Hera, the columns of which can be admired to this day.

The orphans on a trip to visit Paestum, 1949

I managed to get away from Salerno to go to Rome for two days and to register myself with the secretariat of the General Offices of the Conventual Franciscan Order. During lunch the General of the Order – Father Bede Hess – introduced me to the secretariat explaining that they had thought that I had died in the Soviet Union, but that I had managed to escape, study theology with the Jesuits and be ordained to Holy Orders in Beirut.

On a bus in Rome I unexpectedly met Father Michał Zembrzuski from the Order of Pauline Fathers; he was on his way to the USA where he was to become famous later as a great Polish activist and creator of the American Częstochowa in Doylestown, Pennsylvania.

A fight for the children

The IRO in Geneva were planning to send the children to Canada direct from Naples by plane. The Canadian consular officials who were issuing the visas were on the spot in Salerno. But these plans were thwarted by the sudden arrival of Communists from the embassy in Rome. Our month-long blissful idyll in Salerno broke up instantly. We found out that the authorities of the Polish People's Republic had sent to both the IRO and the Italian government notes to the effect that they demanded the return of the children to them and forbade them to leave Italy without the express permission of the Warsaw government. The staff of the Communist embassy obtained permission from the IRO to gain entrance to the camp in order to conduct talks with the children. From then on the Communists started to plague us with their visits. The delegation was led by Dr Kołtonski, and consisted of his secretary Mrs Zglinska – who adopted lady-like airs – and Major Dobrowolski – uniformed, elegant and of nervous disposition. Major Dobrowolski – apparently that was not his real name – argued with great conviction that the children were the rightful property of Poland. We let them have free access to the children and we were not present at the meetings, in order to demonstrate as much as possible our goodwill.

The visitors played on the religious and patriotic feelings of the children, invited them to return to their country and to help with the rebuilding of a Poland that had been ruined by war. They also asked them for a list of the names and addresses of their relatives in Poland, supposedly to be able to send them children's prayer-books and rosaries. But the children, who were exceptionally mature for their age, managed to cope quite well with these wolves in sheep's clothing, who were pretending to be honest fellow-countrymen. The children remembered well the plunder of the Polish Eastern lands, the banishment of their families to Siberia, and the subsequent deaths of their nearest and dearest relatives from starvation, cold and disease.

After the departure of these officials, a certain Mr Pierre Chrysz, apparently a Frenchman, and a Mrs Babinska started to make an appearance around the camp. No one knew where they had come from, who they represented, what their purposes for being there were and who had given them permission to enter the camp. They were very pleasant and cordial, especially Mr Chrysz. He would swim with the children, played with them, joked with them and he tried to soften me up, stating that for such wandering refugees as these children the most natural thing would be for them to return to their native country. In the beginning Monsignor Meysztowicz and I thought that a Canadian woman Mrs Irene Page, a Catholic, who was with us at the time and who was sent by the IRO to be with the Polish orphans for the duration of their stay in Europe, also shared this view. But it soon turned out that we were mistaken. Mrs Page had had several years' experience of bringing relief to victims of war – rather unfortunately named at that time *displaced persons*. These people, with a few exceptions, refused to return to their native countries which had had Communist regimes foisted upon them. Mrs Page knew the reasons for their refusal. She had witnessed the tragic scenes of the forced repatriation of people from Eastern and Central Europe, in particular of Soviet soldiers. I remember her logical argument in defence of the children: the Warsaw government does not have the right to demand the return of these Polish orphans since the native land of their parents is no longer under their jurisdiction. The Eastern borders of Poland from whence the children came are now part of the Soviet Union because this territory was handed over to Stalin by Roosevelt and Churchill in Yalta.

The story of the Murawska sisters

As a result of talks with members of the Polish Communist embassy, two sisters – Czesia and Bronia Murawska – reported that they wished to return to their mother in Poland. The Communists had contact with their mother but it was not totally satisfactory since the mother Wiktoria Murawska was also a victim of Communism. In 1941 she had been deported from the Wilno region together with her three daughters and exiled to the Altai Republic in Siberia on the other side of the Ural Mountains. Bronia was five at the time and Czesia was twelve. The whole family worked in the forests. Their father was sentenced to ten years in prison.

After the so-called amnesty their mother did not have the opportunity to leave the Soviet Union with the Polish army so she left her younger daughters Czesia and Bronia at an orphanage in Bukhara when she heard that those children would be leaving the Soviet Union under the protection of the army of General Anders. Their mother was one of a sizeable group of women who, unable to leave the Soviet Union, put their offspring into orphanages in the hope that in a free world their children would be able to have a reasonable education and lead a normal life. The sacrifice of these Polish mothers is understandable only to those who have themselves experienced Soviet reality and the fate of deported exiles. With this sacrifice the mothers safeguarded the children from being brought up as Soviet citizens – without God or knowledge of their native country, culture or history. Czesia and Bronia made it to East

Africa and to the orphanage in Tengeru. Naturally, any contact with their mother was severed once they left the Soviet Union.

In 1947, after six years in exile, their mother and older sister returned to Poland from Siberia, not to the Wilno region from where they were deported but to ruined Warsaw. Mrs Murawska only found out about her lost daughters when the orphanage reached Salerno. Representatives of the Polish authorities put pressure on her to demand the return of her daughters to Poland. Their mother succumbed to this pressure. No doubt she thought that it was a perfectly natural reaction to want to be reunited with her children after so many years of separation and homesickness. The war was over, the African camps were in the process of being liquidated and any further world-wide wanderings of her children seemed pointless. As guardians of the children we perfectly understood the longing of the mother, so on 18 July 1949 we sent the two girls under the care of Mrs Page to an IRO transit camp in Cinecitta, near Rome. I knew that Mrs Page carried in her briefcase letters from mothers and fathers who had officially asked for their children to be returned, but who in post smuggled from Poland were asking their current carers not to send back the children in the present political climate.

After a week Mrs Page returned to Salerno with Czesia and Bronia, frightened and shaken by the events in Cinecitta. The Communist Major Dobrowolski, whom we had already met – and who appeared to be a military attaché but was in fact an intelligence agent – took advantage of the absence of the older sister to abduct the younger Bronia. He took her away from the camp to subject her to an interrogation in the Embassy in Rome. The disappearance of Bronia terrified Czesia, and when further searches for her produced no result she tearfully approached Mrs Page, who immediately alerted the police. After five hours the major returned Bronia to Cinecitta; but it's not clear if that was due to the alarm being raised or because he had finished his inquiries. Bronia who was thoroughly shaken recalled how he kept asking her "strange questions", for which she did not have the answers. Mrs Page was greatly perturbed by the abduction of the child. Had not both girls agreed to return to their mother in Poland and was not the Embassy already in possession of their travelling documents? After all, the IRO was doing everything in its power to placate the Warsaw regime.

Soon after that Major Dobrowolski tried to abduct Czesia for a hearing at the regime's embassy in Rome. She tried to resist saying that Mrs Page forbade her to go anywhere without her knowledge. Her refusal to go with him angered the officer. In a loud voice he declared that now no one had any rights to the girls – not the IRO, nor the Polish Government-in-exile in London, nor even the Italians. If she didn't leave with him she would have to bear the consequences. Frightened by the tone of his voice and the officer's behaviour, Czesia finally decided to go with him, but first informed a friend where she was going. In the Embassy she was asked many questions, the most memorable being along the lines of: Where were you in Africa? How many Polish people were in Africa and how many are there now? How many children were in the orphanage at the beginning and how many are there now in Salerno? Are there many children under the age of sixteen? Are they well behaved? What is their level of moral development? Do Mrs Grosicka and Father Królikowski speak good Polish? Are they discouraging the children from returning to Poland? During the interrogation the Embassy officials told Czesia not to be afraid and to tell them the entire truth and not to hold anything back from them. While she was answering they would communicate with each other visually and smile ironically, particularly when she praised the British for their kind treatment of the Poles in Africa. They tried to convince her that the children in the orphanage were intimidated and were being taken to Canada against their will. When Czesia returned from the hearing she decided not to return to Poland. She was afraid that her younger sister Bronia would be brought up as a Communist, and that she herself would be sent to Siberia again. Mrs Page empathised with her fears; but she didn't know what to do. The girls' documents remained in the communist Embassy in Rome. Did she have the right to return to Salerno without them? She took the risk, hoping that the director Mr Martynowicz would understand the situation and would accept the girls back. He did. He said that he also had once been pursued by the officials of Dictator Tito.

The Communist Warsaw daily – *Życie Warszawy* – put out its own propaganda version of the events, to the effect that "the girls confused their 'noble carers from London' and the IRO camp officials despite their vigilance, and made their way safely to the Embassy of the Polish People's Republic in Rome and in tears asked to be repatriated to Poland." Mrs Page was accused of kidnapping the girls. The officials never came back to Salerno, but that did not mean that they had given up trying to repatriate the children to Poland. We were informed of their machinations by the Welfare Committee in Rome.

Meanwhile, one night, Miss Dorothy Sullivan, an American from the Catholic Relief Services in New York, who had been involved in helping Catholic children who were war victims, visited Salerno with Monsignor Meysztowicz at the request of the Canadian Bishops. Her arrival had all the makings of a detective story. She parked her car in front of the camp gates in order not to raise the suspicions of the snooping Communists, while the Monsignor came into the camp and got me out of bed. After we left the camp he informed me that I was about to meet a remarkable woman. Miss Sullivan outlined to me the plan of the Welfare Committee in Rome. We were to fly direct to Canada from Naples changing in New York City. When she finished explaining the whole plan she raised up her hands and declared in a thunderous voice, "I will fight, so that the children do not fall into Communist hands." The realisation of these plans was another matter however; they stalled and finally collapsed because of the Canadians not wanting to accept ill and handicapped children and due to the constant sabotaging of the plans by the Warsaw regime.

Dark clouds on the horizon

The carefree stay of the orphans at the Bay of Salerno came to an abrupt end with the sudden and unsettling request by a representative of the IRO to meet Mrs Grosicka and myself for some important talks. We both turned up on the evening of 1 August 1949 at the hotel in Salerno. The children noticed our sudden departure and followed us out of the camp with their eyes full of apprehension and fear, as much for us as for the fate of the whole group. The official from the IRO explained what had happened. The government of the Polish People's Republic had sent the Italian government a formal request demanding that they hand over all Polish orphans on Italian soil. It justified this demand by saying that they only were the lawful guardians of the children and therefore they only should decide to whom they would delegate their care. The IRO officer intimated that the Italian government would like the orphanage to leave the country. In order to avoid an international incident it would be best if we were relocated from Italy to Germany – to the British-occupied zone. Our heads started to spin. Both of us had the same suspicions: that they wanted the children to be closer to the Polish border, and that the IRO was in league with the Communists. On the other hand maybe we should trust this official? We were both shattered. We desperately felt the need to share our fears with our friends, but those in Tengeru were too far away and those in Rome were not very accessible. We thought that the only reasonable solution would be to transfer the orphans to Vatican territory and to ask for asylum.

The children escape from Italy to Germany

Shortly after this meeting with the representatives of the IRO, our sense of Divine protection was restored when our Polish compatriot Count Emeryk Hutten-Czapski, representing the Welfare Committee in Rome, came to visit us in Salerno. He informed us that the idea of transferring the children to Germany was the only sensible solution to the problem. He repeated the same information to our charges in the camp theatre, answering their questions, and reassuring them that both Mrs Grosicka and Father Królikowski would stay with them at all times. This assurance was greeted with hearty applause from the children and both Mrs Grosicka and I started to cry like babies – no doubt releasing the built-up tensions of the last few fearful days. However, at 3 o'clock in the morning Count Hutten-Czapski came back to us with the information that the Welfare Committee was not absolutely convinced as to the safety of the children in Germany, and that the departure of the children from Italy could be a trap set up to ease the transfer of the children to Poland. In face of such a threat the committee would try and have the children accompanied by one of its delegates, who would be constantly on the alert so that no one undesirable would have access to the children. By this time the IRO had already issued its orders, so our escape plan had to be quickly executed.

We tried to disguise our departure from Salerno so as not to arouse the suspicions of the snoopers. A sense of solidarity among the children consolidated and grew. They packed their belongings at night, the boys helping the girls. Early morning, under the pretext of going on a sight-seeing trip we left in buses for Naples without Mr Walczak or Mrs Szyszko.

A sense of exhilaration went through us all, when on the station siding in Naples we caught sight of the IRO train being prepared to take us to Germany. The driver was leaning out of the window of the steam-engine and the railway men were still working around the carriages. In the windows, members of the first-aid team could be seen moving along the train and there was definitely a physician and a cook. We occupied the compartments and the train pulled away from the station. The train wove its way along the Apennine Peninsula passing towns and villages, rushing into tunnels and equally suddenly exiting them and meandering through valleys. During this long journey the train stopped only once in Italy, in the Eternal City, in order to pick up the delegate from the Welfare Committee, Monsignor Walerian Meysztowicz. He was escorted by the ambassador to the Vatican, Dr Kazimierz Papée, Count Hutten-Czapski – whom we had already met – and a group of Poles whose presence contributed to our feeling of being supported. Two ladies whom we knew well – Dorothy Sullivan and Irene Page – boarded the train. We scrutinised Monsignor Meysztowicz, a tall man with military bearing wearing a monocle. I found out later that before he had entered the seminary he had been a captain in the cavalry. His brothers-in-arms, not convinced that he had a vocation, tried to abduct him from the seminary. We referred to him as "the Vatican delegate". He well merited such a title when he demonstrated his diplomatic talents over the matter of our visas at the Brenner Pass, the same pass where once Mussolini had met up with Hitler in the earlier years of the war. The train stopped at that same border-station, which separates Italy from Austria. The Austrian officials demanded visas from us which of course none of us possessed. Moreover the documents of the two Murawska sisters had been left behind in the Communist Polish Embassy in Rome. At least two hours were spent on discussions but because new administrations were only just being created in the whole of post-war Europe and there was no universal set of regulations we were allowed through. From the windows of the carriages we were absorbed by the mountain scenery. After we crossed the border the Italian government could, in all truth, say to Warsaw that there were no more Polish children on its territory.

The train stopped once more – in Innsbruck – among the snow-capped summits of the Alps and then without any more ado headed towards Bremen. In Germany, the results of warfare were evident everywhere. Our escape route was to take three more days. At the railway station in Bremen, to our utter amazement and horror we were greeted by the familiar agents – Pierre Chrysz and Mrs Babinska – who asked about Mr Walczak and Mrs Szyszko. When the orphans replied that they were not with us, they exclaimed that that was impossible!

The town of Bremen had undergone complete destruction as a result of blanket bombing by the allied forces. It was impossible to tell where the streets had once been. We were placed in the Tirpitz Camp, which consisted of a post-Hitler barracks serving as a transit camp for young people of various nationalities who had been brought to Germany during the war as labourers. The director of the camp was of Swedish descent. Among the residents of the camp there circulated a handsome, energetic and meddlesome Russian Orthodox priest in a cassock; he was most certainly a NKVD officer as I had not seen a single priest in all my time in the Soviet Union and certainly not a young one in a cassock! The guards in the camp were Polish.

A diplomatic row

At the same time a storm of protests was unleashed in Poland about the "abduction" of the Polish children from Salerno. The Communist regime lodged a protest with the United Nations in New York. The pro-regime daily newspaper *Życie Warszawy* called Mrs Grosicka and me "kidnappers on an international scale", "modern slave-traders" and "representatives of the London Polish Government-in-exile". According to the expectations of the Communist author, the children arriving in Canada would face the prospect of "brilliant careers as white illegal workers and cheap slave labour for some of the more virtuous Canadian entrepreneurs".

Życie Warszawy mainly blamed the United States, among other things stating that "repeatedly, representatives from Poland, USSR and other truly democratic countries have unmasked the reactionary character of the mainly American-led international agency for the help of refugees (UNHRA), whose true intention is to prevent refugees from returning to their native countries and supplying capitalist countries with cheap labour. But this latest move by the IRO – the kidnapping of 150 Polish children – is something monstrous." Neither was the Italian government spared. "In executing this terrible act of lawlessness, the IRO was helped by the Italian government, presumably prevented from keeping internationally-binding agreements on its own territory."

In many factories around Poland, workers were marshalled – predominantly women – to attend protest rallies, at which resolutions were passed calling for the speedy return of the children to their homeland. Even my own family in Poland acutely felt the effects of this hostile atmosphere towards my person. Some relatives, believing the propaganda about me, cut out newspaper articles and comments and sent them to my mother with the comment, "Look what your son is up to while away from his country".

Manipulation of the people

While all this was happening, Monsignor Meysztowicz and Miss Sullivan were bombarding Archbishop Charbonneau in Montreal with telegrams begging him to arrange visas for all our charges. The IRO meanwhile was trying to segregate those orphans who were over the age of sixteen from the younger ones. This was done in order to give them the status of displaced persons (DPs), which would have meant that each one of them would have had to obtain individual permission to leave for a new country of domicile, without any protection from us. This status would have condemned them to many months of wandering around transit camps and standing for hours in queues. The medical commission of Western countries selected the most fit and healthy people. Even I experienced these "horse-like" inspections, having to stand naked in front of them, perform knee-bends, lift up my arms and bend over. It even occurred to me that maybe the Communist regime was right when it claimed in its accusations that the Canadians were trading in living cargo.

A great blow for us was the threat that visas could be withheld from those orphans who suffered a handicap or had a chronic ailment: a deaf boy, a girl with a palsied hand and two boys with learning disabilities.

In view of the plan for Mrs Grosicka to be reunited with her son in England, the Communist agents used every means possible to separate me from the rest of the group. One of these plans was to transfer the orphans to Bad Aibling in Bavaria to a children's camp, which had its own managerial staff and carers.

The orphans in Bremen. 1949

Armed with Canadian visas

The children received their Canadian visas in Bremen ten days before our planned departure, but I was refused a visa on the pretext that they had "discovered" scars on my lungs, which could mean that I had tuberculosis. There was even talk about a period of quarantine. The scars were the remnants of the untreated pneumonia which I had while in the Soviet labour camp, and which I have already written about. But undergoing a period of quarantine would have removed me from the group, in which case directorship of the orphanage would be taken over by Mrs Szyszko and Mr Walczak, or someone else, who could then declare that the Canadian visas had no validity since these were Polish children and the new carers could demand that the children be returned to their native country.

Only a few days were left until the date of our departure to Canada. We informed Archbishop Charbonneau about the threat that I might be separated from the children. The archbishop decided to accept me into

Canada despite my present state of health. A visa was sent from Ottawa to the Canadian consul Phil Bird who was working in the Fallingbostel transit camp. I had to go to Fallingbostel and back in the one day to collect my visa. I took with me one of the youngsters, Ludwik Burk. Needless to say we had problems and difficulties because of the kilometre-long queues in front of every office. Around three in the afternoon our driver, a German, informed us that he had to go back to Tirpitz Camp and return the car; which he proceeded to do. I continued waiting in line. The consul signed my visa after normal working hours. We had to get back to Bremen by train, but the local railway station was closed at night and the next train for Bremen did not leave until the following morning. We had nowhere to go for the overnight stay. The night was cool and we had only light clothing. From afar we could hear the cheerful music of a brass band and men singing. There was a glimmer of hope that somewhere in the nearby hall a space could be found for us to rest till the morning. But we gave up that idea when we saw revellers leaving the hall with tankards of beer in their hands. Their singing betrayed the extent of their tipsiness and I was uncertain how they might have reacted to us on finding out that we were Polish. We returned to the little station, jumped over the fence and made ourselves comfortable in one of the carriages standing on a siding. We were awoken from our sleep by the hammering of the railway men preparing the train for departure. We were overjoyed when we found out that the train was about to leave for Bremen as we had already bought our tickets the previous day.

On return to the Tirpitz Camp the orphans keenly scrutinised my face to read from it whether or not the trip had been a success and whether I had a visa. How many times in their lives had these poor creatures experienced fear? I confirmed that I *had* a visa and I *could* travel with them.

However I received a telegram from the IRO ordering Mrs Grosicka to be sent immediately to England and that three individuals hitherto unknown to us would travel with the children to Canada. Mrs Grosicka immediately smelt a rat. She refused to leave the Tirpitz Camp. The mystery was shortly to be partially resolved when we left for Bremerhaven to board the American transport ship *General Stuart*

Heintzelman which had been chartered by the IRO. It was sailing for New York and on the way was to drop our group off at Halifax. The day was gloomy and the skies were covered in dark clouds. The ship was literally bursting at the seams due to the number of refugees emigrating to Canada. There were a hundred and thirty of our orphans not counting nineteen of our group who had been held back either because of a disability or because of suspected tuberculosis. They all stayed under the protection of Monsignor Meysztowicz and were later to join the rest of the group in Canada.

After we boarded the ship, stowed our baggage and settled ourselves in the cabins we went up on deck. We crowded round the port side of the ship attempting to keep visual contact with the group of friends ashore who had fought for our departure from Italy to Germany and for our Canadian visas. Among them were Miss Sullivan and Mrs Page, Monsignor Meysztowicz, Ellen Egan – a well- known American journalist from Agency Press – a few Polish chaplains serving as pastors to refugees and Mrs Grosicka, whose heart must have been torn to shreds. A significant way behind them, also on the quay, stood a second group of people. It was those Communist sympathisers who were attempting to disrupt our departure.

Mrs Grosicka and her adopted daughter, 1952

The joy of at last achieving our goal was mitigated for us when for a lengthy period and without any obvious reason the ship failed to weigh anchor. It remained in port for ages and suspense heightened with each passing moment. We asked our friends standing on the quay what was the reason for the delay in the sailing of the ship. They didn't know. Their faces became morose. Meanwhile the expression on the faces of the Communists was becoming decidedly optimistic. They assumed a positive turn of events in their favour.

During those dead-weight moments of waiting, my heart ached with a sense of nostalgia for my country, my homeland. As the crow flies we were only about two hundred kilometres from her borders. Although I felt this longing in myself it was also on behalf of the Polish children, who unaware of the poignancy of the moment were more absorbed at that time with thoughts about going to Canada. Would they be happy there? How would they be received? How would their lives evolve under new conditions in the midst of a different culture? What challenges would they have to overcome? Would their mental condition endure another bout of hardship? Maybe Mrs Page, herself a mother and led by maternal instincts, was right after all and the children would have fared better in Poland looked after by women? Apart from the issue of Communist indoctrination, the women, for better or worse, would have taken the place of their mothers. I countered this latter thought as being naive, knowing full well the cruelty of the Communist system with its need to rule the human heart.

Besides, we were not the only ones refusing to go back to our own country. Thousands of veterans from General Anders's Second Corps, for the most part ex

Siberian deportees, stood by us in solidarity as did a many-thousand strong civilian population who identified themselves as political refugees and who now were Polish emigrants. Nevertheless, everyone had the feeling that regardless of which country they would settle in, they would still be treated as second class citizens. We were also aware of our duty to bear witness to the true nature of the Communists, how they treat people who have different views from their own and who do not belong to the Party. Our witness in the West was crucial and extremely valuable since Marxist propaganda was attracting many sympathisers, mostly among the university elite, who subscribed to the power of human rationality. I suspect they thought that Communism would solve all problems and bring happiness to all humanity.

I was haunted with doubts about my own abilities. In a week I would be reaching the age of thirty. Was I practically prepared to undertake such a hazardous venture as the care of such a large group of children? I would miss the uplifting character of Mrs Grosicka, confidante of my woes, doubts and joys; someone with whom I could discuss the most difficult of problems. I would be alone from now on or with people of a different culture and history.

We waited for over an hour in the port. We were standing on the deck and our friends were still standing on the quay. As soon as we would begin moving the distance between us would only increase the feeling of separation. They say of the Jews that they are perpetual wanderers. Will history be saying the same thing about us: Poles – the perpetual wanderers?

Towards Canada

Eventually after a very long wait, the ship shuddered as the captain was given the orders to raise the anchor. We started on our journey towards Canada; we were not to be enslaved in Stalin's Poland, which resembled a concentration camp. We sang the national anthem *"Jeszcze Polska nie zginęła"*. The children's cheerful faces contrasted in their youthfulness with the faces of the adult passengers and refugees, who had been deported by the Germans for forced labour and who now, like us, had chosen freedom and were sailing westward. After we had pulled away from the quay, Monsignor Meysztowicz remained in Bremen for a longer period to sort out the departure of the remaining orphans. The children who had suspected tuberculosis left for the sanatorium Pro Juventute in Davos Platz, Switzerland. From Jadwiga Romer – the sister of the ex-ambassador to the Soviet Union Tadeusz Romer – we soon heard the news that none of the children had untreated tuberculosis. They only had traces of old calcifications on their lungs and so after a period of quarantine they would be sent to Canada and would join the rest of the group.

It was not until we reached Canada that we found out the reason for the delay of over an hour of the ship in Bremerhaven port. It turned out that the Communists had flown three of their agents to Bremen – Mrs Szyszko and Mr Walczak, whom we had left behind in Salerno, with a third accomplice who was completely unknown to us and remains so to this day. The airport in Bremen where they landed was in the British Zone, but constituted an American enclave. The commanding officer in

198

Bremen, an American, detained the civilians from Salerno, since he had received no intelligence in respect to their activities. He was not the slightest bit interested in their protestations that they were awaited in the port on board the ship *General Stuart Heintzelman* with the aim of taking over the management of the orphanage. They must have been convinced that I was undergoing quarantine and that the orphans were on board the ship alone without a carer. But Divine intervention had played a trick on them. The transport carrier with hundreds of emigrants on board could not wait in the port any longer and shipped anchor.

Compared to the peaceful, sunny journey on the Indian Ocean, the Atlantic crossing was stormy. We were tossed about terribly. All the adults were sick but none of the children. I rarely went down to the dining room. My wards tried to brighten up my life with offerings of sweet oranges. I had no major problems with my protégés, who managed to impress everyone with their good behaviour. But I had a real headache with the small group of seven-year-old "German" children who were put under my care for the duration of the sea voyage. They were designated for adoption in Canada. These were children of various nationalities who had been stolen from their families during the war and given to the families of high-ranking Nazi officers for upbringing. It was impossible to determine the place of their birth and personal details. They had beautiful blond hair and blue eyes, but angry and aggressive characters. For the slightest reprimand they would bite my hand or kick my ankles.

As a boy I was acquainted with Canada through reading the fascinating novels about the first American natives by the German writer Karol Maya. The author had never seen an 'American Indian' in his life and had never been to Canada but he knew how to excite youthful imagination. I also loved to read the magazine put out by the Oblate Fathers about their evangelisation of the Native Americans and Inuits. Now I was to discover for myself that immense, inviting and charming land, which stretches from the Atlantic to the Pacific, and which is larger in area than the USA. My interest in the history and inhabitants of that country was kindled.

On 7 September 1949, after a week at sea we reached the shores of Canada at the port of Halifax, the capital of Nova Scotia. That date is impressed upon the memory of the children for the rest of their lives, because it is also the date of my birthday. I was thirty years old. The French sisters from the congregation Du Bon Conseil (Sisters of Good Counsel) who came out to welcome us moved back a bit at the sight of such a young carer. They imagined that they would encounter an elderly Franciscan with a beard!

In the name of the Archbishop of Montreal, Father Joseph Charbonneau, we were welcomed by Father Jean Caron who had been delegated by him to look after the orphans and by Father Brosseau, a Jesuit, who in the course of his hospital duties was familiar with a range of European languages. The boys looked out of place in their new surroundings. Some of them still wore their wide-brimmed African hats and clothes that were out of fashion. Because of the language barrier the children carefully observed their hosts and the hosts observed the children. What really made an impression upon us were the words of greeting, "*Vous êtes des Neo-Canadiens*" (You are new Canadians).

In Halifax, Czesław Miłosz (1911-2004), the writer/poet and later Nobel laureate, who at that time was an official from the Polish Communist embassy in Washington, firmly demanded that the children should be sent back to Poland. Fortunately he had no influence on the matter.

In accordance with the plan we were to go from Halifax direct to Montreal by train; but on the way we were informed that in the metropolitan city railway station a reception committee of Communists had gathered with sweets and fruit, accompanied by a group of reporters anticipating a demonstration against the "hijacking" of Polish children to Canada. The local press had already written quite a lot about the accusations of the Warsaw regime, while we were still at sea.

In order not to risk unpleasantness for the children the train stopped some twenty miles from Montreal on the magnificent St Lawrence River at a place called Contrecoeur. Our group was put into two summer youth centres; the boys with the Sacré Coeur Brothers and the girls with the sisters of Bon Conseil. We were to wait there until the political storm calmed down.

"Alouette, gentille alouette!"

We felt at home in Contrecoeur – it was as if we were in the countryside. For a while we were assigned a second priest, Father Jacques Larame who was young and very cheerful and who amused the orphans playing on the piano and singing French songs. Everyone got to like the simple tuneful song about the lark – *Alouette, gentille alouette!* (Little lark, sweet little lark...) The song originated in France because on the American continent there are none of those little winged soloists. A few of the older boys could recall that back in Poland those little birds would add charm to their fathers' ploughing with their beautiful strong voices.

September in Canada is the time of the fruit harvest and so we were supplied with basket-loads of tasty red McIntosh apples, oranges, and bananas; we were also offered ice-cream. We were introduced for the first time to tasty Canadian maple syrup. In Canada there are an awful lot of maple trees and they constitute such a rich heritage that the maple leaf has become the national emblem.

In the meantime the ten orphans who had been left behind in Bremen rejoined us: Bolek Kacpur who was deaf and his siblings Maniuś and Stasia and seven other handicapped children. They had left Paris for the port of Le Havre where they sailed by ship to Halifax. They were received in Canada by multilingual Father Brosseau. Some time later Staszek Szwostek also became disabled due to a childhood disease affecting his retina and he started to go blind. He had two older brothers suffering from the same disease. In the turmoil of war one of them landed up in England and another in Australia. Later, when they had completely lost their sight they started to communicate among themselves with the help of tape-recorded messages.

We stayed in Contrecoeur for about two weeks. We organised picnics, short day-trips and boating outings, but often we just reminisced. Browsing through colourful French magazines the youngsters became acquainted with the French language for the first time in their lives, a language which for the majority of them was to become the language of their schooling. We were visited by some distinguished guests from the

Polish community in Montreal, and even some French families who were contemplating the possibility of adopting a Polish orphan. Perhaps I was a bit too cautious in welcoming these guests, who were after all my compatriots, but I was always on the look-out for Communist agents. I received a letter full of abuse from one Polish immigrant, because he claimed I had mistreated him by not trusting him. That is how he perceived it; but I was a person who had already been caught out once and now I was playing it safe.

Like a bolt from the blue

While we were in Contrecoeur, one of the girls laughingly patted Stefcia Kraus on the shoulder during a game of hide-and-seek, intending to eliminate her from the game. Whereupon Stefcia fell to the ground as if hit by lightning. Subsequent tests revealed in her shoulder the presence of a sarcoma, one of the worse types of cancer. The physicians predicted that Stefcia would barely live another three months. This was a huge blow not only for the whole orphanage but especially for her siblings, as she had taken the place of their mother Karolina ever since her death in Teheran. The discovery of cancer in a nineteen-year-old girl dismayed and surprised everyone especially as the group had undergone several medical examinations before their arrival in Canada. Evidently Divine Providence had preserved her to this point in time so that she could leave this world in peace knowing that her charges – two brothers and one sister – would now be able to experience normal living conditions. Stefcia could not come to terms with her diagnosis, so we did not immediately reveal to her the seriousness of her condition, deceiving ourselves that maybe there was some kind of mistake in the diagnosis or even that God would intervene in some miraculous way and cure her. Stefcia was bewildered that following the tests she was directed to a hospice where the majority of the patients were elderly. She noticed that from time to time one of the patients would quietly pass away and this depressed her. She would ask us, "What am I doing here?" It became increasingly difficult not to divulge to her the mortal danger in which she found herself. But she did not pay any attention to this threat to her life; she believed in her robust energy and still had dreams about her future. She had even met a boy and was hoping to marry him. Her inner being stubbornly defended itself against impending death. In order to distract her a little I took her to see the Niagara Falls, so that she could enjoy the splendour of nature. But the attractions and affairs of this world were becoming increasingly less attractive and interesting to her.

We arranged for her to stay at the Polish Centre of the Sisters of the Resurrection instead of at the hospice. There, she helped the sisters with the care of the children, and even for a short while she went to work in the town. Meanwhile, her brother Władek went to Ontario to help pick the tobacco crop, so that he could make some money to buy a car and be able to drive her around the countryside. I also took her to Toronto to attend the Clothing Ceremony of her younger friends who had entered the order of the Sisters of Saint Felix. She had her photograph taken there with the army chaplain of the Second Corps, Father Józef Gawlina. After her return to Montreal from Toronto, there was a day-to-day deterioration in her condition as the malignant cancer made ever greater inroads on her body. She was sent back to the hospital where she needed a lot of special care. She was installed under an oxygen tent. On 15 September at 3pm Stefcia lay close to death. Father Caron visited her with the French sisters of Bon Conseil. I came to her straight after my catechism lessons – but she had already died. Her soul departed to heaven in the presence of her sisters Józia and Stasia Kacpur on 15 September – the feast of Our Lady of Seven Sorrows – in the twenty-second year of her life. She died like Christ on the cross – from asphyxiation. To this day I am troubled by her death. As an orphan she wanted me to be present with her. Her last moments must have been very difficult; missing her mother and father, orphaned siblings, far from her native land, on the exiled-wanderers' trail, without even the possibility of communicating in a foreign language. And yet this could have been simply avoided by my presence, just holding her hand without speaking as a link between everyone and everything that was dear and precious to her.

The death of Stefcia, although anticipated, still came as a shock to the orphans. The girls considered her to be their best friend. They consulted her for advice and she was the confidante of their troubles and cares. Using her figure as a model they carried out their dress-making activities. When her body was laid out in the coffin a scandal almost broke out. Her girl friends declared that "that is not Stefcia", because the body appeared so different. I had to intervene; it turned out that the medical personnel, thinking that because she was an orphan far from her country of origin and with no one to claim her body, had removed from her corpse several body organs for medical research. The management of the hospital apologised but begged us not to inform the press about the incident as that might harm the reputation of the hospital.

There arose the problem of where she should be buried. The family of Father Dostaler came to the rescue. They had bought a plot for their seriously ill father in the well-kept cemetery of Côte des Neiges, situated on a hill almost in the centre of town. Fortunately, their father survived the critical illness and was now in good health again and the plot meanwhile was empty. That is where the body of Stefcia was laid to rest.

Part VII

Canada: Guardianship of the Orphans

Ville Marie

Montreal, a growing metropolis of over a million inhabitants, built in the European style on the large Île de Montréal – Island of Montreal – as the locals fondly refer to it was to become the centre of our life in Canada. In 1535 a Bretonese mariner-explorer – Jacques Cartier – arrived here, searching for the route to India. On the island he discovered an already-established Iroquoian Indian (First Nation) settlement of Hochelaga.

Entering the city we were impressed by the length and size of the iron bridge – named after Jacques Cartier – which spans the royal river of St Lawrence. The wide river gathers its waters from the American Great Lakes, slowly making its way towards the Atlantic Ocean.

We felt at home in Montreal since the Province of Quebec is a Catholic country. The first settlers gave it the name of *Ville Marie*: Mary's Town. Maksymilian Kolbe, who had such a great veneration of the Blessed Virgin Mary, would have been extremely happy on account of this name. The monasteries that he founded were named Niepokalanów in Poland after the Blessed Virgin Mary and Mary's Garden in Japan. Montreal is a city of many churches. The American writer Mark Twain once made the sarcastic remark that if you threw a stone in Montreal it was bound to hit the window of some church. The beautiful name of Ville Marie was changed in time to Mont Royal (Royal Hill). This is the name that Jacques Cartier had given to the elevation. The explorer and soldier Paul Chomeday de Maisonneuve (1612-1676) crowned the top of the hill with a wooden cross which dominated the city. Today, in its place there stands a metal cross.

Two centres

In the city of Montreal we opened two "hearths" (or centres) from which we sent the orphans to schools in the neighbouring towns and hamlets of the Province. In the beginning, for the girls, we took up the offer of hospitality extended to us by the French sisters of the Congregation of

Good Counsel (du Bon Conseil), located in the Notre Dame de Grace district, to the west of the city. After two years I handed over the care of the Polish girls to the Polish sisters of the Congregation of the Resurrection, who had arrived there from Europe and the USA. The sisters opened a hearth in the centre of the city on Ontario Street.

Initially, the boys took advantage of the French educational centre, Mont St Antoine, on the East side of the town, where Father Caron was the chaplain even before our arrival in Canada. When the number of our male students started to decrease, we opened the hearth Mont Thabor for the remainder of them; it was situated at the intersection of St Hubert and Sherbrooke Streets. In the meantime I took up residence in the Parish of the Holy Trinity run by the Conventual Franciscans based in the USA.

The orphans were allocated two more priest-guardians after their arrival in Canada, and therefore we split up our responsibilities. We elected Father Caron as the director, Father Dostaler as his assistant director and because of my knowledge of the Polish language and shared experiences with the orphans, I took over the function of spiritual director. But my fulfilment of this role was not as adequate as the need demanded because the children were scattered around in various schools over a very large area. My visits never fully satisfied their spiritual needs.

The orphaned girls with the Sisters of Bon Secours, Montreal, Canada 1949

Boarding schools

Archbishop Charbonneau expected that the majority of the orphans would be adopted. Prior to our arrival Canadian families had declared an interest in adopting the children even while we were still at sea. In reality the children were too old to be adopted. They had already experienced too much in their lives, and their adoptive parents may have found it difficult to communicate with them in a common language. For people in the West it was difficult to believe – even to imagine – what their childhood must have been like. Therefore we placed most of the children in boarding schools. The Catholic Church in Canada gave financial help to cover their medical costs, clothing and travel. In time, all these costs were taken over by the archdiocese of Montreal, which collected donations for this cause among its parishes. Meanwhile, the cost of supporting the children in the schools was taken on by various religious orders, who willingly took upon themselves this challenge. The older boys and girls who no longer really belonged to the orphanage but who took the opportunity to travel over to Canada with the group were offered help in becoming independent. They took on work on the farms and in factories, in handicraft workshops or as home-helps.

Arrival of orphans from Switzerland

On 23 May 1950 the nine of my charges who had been held over in quarantine in Davos, Switzerland at the Pro Juventute convalescent sanatorium arrived in Canada to the great joy of the rest of the orphanage-family. They were Władek Pieczko, Rysiek and Wanda Cyran, Kostek Janicki, Franciszka and Irek Przychodzen, Hela Kropa, Wala Dubiniewicz and Bronia Paluch. Kostek Janicki had extraordinary good luck; Miss Sullivan took him to Rome for an audience with Pope Pius XII, who bestowed his blessings on our entire group.

Adoptions: exceptions to the rule

In the few cases where adoption did take place I tried to make sure that the children were sent to Polish families. One family had chosen a particular boy, who was the same age as their own son, but we soon backed off from that proposition when the boy confided to me that "my step-mother loves her disobedient and good-for-nothing lazy son more than me, and I try so hard to earn their love; I am the one who does their shopping, washing-up and scrubbing their floors". That same youngster had the opportunity to be adopted twice more, once by a Polish woman and then by a wealthy Canadian furrier family. But adoption never took place. These people kept in contact with the boy almost to the end of their lives and regretted that they had not adopted him.

In the case of some of the girls we did not allow adoption to take place as the self-centred motivation of having a servant around the home or a live-in carer to help with infirmity was patently obvious. Stasia Z was one of the youngest of the children. She was born just before the outbreak of World War II. Her father died in Siberia and her mother in Teheran, shortly after leaving the Soviet Union. Stasia was over the moon at the prospect of adoption and the love was mutual. Stasia clung to her adoptive parents with her whole heart; and they responded to her with the same love, especially her adoptive mother. But Stasia's joy was to be short-lived. Her adoptive mother died shortly afterwards and the father married a woman who had arrived from Poland and who – as it turned out – was jealous of her. Stasia ran away from home. From a sense of misguided shame, believing that her friends would blame her for the adoption fiasco, she disappeared without trace. To this day we do not know what happened to her.

The Italian captain of the ship *Gerusalemme* wanted to adopt Bogusia J who was the second youngest of the orphans. But nothing came of this either. She was later adopted in Canada by a childless couple, the Furmans. Mr Furman was a construction entrepreneur. Later, Bogusia married her friend Staszek Sz. also from the orphanage and the Furmans welcomed both of them with open arms into their family.

Danusia D had an uncle living on the Canadian prairies. He asked whether she could be sent to him. He promised that he would educate her. At the time I did not have the means to set out on such a long assessment journey; in Montreal life was on a constant treadmill while I was trying to place the children in boarding schools and take care of hundreds of other associated matters. So I didn't go and check out the uncle and the environment in which the girl would be living. After two years he informed us that he wanted to deport her to Poland since he could not manage her any more. I demanded that he send her back to Montreal. When she arrived at the main train-station I could tell from her behaviour and manner of dress that she had undergone a change for the worse since being sent to her uncle. Her uncle owned a bar that was frequented by local cowboys. Danusia was told that education was not necessary on the prairies and he engaged her as a waitress. There she learnt to swear, smoke and lie. I placed her in the home of the pre-war Polish consul Mr Brzezinski and his wife, who undertook the difficult task of bringing her up; but they were not successful. She took to staying out later and later at night. Other people also tried to help but to no avail.

Mila W, a seventeen-year-old, was re-united with her aunt in New Richmond, Minnesota. But she was overwhelmed with nostalgia. In her first letter to me she wrote: "I will tell you Father in confidence that I have cried a lot over this letter and I don't really know why. After all I write many letters. Maybe this letter to you is different. Here I live on a farm. The houses are about a mile apart from each other. It's like living on a desert island. Fortunately, there is a large dog here who accompanies me everywhere... It is fifteen miles to the church and twenty to the nearest town. I am glad that the entire household goes to church every Sunday. They are very good to me; and they have bought me a lot of things, but what is the point if I am still homesick for Canada? Please believe me when I say that I will never forget you, the children and the people who showed me so much kindness and with whom I had grown so close... I attend public school and I take the school bus to get there." After a while Mila went to live with another aunt in Biloxi, Mississippi on the Gulf of Mexico. She was to attend school there but these plans were overturned by her aunt's second husband who was an alcoholic; he spent all the savings put aside by the first husband on drink. There was not enough money for the education of Mila and she wrote that sometimes there was not even enough money for food. It transpired that the aunt had brought her down to live with her so that she could cook, clean, wash and generally work as a maid. When I finally went down to Biloxi to investigate the matter Mila was no longer staying with her aunt. She had gone to live with a good Polish woman in the neighbouring town of Ocean Springs. After a few years I lost contact with her.

I informed Mrs Grosicka in England about all the things that were happening and she wrote back that "she would be prepared to be transported over on angel-wings", but unfortunately arranging for her to come proved to be impossible to achieve.

Struggling to learn French

The children were well aware that in the world of trade and technology English was the dominant language. They had already started to learn English in Africa. In Canada they had to learn French in addition. They appreciated its melodic sound but the grammar and orthography gave them a real headache. One of the girls wrote humorously in a letter: "Maybe learning French will stick in my thick skull quicker than last year". Officially Canada is a bi-lingual country, but the children soon realised that apart from the Province of Quebec, the French language was not used in the rest of the country; they also noticed that the English language was ignored in Quebec but spoken everywhere else! Several of the older girls got into English business schools but most of the children had to learn French. In time it was reinforced in my mind that it was the French Canadians who had invited us to their country rather than the English-speaking Canadians. I imported Polish-French dictionaries from Europe and in my circular letters to the children would explain the principles of orthography and pronunciation and the meaning of words. One of the boys decided to put some real effort into learning both languages. He wrote to me: "I will be striving to learn two languages – French and English. When the teacher does not understand my French answers I will try and explain myself in English."

I would find out about their language progress through their letters. Wanda Cyran triumphantly informed me that "Niuśka Murawska, my classmate, came third in a class of twenty-two pupils. Please tell her sister – Czesia. In the beginning I had twenty-five points out of a hundred for catechism tests and now I have got ninety-nine." One teacher, a religious sister from St Hyacinthe, informed me that Krysia Kropa received her Tenth Grade leaving certificate with distinction. All the children eagerly studied French and some even had the inclination and found the time to keep up with the Polish language. I lent them *Quo Vadis* and *The Knights of the Cross* by Henryk Sienkiewicz and other Polish books.

On the whole, the children and youngsters were satisfied with the way the Canadians – priests, brothers, religious sisters and other young people – related to them. One of the girls wrote: "The sisters are very kind and understanding. I feel really at home here. My classmates are well-behaved and polite." The French families who had their own children in the schools would request permission to invite one or two of the young Polish girls to their homes for Sunday.

But in life not everything is perfect. There were also problems. Under normal circumstances parents are aware of the needs of their children, or their children feel comfortable going to them about their problems. On the other hand orphans often hide their needs, embarrassed about their fate. Only the most courageous would speak up for their needs. That is how it was for Staszek Bojnowski. I received a letter from him shortly before he sat his high-school diploma. "I need some money. The two dollars that Father Dostaler gave me I have already managed to spend on cigarettes. From that time I have not had two pennies to rub together; and meanwhile I need to pay for the school gazette, and another newsletter, and there's fifty cents towards the missions and another fifty cents towards the class fund, so that in total it all comes to three dollars. I couldn't even find the four cents to send you this letter. In addition, this year we need to pay for our graduation photographs. Last year it was not so bad as I managed to work during the vacation, and from time to time my friends would send me a bit of money – so I got by somehow. This year I couldn't earn the money myself and I cannot write to my friends as they are also struggling with money themselves. There is nowhere else I can turn but to you. I am not even writing to Father Dostaler because he is French and won't understand me; not that I hold it against him. I really don't know where to turn to with my troubles. Only to you, Father... And by the way, where are my three sisters? I have not had a reply from them to my letter."

I liked to receive such strong, open letters. Of course I helped him. Later, Staszek finished engineering studies.

I was amazed

In Africa, in the middle of the tropical jungle and even during the sea voyage, the orphanage had consisted of one integrated community, forming one family, in which there was one beating heart – a Polish heart. The boys and girls became siblings for each other. But here in Canada that unity was shattered, which resulted in tears and sadness. The majority of children went to various schools, while some of the older boys and girls preferred to start working or went to live with their relatives and a few were adopted. They had been used to communal living and now they had to be separated. In practice, by placing them individually or exceptionally in small groups in one school meant that they were bound to become lonely – something which they expressed in their letters. They had to learn a foreign language and get to know a new country, new customs and practices. I was amazed at how calmly and trustfully they took on this new life experience. Therefore, I consider their comportment to be full of self-denial, reflecting in no small measure quiet heroism.

My friend the psychiatrist Professor Wiktor Szyrynski summarised the attitude of the children in a letter to me as follows: "You, Father, talk about the influence of goodness bestowed on the children through the loving mercy of God. It is a *triumph* of love. Looking generally at the educational atmosphere in Africa and in other settlement areas, the contrast between the forces of darkness and goodness strikes me convincingly. One can clearly see how much the youngsters have gained from the special educational environment found in the various places along their tragic pilgrimage."

Words from the Bible came to my mind: *Can a woman forget her sucking child, that she should have no compassion on the son of her womb? Even these may forget, yet I will not forget you. Behold, I have graven you on the palms of my hands* (Isaiah 49,15).

Getting to know Catholic Canada

I would visit the children regularly in the company of Father Caron. Some of them thought I should visit more often. These visits became occasions to appreciate the charming Canadian scenery throughout the four seasons. I will never forget the winter scenes; the snowy ocean displaying a rarely-seen white hue and the howling blizzard winds reminding me of the *buran* which I had encountered in Kazakhstan. Then there were the tiny village inns where you could get home-made steaming-hot pea soup to warm you up. Pea-soup is almost considered in Canada to be the national dish, which explains why the French Canadians are referred to as *pea-soupers*. Sometimes when the snow drifted onto the road we would have to ask the inn-keepers to help us pull our car out of the ditch with their horses.

The children lived in villages and small towns, the very names of which are testimony to the many generations of Catholic French settlers in New France – for that is how the first settlers, through sentiment, named this newly discovered land. Almost all the villages carry the name of a saint – St Pierre, St Jean, Ste Agathe, St Philippe, St Eustache, St Jerome. Once, I was driving Teresa Kalkstein, the Mother General of the Sisters of the Resurrection, to the pilgrimage site of Ste Anne-de-Beaupré. There were no motorways at that time, so our route was through these small places named after saints. Mother Teresa who knew French very well would prayerfully fold her hands and shout out in delight, *"St Jean, priez pour nous!"* (St John, pray for us) as she named the patron saints of the villages we passed en route. Arriving at Ste Anne-de-Beaupré she asked, "Have we prayed the entire Litany of Saints?"

Frequent visits to the schools were necessary due to the difficulties the children were having in their new environment. Sometimes the French-Canadian community itself was at fault. In the mentality of the Canadians at that time there was still a lot of old-fashioned prejudice towards children of unwed mothers and children who appeared to be without a family. As a result, even some of the sisters treated our orphans in a rather un-Christian way; as if they were second class citizens. They claimed that their very arrival in Canada was in itself a blessing enough for the children, that no harm was being done to them and that they were really very lucky to be where they were. After all, they had come to affluent Canada from countries of the Third World. Janka and Zosia wrote to me about this unfairness: "We thought that after the Christmas holidays our programme would be changed – but not so. We spend even more time in the kitchen – almost all of the day. We do not feel that we are in school at all. When we told the sisters that for this kind of work we do not need the French language, they answered that we would learn the language from just listening and being in a French-speaking environment. But we still don't know any French grammar or how to write in French. What can we learn from scrubbing pots?"

There were occasions when the Canadian girls would be learning something in class and the orphans would be sent to work in the kitchen. Hanka Koryszko hit the nail on the head when she described this prejudice: "Without informing us they were preparing us to work as servants in the homes of the French Canadians". I accidently found out about this thoughtless and un-Christian prejudice towards the orphans when one of the girls wrote to me requesting that I cease calling them "orphans". In two of the schools where there was significant prejudice I requested that the entire teaching personnel and the French youngsters gather together and I spoke to them in an attempt to diminish the overall discrimination. I described the story of the orphans and explained that discrimination towards anyone was something horrible, and in the context of our children particularly hurtful, as these children were victims of the war. Their fathers had died in prisons and labour camps; and their mothers who were exiled to Siberia had died from hunger, cold and disease, as a result of their forced inhuman labour.

No one needs to be shown examples of kindness as much as orphans. I have kept all the letters which the orphans have written to me. Now, as I am re-reading them, this observation appears even truer. I am even more impressed by their unusual sensitivity and loving hearts – their trusting nature and solicitude for others. Perhaps they were not aware of possessing such qualities, and therefore the effect was that much greater. I would read their letters at one sitting. Afterwards I always felt rejuvenated, as if I were bathed in a child's love, which as someone once commented is probably a left-over from our time in paradise which we have now lost. What follows are some short examples from their correspondence which give an idea of the beauty of their young souls. (In some cases I have corrected the grammar!)

The most frequent correspondent was Wanda Cyran. In one of her letters she unveiled in her prosaic introduction her need to share her feelings and to express her affection for everyone, including her guardian: "On the occasion of it being a Saturday I have managed to beg a few free moments in order to jot down to you, Father, these few words which always bring a cheer to the human spirit. Life for me in the boarding-school is fine and moving fast, although there are also some gloomy days full of sadness – but one needs to be patient. After all God did not create us without patience, don't you think? And now I will change the subject. I will alight onto the next flower just like a bee. I would like to know how your job is progressing. Do you have a lot of work? I'm sure you do and is it because of us?"

Wanda Cyran had a younger brother Rysiek. She would mention him in her letters: "I will write to Rysiek... and I will advise him to the best of my ability how he should study and behave. Not much can be achieved by words but I can always pray for him, don't you think? I hope that Father will advise me how to go about it, and then it will be done perfectly." And she signed it "Bothersome Wanda".

In the letters the children would ask me to visit them: "Why don't you and Father Caron have the inspiration one beautiful Sunday and come down to visit us for a few moments – I would not dare to suggest for a couple of hours..."

215

Aniela and Sława wanted to get together with me. Their excuse was to be a play put on by the pupils to celebrate the golden jubilee of religious vows of the mother superior. The girls sent me a special invitation: "Father, we really invite you to come. The sisters would be very sad if you did not come. We will try and reserve our seats next to you, Father, so that you can translate a word or two for us as the spectacle is difficult to understand. We are taking part in the choir. But make sure you arrive early so that we have some time to talk. During lessons, when someone rings at the convent door we say, *'Chére Soeur, c'est peut-être notre pére polonaise!'* (Dear sister, maybe that is our Polish priest!) while sister mispronouncing Father's name, only laughs at us. All right, one day there will be a play about a *bunny-rabbit*. But we really do invite you to come!" (For English readers I have to expand this reference by explaining that my surname Królikowski translates as "rabbit" in Polish.)

The children lavished special care on their guardians. Stasia Kunicka wrote: "Father doesn't want to talk about his problems and worries. But as far as I am concerned, I always know when you have worries. Naturally, I have no idea what is the nature of the problems, but I know that they are big. I would like to make them smaller, but I am powerless. The only help I can give is my prayer. For us you are a father with a mother's heart..."

Another girl had similar experiences to Saint Paul the Apostle: "I am really troubled by some thoughts. I can't really manage with them... *'I want to do the right thing, but I do the wrong one; I cannot distinguish right from wrong'* (Romans: 7,18-19)."

During one of my talks in the home run by the Polish sisters I touched on the subject of Christian love of one's enemies, so that the wounds which the children had experienced would not keep festering in their childish hearts. After that lesson one of the girls wrote: "I see Father in front of me with all your goodness, and next to you a crude Russian Communist. I shouldn't feel hatred towards him but by the same token how am I to like him? I cannot understand that. Please don't be surprised. I can be indifferent towards them, that is, I do not wish them harm, but am I to love them? Maybe I still don't understand that." One girl never stopped thinking about the conversion of Soviet Russia: "Every day I recite a rosary for you and for Russia."

Another wrote disarmingly: "Father knows me very well, so could you please write down a few sins in French so that I can go to confession in school." And here are a few more quotes from the children's letters: "Can Father imagine being on a retreat where you only understand half of what is being said and the other half goes right over your head? I don't know what I would give for this retreat to be in Polish, so that at least I could think and talk in my own language. I don't think I will go to individual confession, because I would say it half-and-half, and if that is to be the case, it is better not to go at all. What do you think?" "There are moments when I stand at the crossroads and I don't know which road to take; which would be the most appropriate way for me, assuring me happiness in this life and later in heaven." "Please pray for me that I may benefit from this retreat; since it is the last before my graduation. I shudder to think that two months from now I will have graduated and that my school days will be over."

Due to the constant changes in their daily lives, some of the children would return in their thoughts to Poland and to their parents. Czesia wrote: "Only now do I appreciate the words of my dying father in Siberia 'All I want to do is to take my daughter to Poland...' That sentence was never finished."

A longing for her native country also caught up with Aniela Szwab, who entered the congregation of the Sisters of the Resurrection, although she later realised that her vocation lay in the married life. She wrote to me from the convent: "I am happy here, but I have to admit that I am increasingly yearning for something or someone – I don't really know what. I am now trying to examine myself to find out the cause for this longing. I think I have now found the reason. It is the feeling of longing for the country we have lost but to which our thoughts and hearts are dying to return. I can confidently say along with the poet Adam Mickiewicz: *Poland! My country! Thou art as good health; How much one should prize you, he only can tell – Who has lost you!* Father will probably be surprised by my saying this, thinking that 'she cannot even remember Poland', yet although I left as a child, how am I not to feel this longing? It is after all my native country. Moreover, this longing is increasing, but no one here understands that. I don't know if I will live long enough, but I ask God to allow me to return one day and kiss that sacred land drenched with the blood of heroes..."

Stasia Kunicka also shared with me her thoughts about Poland. "I often consider going to Poland, but would I come back? I am surprised to find myself so attached to everything that is Polish. If someone wants to hurt me, they just have to say something bad about Poland."

As Niusia Murawska wrote (Niusia, who already had behind her a whole series of sufferings and, who although she did not know it yet, was to be confronted with a new sorrow which her doctors had not yet fully diagnosed): "I really want to pass my high school exams from Class IV. But I do realise that on this earth one needs to suffer, as that is the only way to earn a place in heaven. If God has chosen suffering for me then I am prepared to accept it."

An older boy Zdzich Kulesza wrote as if he were a mentor: " Father Caron has earned the respect and appreciation of the entire orphanage group. Anyone who disagrees is not worthy of benefiting from the care which ensures for us a reasonable existence both now and for the future. The unfailing endeavours of Father Caron will stay with us for a long time. Even if his efforts were not so great, they would become such, since as a Frenchman he has done so much for the cause of a group of people from another nationality. I am not writing this to you as a reminder as you know all about this even better than I. I do not wish to be misunderstood."

Gratitude

The Polish children who had gone through Siberia and who had been rescued developed a great sensitivity and were characterised by a sense of gratitude. One boy wrote: "How can one forget those compatriots who tried to give us the best possible future if not in this life then in the next? It is our duty to remember our guardians who stood in for our parents..." The children would sometimes ask to be forgiven if instead of gratitude they indulged ungrateful feelings. They admitted that they caused us pain through stupidity and lack of understanding.

One of the boys who had for some time been helping a Canadian woman who wanted somehow to express her gratitude said, "Please forget about remuneration. I owe so much to people for their help and concern that I will never be free of that debt."

My relationship with the children

No one is surprised by the words of Jesus Christ: *Unless you turn and become like children, you will never enter the kingdom of heaven* (Matthew 18,3). I have sometimes experienced that spirit which only children possess. At the end of my visit to her school ten-year-old Magda Mazur stood on the tips of her toes and shaking her head looked me straight in the eyes. I asked her, "Why are you boring a hole in my head with that look of yours?" She replied, "I am looking to see if you are crying, because shortly you will not see me for a while".

Her peer Wanda Cyran wrote in a letter: "Would Father be angry at me if I called you *Króliczek* (Bunny-rabbit)? I wanted to call you that when we were saying goodbye last time – Goodbye Bunny-rabbit. Father could then reply to me, 'Goodbye *Cyranette* or even *Tsiganette* (little gipsy)' as I like it when people call me that. What do you think about the idea? If you are in agreement with me then the deal is on. I was praying for all you priests in front of the Blessed Sacrament and I have been going to adoration (of the Blessed Sacrament) during the night. I always pray to God for you."

Aniela and Sława totally succumbed to a wave of healthy humour when they wrote to me: "It's a pity that Father is a little rabbit and not a little bird. For example, you could be a lark and then you could fly over and visit us. You could bring us gossip about our friends from the orphanage and from the outside world. Please do make us a pleasant surprise visit."

The return of Olek to Poland

The boys expressed their feelings differently to the girls. They were more reserved and patient. One of them put into a single sentence the whole range of his feelings: "I am alone among the French. At this rate I will forget how to pray in Polish. Please place me with a Polish family for the summer holidays."

One or two of them would react more sharply but only when they had reached the limits of their endurance. One day during the serving-up of the food at meal-time sixteen-year-old Olek Kuleta, a quiet boy, well behaved, and in addition a talented sculptor, fell into a rage and threw his plate with everything on it in the face of the brother who was serving up the meal. I was concerned at what could have caused Olek's crisis. He was a rather uncommunicative boy, keeping his feelings close to his chest, but he was liked and respected by his peers. I imagine that he was not happy to leave Africa, which he loved and where he had learnt to express himself through his carving, for which he had a talent. He made beautiful primitive objects from wood and ivory.

After this outburst, Olek requested that he be sent back to Poland where his father had apparently taken up residence in the vicinity of Szczecin after he came back from Siberia. We sent Olek to Poland, but not without great trepidation. We waited for news from him daily but none ever came. The boy seemed to disappear into thin air. I discovered later that the Communists took advantage of his return to promote their own propaganda. By twisting the truth they returned to the previous accusations about kidnapping the children and they renewed their campaign at the UN for their return to Poland. They forbade Olek to communicate with anyone overseas and he himself understood the danger in so doing.

When after many years I was able to return safely to Poland I managed to find Olek's wife Zofia and their son Romek. They recounted to me how he spoke very little to them about his past. After some while he left his wife and settled in Wrocław where apart from his professional work he continued to develop his artistic talents in an amateur sculpting club. He would give his work away to all and sundry; I had noticed some of his work in the home of his wife. Eventually information reached his wife that he had committed suicide by jumping from the window of a tall building. All his Siberian experiences, the exile-wanderings, the sudden separation from the orphanage family in Canada and no doubt marital problems all conspired to take away his desire to live. But his death has remained a great mystery for us and it is not beyond possibility that he was murdered.

During the Christmas and Easter holidays we would take all the children who were staying in the boarding schools to Montreal and place them with Polish families. Families, both from new and old immigrations, willingly accepted them and treated the children as their own. They were proud that they could be of help.

I would visit the families who had given hospitality to the children. The youngsters felt happy there and would unwind after all the French lessons. In one of the Polish homes the hosts were amazed at the richness of the children's experiences and memories. The favourite topic of conversation for the children was Africa. They could talk about it for hours. Occasionally they even allowed themselves a lapse into fantasy, and so a particular elephant became all white as if it were made from ivory! Once, a boy ran away from his host family and returned to the Mont Thabor Centre. In response to the question as to why he didn't want to stay there any longer he replied, "Father, those people took me around to their friends and relatives and showed me off like an African monkey. I had enough of that."

Wandzia was liked by everyone, while at the same time being very chatty and sensitive. One Sunday she had a problem. She called me at the presbytery early in the morning and in a hushed voice said,

"Father!"

"What Wandzia, why are you calling so early?"

"Because I want to go to Mass and everyone is asleep here."

"Well then go and wake them up."

"I already have but they told me to go to back to sleep. They explained that they work hard all week and now wish to rest. They said that I also worked hard in school and should go and lie down."

I can't remember if someone eventually managed to go to Mass with her, but I felt sad for her. To this day she always puts God before anything else.

The first year that we arrived in Canada, we organised a Polish Christmas Eve vigil supper (called a *wigilia*) in the home of the Sisters of Bon Conseil, to which we invited our benefactor Archbishop Charbonneau. Among the guests were the Sister Superior of the house Sister Normandine, a minister in the pre-war Polish government Mr Wacław Babinski with his wife Maria, women of various nationalities who had been taken to Germany during the war as forced labour, and our orphans. It was our first meeting with the archbishop. In the presence of that tall man with ascetic features and a warm smile we felt like one large family. After we sang an introductory carol we began the ancient Polish tradition of sharing the *opłatek* (Christmas wafer). Mr Babinski explained to our distinguished guests in beautiful French the significance of the *opłatek* in Polish cultural tradition. The words about the symbolism of brotherly love must have tugged at the strings of the archbishop's heart as he fought with his tears throughout the speech.

Shortly after that the archbishop underwent a great unpleasantness. The press stated that he had been reported to the Vatican by capitalists as a Communist sympathiser because he had stood in defence of striking workers and ordered a collection for their families in the churches. For us, who had been rescued by him from the clutches of communism, this accusation was patently unfair. The campaign against Archbishop Charbonneau became more vocal day by day, so that the Holy See requested that he go to Rome to explain the affair. But he preferred to step down. He left for Victoria in the Province of British Columbia, where he took off his insignia of office and resuming a black cassock started to teach children in school.

I wrote to the Archbishop assuring him of our love, gratitude and respect. He replied: "I thank the good Lord that He chose to inspire Father to write to me a letter in my solitude here in Victoria. I treat your letter as a blessing to sweeten my exile. How well you have brought to life for me the news about the beautiful orphan family in Montreal, informing me about the fate of my boys and girls, and telling me that Christian charity bestowed on them is still manifested to all of them in a motherly way. Dear Father, God himself will repay you for the good that you are doing for all the children. I regret that I cannot be with them to help them, to encourage them – which I really would like to be able to do – but you are with them and that reassures me. I am devoted to you with all my heart, in Christ Our Lord, + Joseph Charbonneau."

Orphans and Father Lucjan with Paul-Emile Cardinal Leger, Montréal 1951

Father Caron visited our benefactor in Victoria, but unfortunately I did not have the opportunity. The archbishop's throne in Montreal was taken over by Cardinal Paul-Émil Léger who assumed all the obligations that Archbishop Charbonneau had undertaken in regard to the Polish orphans. Ten years later Archbishop Charbonneau died. His body was brought back to Montreal where his funeral was a triumph of love; thousands of the faithful took part.

The question of the Japanese mission

During this time I was considering if and when I should go to the mission in Japan. I was assessing in my mind the idea that there must be someone among the Polish elite of Montreal who was by profession better prepared than I to undertake the responsibilities of guardianship of the orphans. Many educated people knew the French language. I made contact with the mission founded by Father Maksymilian Kolbe in Nagasaki. They asked me for an account of my life and a photograph.

Later I found out that the council responsible for deciding whether to accept me or not was wondering if my underlying intention was to add exotic Japan to the list of countries in which I had lived. However, the matter was settled by the church authorities in Montreal who stated that no one could replace me since there was no other person who had lived through a similar fate to the orphans and who could therefore understand them. I accepted this argument as the Will of God and I stopped thinking about the mission. My desire to be a missionary was subsequently fulfilled by God in a different way, which I will recount later.

The Island of Ste Hedwige (*Wyspa Św Jadwiga*)

A great problem for us lay in the organisation of summer holidays for such a large group of boys and girls. The very thought of it gave us a headache. Divine Providence, again watching over of the needs of the children came up with a solution. A certain French notary, whose name I remember as Mr Trambley, had custody over Dowker Island, 25 kilometres to the north of Montreal on Lake St Louis, through the middle of which ran the St Lawrence River. The notary let us have it free for a period of several years. The island has 140 acres and is partially wooded.

For the duration of the holidays the children re-named it St Jadwiga's Island. Once there we found a spacious two-storey house with a glassed-in porch on three sides. We quartered the girls in the house and because the island did not have another house, the boys were put into tents. They understood the situation and never complained. Life had taught them about sacrifice and accepting one's fate if it were impossible to change.

The children were most excited about the freedom and swimming. The state authorities required that a qualified life-guard had to be constantly present when someone was swimming. In order to save money Father Dostaler and I completed the life-guard course. The training was not easy. We had to learn how to hold someone who was drowning, how to dive from a tower four metres high, how to swim a hundred metres in our clothes, how to take off our clothes underwater and how to find and collect at least six plates underwater holding our breath all the time.

So how were these holidays? I pass you over to the voice of Józia Studzinska, one of the girls who in 1951 kept a diary in which she wrote down everything that she considered to be of relevance and note.

"It feels here as if we are at a scout camp. There is no electricity, but we are managing with our supply of kerosene lamps. It reminds us of our time spent in Africa. Going on walks we come across snakes but we are not afraid of them because in Africa they were larger and even more dangerous. We have a chapel with a picture of Our Lady of Częstochowa. Every morning and evening we say our prayers to our heavenly mother who has loved us so much and who shows a kind heart towards children. Our carer is Mrs Aniela Białowska, who teaches us many things and with her experience expands our knowledge. Her daughter Lidka is very pleasant but is nurturing some sadness. But she always has a radiant face and smiles at everyone. Our camp leader Zosia Wakulczyk and her assistants are very fearsome but that is for our good. After they have put on their thunderous expressions, their faces lighten up and become noble. Every day our "Daddy" Father Królikowski who is very concerned about us, comes over. We love him a lot. He does everything to make our holidays as pleasant as possible. Apart from him there are two other priests, Father Caron and Father Dostaler, whom we call Tarzan because he is very strong and athletically built. Our food supplied to us by priests is brought over to us by boats from Montreal. They made a raft by tying together two boats and brought over a piano from Montreal. The raft wasn't very stable and with each increasing wave the piano could have slipped into the water. The greatest pleasure is being able to swim which reminds me of Salerno. When the sky is clear one can see in the distance the cupola of the Basilica of St Joseph. We are in raptures over the sunsets, when our island resembles a Jan Matejko painting. This is how we spend our two-month holidays far from our native land."

On Dowker Island, 1952

Here are a few more interesting observations and experiences recounted in Józia's diary:

"Today we went to the nearby wood to pick wild berries and raspberries. At the sight of them, my memories took me back to images of Poland, and how I would go with all my siblings to the woods, and when that woodland picture dissolved in my memory it gave way to pictures from the African jungle – her secret depths and colourful birds flying from tree to tree amusing us with their trills. Today I have a lot of new material to put in my diary. I have just finished reading Henryk Sienkiewicz's *Letters from Africa.* It seemed to me as if he was describing our own travels in Africa. I was thinking about those illustrations he gave of missionaries who sacrifice themselves in order to serve the poor and tell them about God. They are spiritual guides, but they are also ordinary men who build houses, schools and hospitals. Single-handedly they try and create a civilised society from the wilderness... Today I started reading *The Last of the Mohicans* by James Fenimore Cooper... I like Sundays because there are visits on that day. Many French people came today for the picnic, including our boys and among them my little brother Staś. We organised a hunt for frogs and then we fried them up as they are a great French delicacy. We played volley ball and other games. Towards the

226

evening we took a boat to the other shore to watch a film. We returned after midnight by the light of the moon because the motor broke down... Today I finished reading *The Wolf Hunters* by James Oliver Curwood. The author belonged to an Indian tribe. During his school years he constantly felt the call of the wilderness when he was trying to concentrate on his lessons. He often played truant instead of listening to the droning of his elderly teachers. The wilderness was his companion, even his mother... Father Królikowski introduced us to *The Story of a Soul* by Saint Thérèse of Lisieux."

I also found the following note in Józia's diary: "Today (6.08.1951) Father Królikowski brought us some good news; the Polish Canadian Congress raised funds for our summer camp. They collected more than one thousand dollars. We also watched a new film *A Sentimental Journey*. It contained some very moving scenes so the girls were crying. Even Father Królikowski cried his eyes out... One day the lake filled up with yachts. They looked like seagulls. Later there was a yacht race. An unforgettable sight. In the evening, by moonlight, we held a camp-fire gathering which was led by the Polish guides who had come from Montreal. Our girls also presented their sketches, performances and jokes. The honorary guest was the President of Canadian Poles Mr Gryszówka."

It could have all ended tragically. "One day Father Dostaler left the camp to go with the girls to Montreal. Taking advantage of the fact that there was no priest around some of the girls went kayaking and started fooling about. As so often happens sorrow followed joy. The kayak turned over, and Mila who did not know how to swim sank to the bottom like a stone. Staszek Syjut jumped into the water in his clothes and pulled her onto the shore."

Józia forgot to mention one more event which the vacationers remembered for a long time. Basia G went out one evening through the kitchen into the woods. At the same time at the rubbish bins a skunk – a placid animal similar to a cat – was having a feast. For its own protection the little animal has an awesome weapon – a bladder full of suffocating fluid. The startled animal sprayed all over Basia. The frightened girl ran back into the house filling it with a nauseating smell. We were watching a film at the time and everyone jumped up from their seats and pushed

Basia outside again, because the smell was intolerable. The next day all of her clothing had to be buried in the ground in order to get rid of the smell.

Children cannot exist without pets – and there were two dogs named Princess and Maciuś (Matty). One of them became the exclusive favourite of a little girl with scoliosis and she would confide all her joys and sorrows to him.

Publicity and guests

The whole business about the orphans attracted a great deal of publicity, particularly among émigré Poles living in England, where a large number of Polish veterans from the Second Corps had settled, and also in the USA. The Polish community in Buffalo invited me to give radio interviews on two of its stations. When I was being escorted from one station to the other through the district of Fillmore-Broadway I was amazed at the prevalence of the Polish language on the streets. But as I write these memoirs the situation has undergone a radical change. The old folk have died and the younger generation have moved to other suburban areas, and in the place of the Poles there are Afro-Americans.

In the hearth which was run by the Sisters of the Resurrection in Montreal we hosted two guests very close to our Polish hearts – Miss Dorothy Sullivan and General Bór-Komorowski. Miss Sullivan had fought valiantly for the orphans in Italy and Germany while the General is well-known to Poles as the Military Chief of the Home Army and leader of the 1944 Warsaw Uprising. We marked the visit of these two guests with a group photograph together with the children.

Au bout du monde – At the end of the world

The presence of the orphans in the Province of Quebec attracted the attention of the Ministry of Labour to my person. They asked me for my help in re-settling Poles who intended to establish farms on virgin land on the uninhabited prairies. Several times I went out with an official from the ministry and a Polish immigrant to the so-called "au bout du monde" as Father Caron liked to say. It was a region lying to the northwest of Val d'Or. It was possible to acquire this land cheaply with its abundant woods and fallow terrain overgrown and covered in shrubs and grasses.

At that time Canada was still sparsely inhabited and had a total population of only slightly more than twenty million.

During these resettlement visits I met a Polish farmer who went to live in that area soon after the war. He was young, strong, unmarried and knowledgeable about agriculture. Among the local population he had the reputation of being a rich man because it was noticed that time and again, with the profits that he had made, he would buy more land – a bit of forest, fallow land or access to a lake. The ministry official stayed with him in order to encourage the prospective farmer to settle nearby. On the way back we stopped at the presbytery of a French prelate whose housekeeper immediately started to pester us insisting that we arrange a meeting for her with this farmer, whom she referred to a *jeune Polonaise* (a young Pole). She showed us loads of pots, plates, hand embroidery and clothing, asking us that next time we visited his place we mention her!

The monthly journal *"Ecclesia"*

There was rivalry between the English and French Canadians to attain the higher population figures. In the past the French tried to distance themselves from the English through a "cradle" policy of having large families. After the war there was a race to attract the largest number of immigrants to their provinces. The Montreal School Commission suggested that I edit a monthly for the Polish immigrants. The aim of the publication was to present famous characters from French Canadian history to Polish readers. There were certainly many people to write about, since sixteenth-century France had sent some of its best people to the newly-discovered land. Some of them became saints. In the journal I was also asked to raise topical issues. In short, the idea was that the Polish immigrants should come to know and like the land where they had settled – its language, culture, history and current affairs. I also put in articles about Poland. I did not have a lot of time to devote to the work and there was no correspondence. I put the monthly together practically on my lap and even today I cannot remember why I called it *Ecclesia*.

The School Commission printed the monthly and delivered it to centres in mainly Polish parishes. I was involved in editing *Ecclesia* for several years. I have kept a copy of an issue from which I will quote as an illustration a piece about the mistake of Karl Marx:

"Karl Marx, the father of Communism, predicted in his *Manifesto* that the revolt of the proletariat (working classes) would erupt first in the industrialised countries where the rich were becoming richer and the poor even poorer. Also, according to this prophet and apostle of Communism, the revolution was to occur in England, Germany, France and the USA. Meanwhile it took hold in Russia, an agricultural country, under-industrialised, where poverty had come about as the result of poor management by the Tsars and aristocracy, not as a result of a war between the capitalists and the working classes. Believing in the existence of an evil spirit and his spiteful interference in the affairs of humans, we can only surmise why the 'Prince of this World', as he was called by Christ, should have chosen God-fearing Russian people to become his instrument of war against God."

Religious chats aimed at Poland

Those years were very busy for me. I was persuaded to broadcast short religious talks once a week to Poland from the state-owned CBC (Canadian Broadcasting Corporation) radio-station. From those days I treasure the meetings I had with the Poles who were working in the international department. One of the women there was the daughter of General Anders. The topics of our conversations were varied and informative. But I never had any feedback from Poland. As I subsequently found out, international radio-stations like ours and *Radio Free Europe* were jammed by the Communists. They were considered illegal and listening to them was severely punished.

I would like to mention a talk I gave which reflected the way of life of Canadian citizens. I spoke about the patron saint of the Province of Quebec, Saint John the Baptist whose feast is held on 24 June. This feast which originated from Old France goes back to antiquity and Gallic converts to Christianity. The Jesuit chronicles of 1636 mention that the feast was already being celebrated when there were only a handful of 170 French colonials in Canada. Today the feast has both a state and a religious aspect. In the streets of Montreal a colourful procession takes place decorated with flowers, lights and flags in which every section of society takes part – school children, craftsmen, church organisations and military units. On a decorated float stands a small curly-haired boy representing John the Baptist; next to him is a snowy-white lamb, symbol of the Lamb of God. Manifesting solidarity with the first explorers of Canada, various ethnic groups join in the parade, including the Poles, who always take the opportunity to express their love for their native land.

After three years of working at the CBC radio-station I was released by its director from professing the word of God to Poles in Poland. As a rationale for this move he cited that my native country had regained its religious freedom. At that time Władysław Gomółka came to power; he was a "native" Communist who never stopped being a Communist and who continued persecuting the church.

My role as a censor

In spite of the fact that I had many responsibilities and commitments the Canadian-Polish authorities asked me if I would censor films that were imported from Poland. The films had already been shown in Poland and they all had embedded in them subtle propaganda messages. The Communist party saw to it that the producers and artists impregnated the story-line of the film with Red venom in order to promote a new atheist Poland with an altered history and without a clear identity. According to Communist ideology the whole world was to become a Communist super-state sooner or later... I had therefore an almost impossible task. Actually, no film was appropriate for Catholic and patriotic Canadian-Poles.

Our Lady of Mount Royal

Around that time someone asked me why there wasn't a Polish catechist in Our Lady of Mount Royal School. It was a primary school in a poor neighbourhood, bursting at the seams with children of post-war immigrants. The parents were young people who had been deported to Germany during the war as forced labour. After the war they did not want to go back to their countries which were under Communist governments. They chose an exile and pioneering life instead of returning to their native countries. In this school with its mosaic of nationalities there were two-hundred-and-fifty Polish children. None of the three Polish parishes served by American Franciscans showed any interest in the school. In any case I thought that my own status as an immigrant would help me understand the mentality of the Polish immigrants so I volunteered for the position of catechist. The children were more mature than their Canadian peers. There were fewer problems with them and their keenness to study was greater. I taught religion there for approximately three years. My place was later taken over by Father Jan Bogudzinski who had come from Poland. It gave me a lot of pleasure when years later young couples would mention at the time of their marriage that I had taught them religion at Our Lady of Mount Royal.

Graduating from schools

After a few years of studying the orphans started to reap the rewards of their toil and efforts. Four girls, Zosia Bojnowska, Kazimiera Mazur, Paulina Syjut and Niusia Murawska completed their nursing studies and received their diplomas. The graduation ceremony took place in the presence of Cardinal Paul-Émile Léger. Krystyna Tymicka finished dental studies and Staszek Bojnowski obtained an engineering diploma from McGill University. He paid for his own studies at university by undertaking casual jobs. The majority of the boys finished basic technical training. I rather liked the speech of one of the school directors. He warned the graduates against expecting to be given high salaries immediately, as before their experience caught up with their knowledge the leavers would expend a lot of wasted effort with a consequent loss to the workshop owner. He also characterised the nature of their experiences – namely the sum of errors, mistakes and slip-ups from which they were able to learn positively. What a pertinent definition, I thought, proving itself in the physical world as much as in the spiritual realm.

Visiting one of the orphan apprentices

Other youngsters had different experiences. One of them was Geniu Rusin, who had been saved from the coal-hold on the ship in Pahlevi harbour in Persia by a Polish teacher who had been deported to Siberia. He travelled around Africa with her and her two daughters. He fell in love with Africa to such an extent that although he ended up living in Canada he felt an urge to return to the jungle in Africa. In Ottawa he decided to enter the missionary Congregation of White Fathers, who have their missions in Africa, so that after his ordination that is where he would have been sent. Although he finished his novitiate and two years of theology his superior put an end to his plans by explaining to him that whilst he had a vocation to Africa he did not have a vocation to the congregation. After leaving the seminary Geniu studied political sciences at Montreal University for two more years and then for four years he worked as a lecturer in philosophy. Later he worked for the Canadian Immigration Services. In 1959 he married. He later discovered a cousin in Poznan, thus maintaining his contact with Poland.

After graduating from technical school Michał Bortkiewicz worked for Vickers and Canadair in the manufacture of aircraft. After marrying he evinced a liking for sport. He played tennis and volley-ball but above all he liked to take part in athletics as a runner. His main motivation behind this activity was for health reasons but when he started to achieve favourable results he took part in competitions. He participated in thirteen marathons, in places as far apart as Boston, New York and Montreal, collecting four gold medals. He was also an accomplished chess player.

A vocation to consecrated life

A few of the girls entered religious orders – Stasia Kacpur to the Polish congregation of the Sisters of the Resurrection (*Zmartwychwstanki*) in Montreal, while Stasia Kunicka and Aniela Szwab entered the Polish order of the Sisters of Saint Felix (*Felicjanki*) in Toronto. Today, both congregations have an international profile. Whilst in her chosen order Stasia Kacpur, whose religious name was Sister Alfonsa, fulfilled the two loves of her life – love of her country and love of the Church. She worked for a long time among the Canadian Poles and in Polish parishes teaching religion and Polish language, visiting the sick and helping the immigrants. Later she entered a new phase of her life working with senior citizens in the Copernicus Lodge Retirement Home in Toronto, helping to organise their religious and cultural life.

Stasia started her way-of-the-cross as a five-year-old, when together with her parents and young siblings she was deported to Siberia. The seventh child, Adam, journeyed to Siberia in his mother's womb during February of the harsh winter of 1940. After his birth a blanket tied between a stove and a bunk-bed served him as a hammock-style improvised cradle, but because it was impossible to live on love alone little Adam died shortly afterwards. Fate dealt cruelly with the Kacpur family –and it was simply because their father fought against the Bolshevik invasion for the freedom of his country in 1920. In the interior of that inhuman land, after the death of their parents and older brother, the three children under the care of twelve-year-old Bolek who was deaf, found their way miraculously to a Polish orphanage, which was eventually transported by lorries through Meshed and Karachi to the port of Basra in Iran. From there the orphanage left by ship for India. During long stopovers schooling was organised for the children where they were taught to read and write on the sand. The Soviet hell was still making itself felt in their young bodies and as a result they came down with scurvy, mumps, night-blindness, typhoid fever, malaria and scarlet fever. Many children ended up in hospitals and sanatoria. In India,

Stasia was accommodated in the Jamnagar camp and later in Valivade. When these camps were closed down the Kacpurs transferred by ship to Mombasa and from there to Tengeru in Tanganyika where they were greeted with shouts of "the *Indians* are coming!" After various adventures in Canada and after she had finished at St Ursula's High School Stasia entered the congregation of the Sisters of the Resurrection. She did her novitiate in Grottaferrata in Italy in 1995 and returned to Canada where she spent her time working with children and young people. She was decorated for her services by the Polish Canadian Congress.

God called Stasia Kunicka in a very prosaic way. While still living in lodgings in Montreal next to a home for the elderly Stasia witnessed an engaging scene. One of the sisters went up to an elderly woman frozen in a stupor with inertia and gently running her hand over her cheek brought her back to consciousness. The eyes of the elderly woman came back to life and a grateful smile covered her face. Stasia who was always sensitive to any demonstration of overt goodness took that event as a sign from God. She entered the Felician sisters with a huge background of experience. She came from a large family, and her mother had died a year before the outbreak of war. After the Red Army entered Poland they arrested her policeman-father and all trace of him disappeared. With her four siblings she was deported to Kazakhstan, but after the so-called "amnesty" good fortune smiled upon the youngest two Stasia and Alfons, enabling them to escape from the Bolshevik paradise. In order not to become separated again they went through two camps in India holding each other by the hand. Finally, they ended up in the orphanage in Tengeru in East Africa.

A test of strength

The school years came to an end, and the children who were now young men and women started to become independent and to test their strengths. Rarely did we have to adopt the stork's method – pushing someone out of the nest so that they could be convinced of the strength of their wings. If there was some tardiness it was because of the fear of having to break ties with the orphanage family, but it was often necessary to leave in search of work in other towns or other Provinces or in the USA. On the whole everyone managed to find their own work and accommodation. The boys were assured of work due to their vocational and technical training and some of them found work in airline repair workshops. They were not particularly socially involved in the Polish community with the exception of two of them – Zdzisław Kulesza and Kazik Majewski. Zdzisław came from the Eastern borders of Poland and lost his entire family during their wanderings in exile – his father in Russia and his mother, brother and sister in Iraq. Interestingly, he was also in Kara-Su where I had finished my officer-cadet training in the artillery. He attended school in Northern Rhodesia (today's Zambia). The amalgamation of dwindling orphanages meant that he was brought over to equatorial Africa and finally to Tengeru. In Canada, Zdzisław quickly became independent from the group and settled in the Province of Ontario in Windsor, a town on the banks of the Detroit River which separates it from the American city of the same name. He married Stasia, an orphan from the Jamnagar orphanage in India, which was run by Father Pluta. While in Windsor, Zdzisław was involved in his capacity as secretary of the Polish Canadian Congress in erecting a monument to Nicholas Copernicus.

The second interesting person was Kazik Majewski from the Podola region of Poland, who as an eight-year-old had been deported with his whole family to Siberia. After the so-called "amnesty" his father entered the army of General Anders while the rest of the family made their way to Northern Rhodesia. After the death of both of his parents Kazik found himself in the orphanage in Tengeru. His older brother entered the Franciscan order of Capuchin friars, while Kazik himself displayed a lot of initiative and energy. He became a well-known promoter of Polish culture and founded the Neo-Canadian Club. Later he moved to the USA and settled in the charming town of Milford, Connecticut. There he immediately spread his wings. He spoke fluent Polish, French and English; he took an active part in the social and cultural life of the Polish émigrés. For a while he was correspondent for the New York-based Polish-American newspaper *Nowy Dziennik*. He was president of the Educational Trust and initiated the teaching of Polish in local universities, he was a member of the Polish Heritage Society and co-operated with the Polish Saturday schools. He organised various cultural performances and was a member of the Union of Polish Clubs of Bridgeport. In 1973 he set up a Polish radio programme *Poland in Music* and Song, currently also available through the web, and which he runs to this day. After the fall of Communism in Poland he made contact with the Polish Ministry of Education and he attended gatherings in Poland of the Under the Baobab Tree Club (an organisation of Poles who had passed through Africa during World War II, Klub pod Baobabem). His energetic activities resulted in his receiving many awards. Kazik is much liked and his work is appreciated as much by his orphanage family as by the Polish Diaspora, and this is due to his uncomplicated approach to people and his humility.

On the whole the young people preferred the quiet and peaceful life to one involving fame, career or riches. This approach to their life was due to their experiences of the insignificance of the things of this world and its structures. Botanically, they prefer to be daisies and cowslips shimmering in the fields rather than roses or tulips in the parks.

Tying the knot

The majority of boys and girls chose the married state. I quote the words of a girl who was engaged to be married. She wrote to me: "Praise be to Jesus Christ. I am writing this short letter to Father to ask for your blessings on my married life. I have found a companion for my new way of life and by the help of God and with His blessings I wish to find my happiness there. I wish to thank you for all the good that I have received from Father and I ask also for forgiveness if I have done some wrong. I will repay you with prayer to the Lord God, and ask for the same because we are always in need of it."

Vestiges of Soviet experiences

In spite of having regained their freedom and enjoying a better standard of living many of the children still could not put behind them the memories of the Soviet experience. Irenka poured out her feelings on paper stating: "If a person does not have reasonable health then nothing will cheer them up. I was eight years old when I was deported to Russia; Tadek was four, my sister Czesia was thirteen and my older brother Władek was sixteen. I have constantly in my mind the scenic beauty of the land where I was born and where I used to run across the meadows gathering forget-me-nots and cowslips... I would pick large bouquets for my mother to put on the table. I remember those woods where we would go to collect hazel-nuts, mushrooms and raspberries. They were wonderful days in my childhood in Poland, and after that came those terrible years in Russia, especially in the orphanage of Karkin Batash. It was a terrible shock for a child. But we endured all of that and we are still alive, for which we thank God for His protection over us during these awful times. It is hard to believe that we could have been so hungry and treated so badly. That tragedy cannot be eradicated from our hearts. Those memories will stay with us to the end of our lives. Meanwhile in my mind, Poland will always remain a gorgeous land and I don't want its memory to fade or be destroyed until I die. I would like to get to know my native land, the place where I was born between Nowogródek and Baranowicze, but that part of Poland now belongs to Belarus."

Many children passed through the orphanage, later becoming independent and entering the labour market. But the nightmare of that Soviet hell never leaves them and its traces become evident in many different ways. An example of how this can happen leads me to express my thoughts in the following way:

We are back in the Soviet Union. The death of a mother orphaned three daughters, of whom the eldest was twelve years old. I will call her Aniela. The responsibility fell on her to act as a substitute for her dead mother to her younger sisters. Her maternal instincts came to life. I don't know all the particulars of the case because over time they have faded in Aniela's mind. She undertook enormous efforts to ensure all three did not die of hunger, frost or disease. She turned for help to grown-ups. Aniela would cling to anyone who so much as gave them a piece of dried bread or a bit of porridge. She turned her attention to a Polish man who had been freed from a labour camp, thinking he that could replace their father for the three of them. The little girls survived thanks to sporadic well-wishers and made their way with the Polish army to a Polish orphanage in India, ultimately arriving in America where after finishing their education they all married. But in Aniela there remained a scar which one can only call possessiveness. Through fear that she might lose her husband – although I knew him to be a responsible and loving man – she would often accuse him of not coming home straight from work but dilly-dallying, heaven knows where. Her American husband had an elderly mother and various siblings whom he visited. He considered it to be his family duty, especially when his mother became seriously ill and close to death. Aniela would say, "You're not fit to be a husband. You still need to cling on to your mother's apron strings." Her possessive streak lasted for several years. She did not want to face up to it since she had long forgotten when and how she had adopted that behaviour.

I don't have a mother

Another example illustrates a tragic experience. After leaving Russia many children disappeared without trace, thus generating an avalanche of searches for those who were lost. Enquiry letters concerning missing individuals were sent to the International Red Cross, to orphanages, to army archives and to consulates. I myself received several such letters. One letter happily found its target. One of my charges called Sława was being sought in Poland by her cousin Jadwiga. They had shared exile together in Siberia and had both made it to Africa; Jadwiga went to the camp in Masindi in Uganda and Sława went to Tengeru in Tanganyika. Jadwiga was in Africa with her mother and after the war they both returned to Poland. Jadwiga made contact with her aunt (Sława's mother) and found out that after the death of Stalin she returned from Siberia to her home in the old pre-war Eastern borders of Poland, now incorporated into the Soviet Union. I sent Jadwiga a telegram with the information that Sława was in Canada and that I would send further details in a letter.

Delighted, I immediately telephoned Sława. She was married and had a family and lived in Pointe Claire, near Montreal. The conversation went something like this:

"Sława, if you are standing up, sit down. I have great news for you which is pure dynamite. It may knock you off your feet."

"What's happened?"

"Your mother has been looking for you and has found you. She is living in the old Polish lands now part of the Soviet Union. She has been praying for you every day from the time of your separation. Isn't that wonderful?"

Stony silence. Sława was unresponsive. So I repeated the news. After a long pause she replied in a sepulchral tone:

"I don't have a mother."

"How silly of you to say, 'I don't have a mother'; everybody has a mother."

"I don't have a mother."

In Sława's voice there was so much sadness and indifference, that I was shocked, and I curtailed the conversation. Then having thought through her behaviour I called her again a few days later.

"Sława, can you tell me when and how you separated from your mother? How old were you?"

"I was four years old. My mother worked on a collective farm near Bukhara in Uzbekistan. One day my mother hired a wagon and donkey and putting my younger brother and me on it drove it to the orphanage in Karkin Batash. She said we would be better off there and maybe we would be able to leave the Soviet Union with the Polish Army."

"What memories do you have from the orphanage?"

"It was night-time. It was dark inside and we could only hear the sobbing of children."

"And your mother?"

"The next day she returned to the collective farm. I ran after the wagon crying and screaming, 'Mummy take me'. And she turned around and said, 'You will be better off there'. I couldn't keep up with her, and she disappeared from view. Behind me was a carer. She picked me up in her arms and took me to the orphanage, and I went with them to Persia. My brother became ill and did not leave with me; he must have died."

Now I understood why Sława said that she did not have a mother. During all the years of separation she was absolutely convinced that her mother had rejected and abandoned her. That is what the Russian carers would often say to the orphans. At that time Sława did not yet understand about the Communists; she did not remember the deportation to Siberia nor did she know about the Soviet Union. All she knew was that her mother had stopped loving her. Apart from that there was nothing else to know.

A long time passed by before I could explain to Sława, an adult woman, that her mother had made the ultimate sacrifice, which no mother living a normal life in the West could ever understand. Sława's mother condemned herself to a solitary life, and possibly death, under inhuman conditions in the Soviet Union, in order to give her child the chance of growing up in freedom and financial stability. Sława had been incapable of understanding, and had harboured that hurt for forty years, with a deeply wounded heart full of grievances and even defiance.

I pressurised her into writing the first letter to her mother. Apart from describing events previously unknown to her mother she included in her letter Christmas greetings as it was approaching that time of year. Sława gave me the letter to read. And even though I don't have a copy I remember its content very well. Sława had a way with words and a poetic talent and she wrote:

"Dear Mother, may this letter like the star of Bethlehem make its way to you through the twilight of the lost years. May it brighten and warm up the interior of your little house and illuminate your face with its brightness as it brings to you the glad tidings that your child is alive, is keeping well and is grateful for your prayers..."

However, after re-discovering her mother, Sława became severely depressed. The mental injury sustained in her childhood called for psychiatric intervention. To this day she is on anti-depressant medication. She never saw her mother again. She was terrified of going to the Soviet Union while her mother was too old and worn out with her own way of the cross... Sława sent her parcels of clothing and food, and several years later while she was in Poland she met her older brother who came from her mother to meet her. As I write this, both her mother and her brother are no longer alive.

The various fates of the children

To this day I don't really understand the case of one of our most talented boys. In a very short span of time he mastered both French and

241

English, and then he was arrested for shoplifting. Some misconceived hunger after knowledge prompted him to raid bookshops and make off with books in his coat pockets. The judge let him off when he found out the underlying reason for the thefts. Shortly afterwards the boy became a patient in a psychiatric hospital and was held there indefinitely.

Despite brotherly ties my young adults underwent a great deal of suffering as a result of loneliness and displacement; for the weaker ones there was always a pint of beer in which they would drown their sorrows. This would last for a while, and then they would get the better of the addiction. In two cases the reason for an unproductive life was a form of developmental delay, which was confirmed as such by psychiatrists. From a social perspective a person's life may be considered to be unsuccessful, but for God every life is of enormous value. This concept is greatly emphasised these days among volunteers working with people who suffer developmental delays or are handicapped. Sometimes I would blame myself and conclude that the disabilities of my charges occurred because of something that I had done. Dr Szyrynski, who knew my youngsters, said that in any society about ten percent of the population may have some form of disability. In my group there was also a high mortality rate, which was explained by their malnutrition and lack of proper medical attention during their childhood.

Pastoral and social activities

For me, as one of the first Polish-speaking priests in Eastern Canada, the post-war wave of immigration made huge demands on my work-load. The scouts wanted a chaplain, as did the veterans, dancing groups, Living Rosary Associations, parish organisations and the Catholic Intellectuals' Club (*Klub Inteligencji Katolickiej*). I have fond memories of the Canadian Kaszuby, which is located in Ontario. At the beginning of the 19th century, during the first mass wave of Polish immigration, Kaszubians from the North East of Poland settled in the hilly lake country of their new homeland. The terrain reminded them of home. They named the first settlement Wilno in honour of their beloved priest who originally came from there. In the woods separate from the church the Kaszubians liked to point out the traces of their first place of prayer, which some claim was burnt down so that a new brick edifice could be built. From the rebuilt church there is a gorgeous view over the deep forested valley below.

The residents demonstrate painstaking care over the preservation of their Kaszubian dialect. Once, during my time in Canada, when there was no native priest, the Kaszubians accepted a Silesian, Father Kondziołka, who in order to give them pleasure delivered his first sermon in Kaszubian. After Mass the elders of the parish faced the priest with a grievance. The Word of God should be delivered in good, clear, Polish language; dialect is used only in the home, talking over the fence with neighbours and in arguments! The pulpit in their church was at the same height as the chandeliers. The vergers would trundle it out on wheels into the middle of the church every Sunday for the sermon and place it in front of the altar-railings. Otherwise, its normal place was alongside one of the walls.

Father Raphael Grządziel, a fellow-Franciscan and a chaplain in the Second Corps, who during the Italian campaign was one of the first to enter Bologna, was attracted by the charm of Kaszuby. The Kaszubians sold him a plot of forested land on which he built a chapel in the Polish mountain-folk (*górale*) style. I visited him while the chapel was being built. He led a truly Spartan life; his little rooms were unheated and we ate dry bread and sardines. In time Father Raphael developed a Polish cultural centre there and established a post-office with its own official stamp stating: *Kaszuby*. Postcards which were sold there had printed on them: Kaszuby will never be lost (*Kaszuby nigdy nie przyjdą do zguby*). Next to the tiny church, on a podium among the pine trees, he placed an enormous picture of Our Lady of Częstochowa. Every Sunday Mass was said in front of it for visitors and the permanent inhabitants of Kaszuby.

During my time in Canada the Kaszubians from Wilno (in Ontario) and Barry's Bay started to sell plots of land along the lakeshores to Poles from Montreal and Toronto. They came to the area in great numbers. They built summer houses and spent their summer months there. An added attraction for Polish families were scout and guide camps and a permanent campsite for the older ranger scouts.

Shortly before the arrival of our children in Canada a Russian baroness Catherine de Hueck Doherty founded an apostolate for the poor in the small village of Combermere on the outskirts of Kaszuby. She called it Madonna House. Her vocation was kindled during the Bolshevik Revolution, and when she left Russia she wanted to continue to serve the poor. She sought them out in the West in order to prevent any Communist ideology being transplanted there. She carried out her search for them in Toronto and also in Harlem, the black Afro-American district of New York City. When I used to visit Kaszuby I liked to call in at Madonna House and re-energise my spirit in the centre's chapel. For Catherine the chapel was a sort of hermitage, and it was where she most often encountered God. As I am writing these memoirs, Catherine is now reunited with God; she died in the odour of sanctity in 1985 and her canonisation process was officially opened by the Diocese of Pembroke in 2000.

A town called Wawa

Polish labourers working in the northern part of the Province of Ontario mining for minerals such as gold, silver, metal and copper invited me to deliver a series of retreats for them. They were a team of mobile miners who moved from place to place in the overall direction of Hudson Bay. They did not need to build mine shafts as minerals on the Canadian plain lay right under the soil, which from the time that the earth's crust had cooled down had not been affected by mountain-forming activity. This plain spreads throughout the Provinces of Quebec and Ontario. While this represents huge wealth, it is necessary for its extraction to have modern technology and a huge outlay of capital. Canada is too sparsely populated to exploit mineral deposits on a grand scale. At the same time she does not want to become dependent on help from the USA.

The workers created a village on wheels for the duration of the mining in the area, after which they would move on. In the forest where the engineers had decided to cut into the rock – pulverising it and sieving the metal ore – they had built a wooden hut in which were located a tool-room, office, community hall, chapel and kitchen. The teams of workers lived in camper vans. The high wages were an incentive to do this work but in the long run the feeling of loneliness and remoteness from one's family and normal society proved to be a temptation to drunkenness.

244

On the way to this unusual strip mine I stopped in a small town with the peculiar name of Wawa. I asked the inhabitants of the town about the significance of this name. They pointed to a splendid steel monument in the town square representing a huge Canadian goose. She had her wings outstretched as if ready for flight. But I still did not realise what the word *wawa* meant. The indigenous people – the Hurons – who once inhabited this land, used the word *wawa* in communicating with the early European settlers, mimicking the drawn-out honking of the birds. A wild Canadian goose is larger than the domestic variety. It is colourful, has a long neck and has a unique majestic gait. In the autumn huge flocks of Canadian geese in V-formation transfer to warmer climates with a lead-bird at the head, bidding farewell to the local inhabitants with its characteristic honking.

The O'Sullivan family

In the course of my work I started to feel the lack of my command of the English language. In the Province of Quebec its use is limited. The Quebecois are of French descent and after losing their independence in 1759 they now leave no stone unturned in trying to keep alive the language of their ancestors. In the shops the assistants are told to speak only in French to their clients, even if they are American. Only after an unsuccessful second attempt are they allowed to speak in English. I was embarrassed by my lack of knowledge of the English language especially when I had guests from the United States. Meanwhile the French pretended to be offended when during a banquet I addressed a few words in English to the Americans.

I did not really have the time for English lessons, as I was constantly on the move at meetings and conferences. I learnt the language when I could, familiarising myself with individual words from advertisements and from notices read on trams, checking their meaning in a dictionary. On Sundays I would devour American comics, as they were perfect for my requirements; short sentences, colloquial words in current use and at the same time describing comical situations. But this was not sufficient and so I became friendly with the family of John and Ady O'Sullivan who had Scots and Irish roots. Through its sufferings the Irish nation is similar to the Polish nation. During their persecutions they lost their Celtic language but kept their faith. The couple were in their fifties, had strong

Celtic features and they were proud of their origins. On the feast of their national patron saint – Saint Patrick – they would invite me to a formal dinner; in a word they adopted me. I indicated my spiritual bond with them by adding to my name the prefix O' – O'Królikowski. Their son Terry who was married to a Cree Indian was a lover of nature and he lived in the woods in the North. Their daughter Marcella still lived at home with her parents. The O'Sullivan family truly formed a small church. In their family God was always put in pride of place. At home they had a well-stocked library which explained their wide knowledge of religious issues.

Although I really wanted to practise English conversation I didn't actually go to the O'Sullivans that often due to my busy schedule. I felt the lack of sound grammatical principles and knowledge about Anglo-Saxon literature so my hosts introduced me to Betty McCabe, a high school teacher, also of Irish origin. She took to teaching me with true educational zeal. She would bring me books of English literature, and set me homework to do. But after a few lessons I had to give up her services because I would come to the lessons unprepared and this put me to shame.

A trip to the USA

When everything in the children's lives in Canada had settled down I decided to make a trip to the USA. Everyone is fascinated by this huge country. I visited the country twice in the company of Father Dostaler, a tall athletic man with a child-like disposition. He offered to be my guide, translator and driver. We had to be careful with our money as Father Dostaler did not save much from his high-school teacher's salary spending most of his earnings on his hobby – amateur photography. He freely developed the photographic work of his students.

Going by car gave us greater freedom. We took with us dry groceries. A paraffin stove allowed us to heat up water for tea and soup from a tin. We stayed mostly in Franciscan friaries, as we did not have enough money to stay in motels. However, if the night was hot we slept in the car.

The first impression I had from looking at America was the perfect order and cleanliness of the place. But most of all I liked the people – their courtesy and willingness to anticipate the needs of other people and their willingness to be occupied with someone as if there was no one else. I was especially taken by the young people. As I was identifiable by my dog-collar, Catholic children and youngsters, not to mention grown-ups, would greet me formally with a smile saying, "Good morning, Father" or "Good evening, Father". What a wonderful country, I said to myself, almost heaven on earth. Today, writing fifty years later I have a different idea of this "vestibule to heaven"; the population is polarised, it is extremely liberal, the youngsters often seem lost and there is much litter around.

Using the motorways alternating between uninhabited areas and sprawling towns growing like polyps, we reached the foothills of the Rocky Mountains. One evening we stopped in Denver, Colorado. Not seeing any other alternative we rang the door-bell of the Bishop's residence asking him to put us up for the night. Father Dostaler was against the idea, saying that it was not the done thing. I tried to explain to him that in Poland it would be the most natural thing for a Bishop to do – to accommodate transient priests overnight. It was a Saturday. The bishop, in black trousers and a snow-white shirt, opened the door himself. When we told him our reason for being there, he was so amused by the explanation that he burst out laughing and could not control himself for a long time. With a great deal of warmth he said, "What will I do with you boys? My housekeeper is on her day off and I don't know how to do anything around the house; I cannot even make a bed and I don't know where the sheets are kept, I haven't a clue about cooking and I am sure that you are tired and hungry from your time on the road. But wait a minute. After all I can't shut the door in your faces." Showing us inside, he left us for a while. When he came back he said: "I have called up some sisters who work in a hospital. They will gladly take you in and offer you their hospitality. The healthier patients are sent home for the weekend to their families, so there are free beds. There is also a chapel where you can say Mass. They won't let you go hungry either. Go there with my blessing."

The American sisters were moved by our unusual visit. First they served us a quickly prepared supper and then showed us the hospital rooms. In my whole life I had never seen such order, various electronic monitoring equipment and intravenous therapy poles and bags of fluid. After Russia, we felt we had reached the threshold of heaven. Everywhere cleanliness and order reigned. There were no unpleasant smells. The next day after celebrating Mass in the beautiful hospital chapel we were invited to the dining-room. The sister superior was very interested in my experiences in the Soviet Union under Communist rule. It was the first time she had met a real Siberian exile. She asked if after my Soviet hell I had undergone intensive tests by a doctor. During that long odyssey some micro-organisms could have entered the body. She suggested that I stay at the hospital for a week so that the medical staff could examine me from head to toe. She urged me to take up this free offer. But we had duties which we had to get back to; I needed to return to Montreal and my parish duties at a determined time.

At Albert Einstein residence

The second trip to the United States was notable in other ways. The places we visited were always of less importance than the people we met. One morning we were tearing down the New Jersey motorway in pouring rain. Father Dostaler was overtaking other drivers when all of a sudden a car in the middle lane began to cut up in front of us in order to exit the motorway. The driver obviously had not noticed us and there was a collision in which I smashed my head on the windshield. One of the wheels fell off. The car which ran into us was carrying several Afro-Americans and their windows were dirty and covered in mud, so they didn't see us. The police and ambulance arrived immediately. We were both shaken but otherwise nothing was broken. The car-rescue company hauled away our vehicle to a garage. The repairs were to last a few hours. We were undecided what to do with the free time or where to go. As I stood on the edge of the pavement outside the garage repair-shop a car stopped in front of me. The driver asked if I needed to be taken somewhere. I explained the situation and we engaged in a pleasant conversation. He said he was descended from the Huguenots and his ancestors had arrived from France several generations ago. He himself was a freemason. I was surprised at his Christian charity. As everywhere God encourages people to do good and at the same time draws them to Himself. He said that we were in the famous New Jersey town of Princeton, the residence of the physicist genius Albert Einstein.

He was a professor in the local Institute for Advanced Studies. I was overcome with a desire to see the professor and if possible to shake his hand. My curiosity went even further. Did he believe in God?

I am convinced that real scientists are believers and only half-baked intellectuals have doubts. With the aid of the helpful American I made my way to the district where the professor lived which was barred to wheeled traffic. I rang the door-bell. The door was opened by a secretary who said that she was sorry to tell me that Professor Einstein was away in San Francisco at a conference of the United Nations. I asked her if I could look at his library. She graciously escorted me there. I was curious to know whether he had any books about God. Of course he had several. Later I came across several of his deep reflections about God. I remember one of them: "The cause of our complaints lies in the fact that we spend too much time in laboratories and not enough time praying."

The garage workshop could not repair our car the same day, so we had to shorten our holidays and return to Canada.

Meeting with Melchior Wankowicz

I was not fortunate enough to meet Albert Einstein, but Lady Luck smiled on me in another way. I was visited by Melchior Wankowicz (1892-1974) who was acknowledged over many years as an excellent Polish journalist and writer. He left behind for the soldiers of the Second Corps a superb documentary monograph *The Battle of Monte Cassino*. But I immediately had my suspicions as to why he had come to me. He was interested in the saga of the orphans and he asked me for a brief account of their odyssey. His eyes glowed as he listened. I spent several hours with him. He asked for another meeting with me to look at some notes and photographs. Fearing that he might use the material for his own ends I didn't reveal too much to him. He suggested that he was willing to write a book about my orphans if I had no objection to the idea. I replied that I was thinking of writing such a book myself. Then he asked me sarcastically, "Has Father ever written a book before?" The question nettled me somewhat, so I stated equally sarcastically, "No doubt you started somewhere with your first book" adding, "I will be writing as a witness to the events, while you would write in a far more literary style, but as an ordinary commentator."

Wankowicz motivated me to record the orphans' story. I am therefore an accidental writer, never having had any writing ambitions, but I felt that as a witness to dramatic events I had a duty to write them down. I was aware that very few people had seen what I had seen, lived through what I had experienced or had been to so many countries. The topic was engrossing and I was inspired by the words of Adam Mickiewicz that "it is harder to live a day well than to write a book".

I gave the book the title – Stolen Childhood (*Skradzione Dziecinstwo*). I chose this title from among many; it was suggested by Dr Szyrynski, the psychiatrist whom I have already mentioned several times in this memoir. Writing the children's epic was not easy. I worked on the book when I could, in the few free moments I had and with large breaks in between. The book recounts almost a decade in the life of fifteen thousand exiled children dispersed all over the world. There were no computers around at that time, which would permit you to move paragraphs around, delete mistakes, add words and edit whole sentences. So I was buried under papers and it involved a lot of hard work. I wrote in the National Library in Montreal on Sherbrooke Street opposite Lafontaine Park. It was an ideal place; perfectly isolated and where I could concentrate and easily check facts in official documents and encyclopaedia. Even people closest to me did not know about my hide-away. Several people read the manuscript for me. From them I received valuable comments and corrections. Hieronim Szumowski, a teacher from Tengeru, gave me several photographs and recounted personal memories from the Soviet Union. The first Polish language edition was published in London, England by the Catholic Polish Publishing House, Veritas (*Polski Ośrodek Wydawniczy Veritas*) in 1960.

The introduction was written by the Polish Field Army Bishop, later protector of émigrés, Father Józef Gawlina. He in turn cited the words of an eminent Catholic lay-person: "Some of the pages of the book are so uplifting and so good that I would like my children to memorise them and accept them as way-marks for their lives." I dedicated the Polish book to young people. The second expanded Polish edition came out in the USA in 1983, while the third edition was published in an already free Poland by the Jesuit publishing house WAM, in Kraków, in 1991. All the proceeds from the sale of the books went towards helping orphans in Poland. I had difficulties in publishing the oversea editions; I had to pay up front and I had to arrange advertising and the distribution of the book to readers. Several notable Polish émigré writers such as Zofia Kossak, Zygmunt Nowakowski, Jan Bielatowicz and others expressed surprise that my book had such a huge success.

Zofia Kossak, writing in the London Polish weekly *Wiadomości* (22 January 1961) was struck by the "...realism of the descriptions, at the same time their restraint, which is illustrated in sentences such as, 'Poles would recognise each other by their wolf-like appetites, by their eczematous sores all over their bodies and by the lice weaving their way into the seams of their clothes'."

In the London-based émigré newspaper *Dziennik Polski i Dziennik Żołnierza* (The Polish Daily and The Soldier's Daily) on 24 November 1960, the émigré writer Zygmunt Nowakowski observed: "In our national hymn there are the words that we will be Poles even if we have to cross the Wisła (the Vistula) and Warta rivers. But these children could easily change the text and insert hundreds and hundreds of other river names. They had crossed the Volga, Yenisei and the Ob' Rivers, they crossed the Tigris and the Ganges, they sailed down the Nile and stood on the banks of African lakes; they found themselves by the Tiber and in the port at Bremen; by the Vesera River and in Canada on the St Lawrence River. But will they be Poles? I don't know. Maybe they will, but not all of them. They have had not only their childhood stolen from them but also their nationality..."

The book was also highly praised by the well-known and much acclaimed Dr Zbigniew Brzezinski, who was adviser for National Security in President Carter's administration. I baptised his child in Montreal. He wrote of the book that it is "a compelling and moving account of a little known chapter during the Second World War; a story about 380,000 Polish children deported to the Soviet Union during the years 1939-41... It is of huge historical significance, as a document about charity, courage and a rare human tragedy."

But it was the comments of my orphaned children which were most interesting. Zdzisław Kulesza wrote: "The book is great. That's not a compliment, but an honest opinion – and not only mine... As far as I'm concerned I was shocked and I'll tell you honestly I did not expect such a succinct and interesting book. Father obviously reads our thoughts."

In 1983 the book was translated and published under the English title *Stolen Childhood*. It was translated by Kazimierz J Rozniatowski from Winnipeg. Both Professor Catherine Morrisey from Dunkirk in New York State and Dr Calvin Smith, dean of English literature at the State University of New York in Fredonia, were my advisers. I dedicated the book to his Eminence Joseph Charbonneau. Today this edition can be easily bought over the internet.

Displaced Persons

Increasingly, after our arrival in Canada we would hear the expression Displaced Person (DP for short and for the plural of DP the Poles would say *DeePeeshee*). This was the term given to anyone who as a result of the war had been moved to a free/safe country. Another term commonly used was *refugee.* When the term DPs was used it was generally said in a mocking tone of voice and with a sense of superiority. In relationship to myself and the orphans both terms were insulting, hurtful and stigmatised us onto the margins of society, treating us as second class citizens. We would defend ourselves against these taunts, because in reality we had had to leave our native country in dramatic circumstances for reasons completely beyond our control. We had no intention of wandering around the world and beginning life all over again. We did not return to our country at the end of the war because our enemy had taken over our culture and our faith.

A story about a young DP

I had the opportunity to know just how damaging and inhuman the label DP could be. I was once called to the Bordeaux prison in Montreal, where a twenty-one-year old man was in jail accused of murder. The press gave him another label – that of "wild man", because he was so strong that when he was arrested he threw off the policemen like a wounded bear would throw off hunting dogs. The prison guard wanted to accompany me in the cell, over the entrance of which hung the sign "special prisoner". They told me that although he was shackled he could still be dangerous. I thanked them for their concern and entered on my own. His name was Maksymilian C. He had a handsome young face, with clear Slavic features. He was sitting on a bed with his head hanging down.

I visited him once a week for two months. He didn't utter a word, while I almost coughed up my lungs in the effort of talking to him. Only after many visits, as I was leaving after yet another discouraging meeting, he mumbled, "Father forget about me". Up until then he had been distrustful and closed in on himself on account of his hurtful experience of life. But the fact that he said something was a breakthrough and it was the beginning of a human friendship. I found out that he was a good man and another war victim. The Germans had shot his parents in front of his house; and as a ten-year-old boy he escaped through the window and hid in the bushes. Not having any close relatives he fled to the woods to join the Home Army partisans, where he served them as a runner. The war ended and he joined an organised gang which lived off robberies. He remained illiterate. But something of his family upbringing stayed with him for one Sunday standing on a slag-heap somewhere in Silesia he observed people smartly dressed going to church and greeting each other with the words "Praised be the Lord Jesus Christ". At that moment he thought to himself, "Why am I different to these people?" Then he spent some time in prison for a raid on a bank. After the amnesty he promised himself that he would try to lead an honest life. For his exemplary work in the factory he received congratulations and awards. But he wanted to get out into the wider world and he devised a plan. From his wages he bought flippers, a swimming cap and a piece of *halva* to eat. In the vicinity of Szczecin he managed to avoid the border-guards on the Baltic coast and swam out to sea. In the morning after he lost sight of land he rested on the wreck of a ship which was partly submerged; then he swam on. On the third day, half dead, he was hauled out of the sea by a Danish fishing boat. He asked for asylum and was accepted in Canada.

So – a new country a new start in life. He decided to be a model citizen. But his conscientious and exemplary work provoked a jealous response. He heard himself referred to as "that damned Pole". But he didn't understand. From the anger in the eyes of his co-workers he read hatred and jealousy because he was outstripping them in their work. Get back to your own country, they taunted him. He took to living on his own; he knew how to survive. He squatted in an abandoned summer cabin where he found a rifle. He sawed off the barrel and went to nearby farms to steal eggs. One day he went into a grocery store and demanded money from the shop-keeper. Her screaming brought her husband to the scene. There was a struggle and the gun went off. During the hunt for the murderer the farmers informed the police that their eggs had gone missing. That was circumstantial evidence, a manhunt was organised and he was sent to jail.

He hoped that he would be forgiven, as he was young and a war victim. The Polish Canadian Congress lobbied to have his sentence overturned, but in vain. He was a DP. Meanwhile I taught him the articles of faith from the mysteries of the rosary. He was glad that I could teach him to read and write. I supplied him with chalk. He sketched symbolic scenes from his life.

We did not manage to save him. I spent the last day of his life together with him behind bars. Bishop Trudel of Tabor (near Montreal) accorded him the sacrament of Confirmation. A poor cleaning-woman offered him a small cross and spent an hour in adoration before the Blessed Sacrament in his intention, from midnight to one o'clock in the morning. Men from the Polish Canadian Congress came to say goodbye, among them the father of Zbigniew Brzezinski, as did simple prison-guards. He stood in front of them radiant with wide-open eyes like a child. He didn't touch his meal, but he took an orange into his hand and said, "None of the policemen who captured me have stopped to say goodbye, even though they are passing the bars of my cell all the time. I know what they think of me, that I am a thug and will always remain one. But this orange is a sign of God's love. It was sent to me from far away, perhaps even California. It passed from hand to hand, many hundreds of hands, until it reached the prison kitchen. Through this orange God wishes to sweeten the last moments of my life."

As the hour of the execution drew closer he started to get impatient since the visitors were taking up too much of his time. He asked me to read from the New Testament about Christ's way of the cross and death.

On Friday, the feast of Our Lady of Sorrows, 27 March 1953, at twelve midnight the prison chaplain celebrated Mass so that I could do the readings and prepare Maksymilian for his first and only Holy Communion. After Mass I shook his hand and I said, "Maksymilian, until we meet again in heaven." He answered by taking my hand in his strong hands and saying, "Father, don't be afraid. So long, until we meet in heaven." Tears gathered in my eyes. Minutes later the condemned man was hanging from the gallows. On his exposed chest hung the rosary, which had prepared his way to God.

The article which I wrote for the French and English press *A murderer discovers God* eventually raised a hornet's nest. Alongside positive letters to the editor there were also words of outrage; how dare I call a DP a converted man – a good man; as if there never were conversions, as if God did not draw people to Himself. In their eyes he remained a DP to the end.

Winding up the work with the orphans

Around this time my work with the orphans came to an end. However, the completion of their education, their integration into society and their marriages and subsequent families did not signify the disintegration of the orphan family. With a few exceptions they remained a tightly-knit group which stood in place of everything they had lost – their country and their own families – and offered support in exile. Just as the wandering-nomad always prays in his mother-tongue so his heart remains loyal to those who are closest and dearest to him in his youth. Compared to natural orphans, our children had additional reasons for maintaining spiritual and psychological bonds. They had shared experiences and the same life trajectory of exile and wanderings. No one understands them as well as the person who like them has touched the abyss of life and has miraculously survived.

An early meeting with the grown-up orphans and their new families

Acknowledging the help and care extended towards the orphans

I would like to express here my heartfelt gratitude to His Excellency Archbishop Joseph Charbonneau, to Cardinal Paul-Émile Léger and to the male and female congregations for the unselfish Christian support which they extended to us over several years. I remember that when Cardinal Karol Wojtyła was elected as the successor of Saint Peter, Cardinal Léger asked me to remind the newly-elected Pope of the Samaritan-inspired kindness which French Canada had extended to the Polish orphans. Indeed, many French and Polish families became friendly with the children, especially Louis and Jeanne McComber and the Rzemien family who offered their help for many years. They treated several of the boys as if they were their own sons, spending holidays and feast-days with them. A special recognition should go to Dr Verschelden, who for a goodly number of years provided cost-free care for the orphans. In some instances at my request he treated poor Polish families without recompense.

I would like to go back to an earlier time here, in order to express my thanks to the NCWC (National Catholic Welfare Conference) which equipped each settlement-camp in Africa with a community centre, educational material, library, liturgical vessels, sanatoria, nursing-homes and scout huts. As a matter of interest an employee of NCWC, an American of Polish descent called Józef Wnukowski, chose as his wife a girl from Tengeru, Regina Szczygieł.

Part VIII

Canada: Pastoral Duties

In March 1959 a telegram arrived from Poznan informing me about the death of my mother. For everyone the death of their mother is a great blow; because after God your mother occupies the second place in your heart and you consider her the best person in the world. I never called my mother anything else but "Mummy". In this word I tried to encapsulate all the love that I could muster. The circumstances of her death were that she and her six-year-old grandson Luke were standing outside a shop in a queue for bread and butter. In Communist Poland at the time queuing for groceries was a daily occurrence. The Communist system was attempting to introduce heaven on earth in such a way that it couldn't even guarantee basic foodstuffs for its people. When the shop assistants opened the grocery store the people from the back of the queue pushed their way to the front because they were afraid that they would miss out. In the ensuing rush my mother had a stroke. People asked her whether they should call for a priest but she answered, "No. I have just left church and I have just received Holy Communion." At her request they took her home and not to a hospital. She was still able to talk with her daughter – my sister Władzia – but after a few days the paralysis affected her speech. She died shortly afterwards, having lived sixty-four years and having survived two terrible wars.

She carried her heart on her sleeve, so to speak. Forgetting about her own most basic needs she sacrificed her entire life for the family. She received the strength for such unselfish love from her deep faith. I still have vivid memories of her mother – my grandmother – in deep prayer; and similarly of my mother. It had been eighteen years since I had last seen her when I had gone home for the summer holidays from Niepokalanów a year before the outbreak of World War II. This lengthy separation was caused not only by my deportation into Siberia and subsequent post-war wanderings, but also because the Communists had taken control of the government in Poland with the back-up of Soviet military might.

While my mother was still alive it was impossible for me to return to Poland for many years. The regime had revoked my Polish citizenship and even threatened me with punishment for "abducting" the orphans to Canada. At the time of my mother's death I had been a priest for ten years. She had never seen me at the altar or heard me proclaiming the Word of God. I wrote to her when I could, but my letters had to be bland and non-committal because of state censorship and surveillance. This was also the reason why our correspondence was so sparse. Both of us offered this sacrifice to God. Even the death of Stalin did nothing realistically to change Poland. The road back to my country was still closed. It would be another fourteen years from the time of the death of my mother to the easing of some of the rigours of Communism before I could dare go back to my country for the first time.

Parish work

My religious superiors were aware that the children had finished their education and had become independent. Practically speaking, the orphanage no longer existed and I was free. Father Jerzy Roskwitalski, superior of the American Polish Franciscan province summed up the situation by saying, "You are still technically a member of the Polish Franciscan province which ties my hands. I cannot use you in one of our parishes because you are waiting for the collapse of Communism to return to Poland. How long can you wait? It doesn't look as if Communism is about to collapse in the near future. Rather, it is spreading in the world and some are even prophesying that it will last a thousand years. Get yourself transferred to the American province of Saint Anthony of Padua so that I can benefit from your life experiences. And if Poland frees herself from Communism we will not stop you from going back. Moreover, in the event that your Polish brothers should say to you, 'He spent his youth in the pleasant West but brings back to us his old bones for care and treatment', then we are prepared to take you back!" After I received permission from Poland to transfer my affiliation I became a member of the American province. Father Roskwitalski moved me from the parish of the Holy Trinity, where my presence was essentially that of a resident, to the parish of Our Lady of Częstochowa on Gascon Street in Montreal in the capacity of curate to the parish priest Father Fredryk Bałdyga.

Father Bałdyga monitored me for a long time because of his prejudice to DPs. As with many Americans he was a pedant aspiring to the German principle of *Ordung aber müss sein* – Come what may, there must be order. Since I had been allocated to this new work I mustn't hark back to my previous assignment; that was the opinion of the parish priest. But my position was exceptional. My contact with the orphans continued to be active and familial. One day quite by chance, I overheard a telephone conversation involving my parish priest. From the answers I guessed that I was the subject of the conversation and that the person calling was one of my former charges. The priest's words were harsh and for the listener they were simply ruthless: "He's not with you anymore. He has been moved to a new assignment. Forget about him and leave him alone." That statement hurt me a lot, and presumably hurt the person on the other end of the phone even more. I was terrified that the words of the priest would spread around the orphan family. I was in anguish over not being able to do anything about the matter. Can you forbid someone to love? To keep in touch? As a matter of principle pastoral work should not be restricted by administrative boundaries.

I came to like working in the parish, especially with the children and young people. Every Sunday afternoon I organised games and recreation, and screened comedy and cowboy films and also religious films such as *The Song of Bernadette* about Saint Bernadette Soubirous. In the evenings I took the youth people to social gatherings and dances; while during the week I acted as chaplain to the various meetings for adults.

I must pay tribute here to an amazing couple – Władysław Stępien and his wife Agrypina. Both had been members of the Polish Home Army (*Armia Krajowa – AK*). In the parish Mrs Stępien acted as the co-ordinator of the Third Order of Saint Francis (now referred to as Lay Franciscans), while her charismatic husband took over work with the youngsters and organised a dance group. Both of them extended their care to include the elderly, the lonely and the ill. The Society of St Ann (*Towarzystwo Św Anny*) was extremely active, as was the Living Rosary Association. The Sisters of the Resurrection organised theatrical performances with the help of the children, many of which resulted in comical situations. I still recall scenes from one such play *The Defence of Częstochowa*. During the play the boys – dressed up as soldiers – were energetically firing muskets so that the whole monastery was filled with smoke. As the curtains came down a little boy, half-Polish half-Italian, jumped to the front of the stage calling out to his parents in the audience, " Mummy, Daddy don't be afraid. It's not a real war."

From time to time I would accompany outings to Ste Anne de Beaupré in northern Quebec, Midland in Ontario and Auriesville in the USA, (all places where the Jesuits Jean de Brébeuf, Lalande, René Goupil and Isaac Jogues had been martyred). The youngsters were learning about the religious virtue of courage. For Indians, courage and bravery were considered to be the most important of all virtues. During the burning of Jean de Brébeuf at the stake the Mohawk leader was so impressed by the bravery of the missionary who was singing and praying for their conversion that he jumped into the flames which had engulfed the missionary and cutting into his chest pulled out his heart and proceeded to eat it. He believed that by so doing he would also be as brave as the missionary. On many occasions we would go to the largest Basilica in the world dedicated to Saint Joseph – Oratoire St Joseph in Montreal. The Oratory was built thanks to the efforts of a humble brother of the Congregation of the Holy Cross, Brother André Besette, who was canonised by Pope Benedict XVI in 2010. Saint André never finished his basic schooling, had no skills and was constantly ill, but he possessed a remarkable gift of prayer. His parish priest encouraged the superiors of the Congregation to accept him saying, "He will be praying for you all". We would also visit American Częstochowa and Philadelphia.

In a stateless situation

After the conclusion of military activities, the Communist regime installed in Poland by Moscow urged all Poles who had remained abroad to return to their country, especially officers and soldiers of the Second Corps of General Anders who for the most part were ex-deportees to Siberia. Presumably, Stalin couldn't stand the thought that witnesses of the Soviet atrocities had managed to escape from the Soviet Union and had fought for a different Poland than the one he imposed on them. The Katyn murders were not yet widely talked about. In 1946 by order of the

Council of Ministers the Communist regime revoked the citizenship of several high ranking officers of the Polish Armed Forces, and of many others who also could not return to their country. This was also the case with me. I considered myself to be without a country from the time that I was called a "kidnapper" of Polish orphans. The call to return was a treacherous game played out on patriotic emotions. They tried to entice Poles to return from abroad in order to imprison or to eliminate them. Many of them, especially officers living abroad, asked in their testaments that they should be cremated and that their ashes be buried in Poland.

My position of "statelessness" prompted me to obtain Canadian citizenship, for practical reasons if none other, so I could travel to other countries. My citizenship examination was conducted by a French Canadian official. He was delighted that I had such a good command of the French language. He didn't ask me about the Canadian Constitution, history or social affairs of the Province of Quebec. The subject of our long discussion was the Soviet Union, Communism, the Gulag Archipelago and my stay in the Middle East and Africa.

I only regained my Polish citizenship in 1989 after the fall of Communism and the change of the system of government.

Who is the boss here?

The Polish community in Montreal, as everywhere else in the world, was divided into the New and the Old Polish émigré communities. The old Polish community had formed before the First World War while the New Poles were made up of a mosaic of various asylum-seekers after the Second World War. The old Polish community had spoken Polish at home and in their Polish schools. But their language knowledge was not sufficient. In time they preferred to use the English language, especially for professional purposes. The arrival in Montreal of Polish speaking Franciscans from the United States developed in them an even greater desire to move to the English language. For a few who were already experiencing problems with the Polish language Father Fredryk Bałdyga decided to introduce one Mass on Sunday in the English language. Being aware of French-English antagonism, I warned him not to do it but he took the risk. Meanwhile, the request of the parish priest surprised the diocesan chancellor, who reasoned that if the French were fighting

261

so hard to maintain their national identity and language then the Poles should do so also. It surprised him that in a French province the Poles were moving more willingly to the use of the English language. He recalled that the first pastors among the Poles (who were not Franciscans) kept all their parish books in French. But in America the Polish Franciscans had adopted English. Could it be that the Poles had lost their language? He commented ironically that for those who so badly wanted to have an English liturgy the simplest thing to do was to sign themselves up to the English parish of Saint Patrick; thereby reminding Father Bałdyga who was boss in the Province of Quebec. He declared that Poles in their Polish parishes could only introduce French-language Masses. So the project failed dismally.

Pastoral work in the Polish Parish, Montreal

Several first class artists emerged from among the new Polish community (*Polonia*). In our parish both Stefan Kątski and Jan Mental produced some interesting work. Kątski was an experienced artist in the medieval Moorish art of painting on leather. Rarely encountered in the Americas it is called Cordovan leather painting after the Spanish town of Cordoba. The paintings which are executed on pressed goat-skins are exceptionally durable. The artist decorated the tabernacle, altar, pulpit and communion-rails with Cordovan leather and also designed a triptych at the back of the church. Meanwhile Jan Mental, who originally came from the mountain regions of Poland, left behind a beautiful crucifix and several sculptures placed by the altar and communion-rails. Thanks to the Cordovan leather-work the parish church of Our Lady of Częstochowa was formally included in the guide to sacred monuments in Montreal.

In the post of parish priest

In June 1964 at the age of 54, Father Fredryk Bałdyga died of emphysema. The immediate cause of death was a weak heart, damaged by his addiction to tobacco. In spite of warnings from doctors that he would end up in a wheelchair he didn't have enough will-power to quit the habit. After the funeral the Father Provincial, Jerzy Rozkwitalski, appointed me as his successor. Elevating a DP priest to this position had repercussions among the other priests of the American Franciscan province. Perhaps more than one dreamed about taking over that foremost Canadian parish.

My life experiences helped me in running the parish. Due to the earlier chronic illness of Father Fredryk I had been standing in for him in almost all his parish activities. I only regretted that the administrative position of parish priest took me away from pastoral duties and forced me to become engaged in organisational matters, administration and church repairs. It saddened me because my life had really prepared me to engage with people.

The post-war Polish émigrés considered my nomination to be evidence of their social advancement. Meanwhile the old Polonia was disappointed, although they did not say so explicitly. They would have preferred as their parish priest a Franciscan who was born in the United States. They felt closer to the Anglo-Saxon faction. Although the parishioners spoke Polish they actually found it easier to communicate in English. Among them were specialists from many different fields. However, these social divisions did not constitute a barrier for me in carrying out my work. I loved and valued everyone and gave to each what they needed.

For a long time I was alone without a curate, which made my work very difficult; so I was delighted when I received a letter from Fr Łucjan Wojciechowski from Poland who was visiting his brother in Toledo, Ohio. As a professor in the Sandomierz Diocesan Seminary, he wanted to take a closer look at French Catholicism as practised in the Province of Quebec. He requested if he could share our hospitality for some time. I considered the request to be a blessing from God and took him in like my own brother. Over the several months that he stayed with me he had the opportunity to study the colourful history of the Catholic Church in Canada and to meet several outstanding people, lay as well as clergy. Together with him I visited General Kazimierz Sosnowski, Chief of the Polish Armed Forces at the end of the Second World War. At the time he was retired and lived with his wife on a farm outside Montreal. When I presented myself to him as an ex-artillery officer-cadet and later chaplain at the military hospital in the rank of Captain, he asked me playfully tongue-in-cheek whether I carried a hunting-gun under my cassock like Father Robak in *Pan Tadeusz*. I recalled that he made the same joke at my expense when we had met in Beirut in 1943!

Father Wojciechowski – a charismatic priest with many talents – helped me to revitalise the parish. He delivered popular lectures on religious topics based on Christian apologetics. The Polish émigrés reacted positively to this rarity. Every week the parish hall was filled to bursting point. This free continuing education course was compared by some to a people's university. The professor was also an excellent preacher so that services with the exposition of the Blessed Sacrament would make all the faithful tearful – including the main celebrant! His "spiritual labour" united us together for the rest of my life.

In 1966 Polish émigrés all over the world – and therefore also the Polish parishes located outside Poland – were preparing to celebrate the Millennium of Christianity in Poland with a nine-year novena. I don't know of any other country where the birth of a country's statehood coincides with its official Baptism (acceptance of Christianity). But that is how it was in Poland.

Since Father Professor Wojciechowski had by then returned to Poland, the extra work involved in the Millennial celebrations persuaded me to bring over from England my friend and companion during the Soviet years, Father Rysiek Gruza. Up to then he had been serving as a parish priest for the small Polish community in the port town of Bristol in the West of England. He accepted my call with enthusiasm.

An unusual guest

For several years during the summer months the modern Polish transatlantic liner M/S *Batory* which was built just before the Second World War used to call at the port of Montreal. Ocean liners could visit the port because of the latitude at which Montreal is situated and the depth of the St Lawrence River. The *Batory* brought over from Poland many compatriots; and the seamen would augment their sparse Communist salaries by selling amber and spirits.

Due to the proximity of our parish to the port, many visiting priests would stay at our presbytery. Among them was one unusual guest – Father Wojciech Turowski, Superior General of the Pallotine Fathers. He stayed with me for several days. In the evenings he would tell me stories from his interesting life. During the First World War as a German officer he commanded a hospital unit in Gdansk, later fighting at the front. Only after the war did he enter the seminary. As a priest he worked in various ecclesiastical capacities; as a lecturer in moral theology and homiletics, as a parish priest and pastoral worker, as a retreat master, as a rector of a seminary, as a novice-master and finally as an adviser to the Father Provincial of the Pallotines. It was a life as colourful as a kaleidoscope.

He recounted one particularly shocking story to me. In 1950, while performing his duties as Superior General of the Pallotine Fathers, he was nominated by Pope Pius XII as auxiliary bishop of Częstochowa in immediate succession to Bishop Teodor Kubina. With the papal document in his hand he set off for Poland. The nomination was to be announced by the Polish Primate Cardinal Stefan Wyszynski and he was to ordain him as bishop. He landed at Okęcie airport outside Warsaw in the middle of the night, where functionaries of the secret police (*Urząd Bezpieczenstwa – UB*) immediately approached him. They informed him that they knew the purpose of his visit to Poland, but that as he was *persona non grata* he was not viewed favourably in the People's Republic and therefore he must return to Rome that very night. Moreover, in a spirit of generosity, the highest authorities (in Poland) were graciously allowing him to visit the Polish Primate, Father Wyszynski. A secret police patrol wagon drove Father Turowski direct to the Primate's residence. He found him in a state of great agitation. The cardinal cried at the sight of his visitor from Rome, asking him to inform the Holy Father that he was barely managing to carry his cross and that he was requesting that someone else should replace him. The police wagon took Father Turowski straight back to the airport and that same evening he returned to the Eternal City, where he felt forced to resign from the bishopric.

In the home of Rafał Malczewski

Rafał, the son of the famous Polish symbolist painter Jacek Malczewski (1854-1929) was also a painter and he settled in Montreal. In exile he had already passed through France and Brazil before arriving in Canada. His wife asked me to visit him when he was already ailing and had become bedridden.

When he saw me in my clerical collar he shouted out, "Get away from me". He pointed with his finger to the door and angrily turned his face to the wall. After a moment he glanced around again and seeing that I was not leaving, shouted again, "Get away from me". I was amused by this reception and in slow measured steps I approached the aging artist. I guessed why he was treating me that way. He was angry at God for paralysing the right hand which he used for painting. He had a childish conception of God. So I took off my clerical collar and asked him, "Is this better? Will you accept me now?" I visited him weekly and he got to like me. I took him books and wine and we would discuss various topics, but

266

he stubbornly avoided any conversation about theology. I urged him to become reconciled with God. I told him that there was nothing to be embarrassed about since even in the media today people talk about their most intimate human failings, while for the Merciful God no human activity is so appalling that it could not be forgiven. I visited him up to the day before his death in 1965. He refused to the very end the Sacrament of Reconciliation; but he was a good man. Like many others he had neglected his religion; but God also loves people like that.

Blessed Kateri Tekakwita

Among the notable guests to the presbytery were Father Rafał Grządziel, a Bernardine friar, and the Reverend Dr Zdzisław Peszkowski, a survivor of the Katyn massacre and a former scouting instructor for the Polish youth in India. He subsequently entered the Polish seminary in Orchard Lake, Michigan. Many years later he was to become famous as chaplain to the association of families who had been deported to the Soviet Union and of the families of the murdered Polish army officers from Katyn, Miednoje and Charkhov.

Both guests were from the Polish seminary in Orchard Lake. Both had been scouts for years and as young scout-masters had taken part in the international scouting jamboree in Spała, Poland in 1935 just a few years before the war. They had ventured up to Montreal in search of the grave of the young Indian woman Kateri (Catherine) Tekakwita who had died in 1680. I was intrigued by their quest. As Poles where did they get the idea to visit the grave of an Indian woman from the warrior tribe of Mohawks, belonging to the Confederation of six nations (tribes) called the Iroquois? Although the English referred to the native Indians in the same way as they did about the Africans – that is as people of a lower category – the Indians had established a powerful federation consisting of the Mohawk, Seneca, Oneida, Onondaga, Cayuga and Tuscarora! Apparently young Kateri had appeared to one of them in a dream or vision – in a fringed Indian leather skirt. She foretold the terrible sufferings that the Polish nation was shortly to experience on account of a new war, an ordeal from which they would emerge with honour.

The newcomers came to the right place. The grave of Kateri is located in the Indian reservation Caughnawaga, close to Montreal at the mission church of Saint Francis Xavier. Kateri, the daughter of the Mohawk leader Konhoronkwa, was born in the Ossernenon settlement, close to today's town of Amsterdam. The settlement was built high on the banks of the river Mohawk, so that the warriors could control the flow of craft (*pirogues*) on the river below. They encircled their settlement with a palisade. Kateri's parents fell victims to a smallpox epidemic, which the Indians attributed to the spells of the missionaries. The little girl who was four years old at the time was also slightly affected by the disease but she survived. She was taken in by her maternal uncle and at the age of nineteen she received baptism from the hands of the Jesuit missionaries, who in time were to become martyrs. The responsibilities of a Christian did not allow her to live a fully integrated Indian life, and this meant that she was persecuted by the tribe, especially by her uncle who wanted to kill her. To protect her from their revenge the missionaries decided to send her to the St Francis Xavier Mission near Montreal, about three hundred miles away. Taking the opportunity of the absence of her uncle three Indians from the Huron nation led her away from the settlement during the night. For a while they travelled by *pirogue*, later making their way through the woods. Kateri's uncle and his companions immediately set out in pursuit of her. After many adventures Kateri finally made it to the Jesuit mission in Caughnawaga. There she received her first Holy Communion and later taught Indian children their catechism. She died at the age of twenty-four. After her death her face lost its scars and became so beautiful that the Indians referred to her as the Lily of the Mohawks. Pope Pius XII bestowed upon her the title Venerable Servant of God, while Pope John Paul II declared her Blessed in 1980. Pope Benedict XVI is to declare her a saint of the universal church in the autumn of 2012.

Rumours

For a brief time there were rumours about the establishment of a bishopric for the Polish diaspora in Canada, at the disposition of the Canadian bishops who had Polish parishes in their dioceses. I did not think that creating such a separate position was possible, necessary or even practical. Pope Pius XII produced a beautiful Apostolic Constitution – *Exsul Familia* (1952) – concerning the spiritual welfare of immigrants, but the Canadian and American bishops ignored it. In time, life itself helped in the obliteration of ethnic distinctions and in the integration of immigrants into the host society.

Second Vatican Council

My memoirs must inevitably touch upon events from the twentieth century – a century in which the maxims of the Enlightenment acknowledging the priority of human reason had deprived many of their faith. The human ideologies which led to the turning away from God and his Commandments was responsible for two World Wars, three totalitarian systems, concentration camps, heaps of corpses, seas of blood and millions of people thrown out of their countries.

In 1962 the Catholic world accepted with joy and hope the opening of the Second Vatican Council by "Good Pope" John XXIII (now counted among the *beati* as Blessed Pope John XXIII). The council was a great blessing of God for the Catholic Church and the world; a gift of our Saviour Jesus Christ himself. The church needed to be reformed in order to continue having its sacred influence upon the world. After the Council of Trent (1545-1563) the Church turned into a closed fortress – a fortified depository to preserve the Holy Faith. Blessed John XXIII saw, that as a result of this self-enclosure, people living outside the Church without spiritual guidance were becoming increasingly paganised. In order for the Church to move closer to them he threw out the catchword *aggiornamento* adapting and modernising the *human* structures of the church. He described it in a picturesque way saying that it was like "opening the windows and airing out the interior of a musty church".

Liturgical changes in my parish

At the parish level the changes affected primarily the Divine services, that is – the liturgy. There was the transition from the use of the Latin language to the use of the native tongue – the vernacular. Most of the people in my parish eagerly accepted the use of their native Polish language because they could understand the word of God. But there were others who regretted the loss of Latin on account of its unifying and universal character. It allowed Catholics to feel at home without regard to which country they were in. They felt that the Latin language evoked an atmosphere of mystery and a sense of *sacrum* – the sacred.

Other changes were less significant. They concerned the altar, tabernacle and singing. According to the new liturgy the cross which is placed by the altar symbolises the Resurrected Christ, the Lord of History – who is with us. It is He who now takes over the leadership of His people and leads them to the house of His father. The priest is His helper.

The Blessed Sacrament was taken from the central altar and given shelter in a tabernacle for adoration by the faithful and for the sick. A tabernacle is the Arc of the New Covenant. In our church there was no separate chapel where one could put the tabernacle with the Blessed Sacrament for adoration; so we placed it in a side-altar but this led to disorientation for some the parishioners.

The council desired that the entire parish community should express its faith and love through communal singing. On the whole Poles enjoy collective singing but in my parish the introduction of singing by all the faithful was not approved of by members of the parish choir. We had to go for a compromise – one Sunday the choir would sing and on the other Sunday the congregation.

My country Poland managed to avoid many of these experiments thanks to the Polish Primate Cardinal Stefan Wyszynski. He was aware that even the smallest misunderstanding in the church could be used by the Communist authorities to break up unity and damage the church, and therefore he would not allow any changes without his explicit endorsement. Therefore changes were prepared by experts and introduced with great caution.

Felix culpa

Around this time I experienced a period which was very difficult for me. I underwent a crisis with regard to the responsibilities I had resulting from my vocation. Up until then I had always been convinced that my life experiences, together with my ability to confront temptations head-on, had helped strengthen me in my priestly vocation. But it wasn't that simple. The rapid pace of wartime activities and post-war events, the fast-forwarding of my theological studies and the large – possibly too large – engagement in parish work, undertaken within an atmosphere of antipathy towards DPs, all contributed to undermine my spiritual life. I neglected my prayer-life and there was a decrease in my contact with God – the source of my strength. Confident of my own strength, I forgot the warning of Saint Paul: *Therefore let anyone who thinks that he stands take heed lest he fall* (I Corinthians 10,12). Being young and sure of my own powers I did not take to heart the words of Christ ...*apart from me you can do nothing* (John 15,5). The sin of activism meant that due to lack of time, I didn't prepare my sermons and homilies properly. Overly busy with other things I did not take seriously the warning voice of God; I saddened God by this activity, although I never stopped loving Him.

According to the catechism, violating the law of God is called a sin. But the word in and of itself means very little; perhaps that is why it is unpopular today. It is better to consider the nature of the relationship of man with God. Then, sin becomes a matter relevant to the nature of our love and about breaking the covenant. That love can be – to a greater or lesser extent – betrayed, forgotten, neglected, affronted and even sometimes can change into the opposite of love and in its place enters enmity and hatred. As far as my relationship with God was concerned, I could be more open since as sinful beings the need to acknowledge our weaknesses and downfalls is always great. This was demonstrated in concentration camps where the prisoners, not having the opportunity for sacramental confession, would confess their sins to their companions in penal servitude. Under normal conditions human sensitivity is diminished so it is easier to forget that God is everywhere and sees everything.

In discovering the faults and slip-ups of our neighbours we have the tendency to proclaim harsh judgement about them; we notice the proverbial log in their eye, while attributing to ourselves the smallest speck (Matthew 7,3). And when we rely solely on the harsh justice of ...*eye for eye, tooth for tooth*... (Exodus 21,24) how many of us overstep the boundaries of justice, so that we are without mercy towards our neighbour? This merciless stance of humans provoked King David to say the words: "...*let us fall into the hand of the Lord, for his mercy is great; but let me not fall into the hand of man*" (II Samuel 24,14).

My failings prompted a crisis, the cause of which lay in my heart. It was a matter of Love. I did not recognise myself. It felt as if some outsider had entered into my life and disrupted the calm, introducing a sense of disorder. As a child and as a growing lad I always loved God, and I had the awareness that I belonged to Him, that I was developing in the light of His mercy for Him alone. This spiritual crisis brought to my mind the fall of Saint Peter the apostle. The Master forgave him his betrayal and gave him another chance – entrusting to him the welfare of human souls. To the end of his life Peter did not stop lamenting over sin. The pulsating repentance felt in my soul is similar to a continuing dialogue with the Lord, which in my case always finishes with the words "Lord have mercy upon me".

How often one would like to throw away periods of weakness, to get rid of painful wounds, scars, and embarrassments – and attempt to erase them from memory. Meanwhile the fight and escape from the clutches of the devil should be seen in keeping with the Easter hymn *The Exultet* – as a happy fault – *Felix culpa*. It evokes God's greater love and moves Him to demonstrate an even greater love and omnipotence. It is worth reconsidering from time to time the parable of the Prodigal Son.

The mercy of God changed me, above all it stimulated me to a greater love of God, and to a greater vigilance over my own salvation and of those whom Divine Providence had entrusted to my care. Zeal is the resultant consequence of loving God and loving people.

Solzhenitsyn and academics

In the context of the revolution occurring in the civilised Western world, and examining my own weaknesses, I contemplated human propensity towards sin stemming from the fall of our first parents. Without the grace of God, humans are so insignificant and frail; they can commit the most serious of sins given the right set of circumstances and in the right context. An example of this would be Hitler, Stalin, Mao Tse-Tung and many others. Humans are capable of committing a list of all the most grievous sins; they can become murderers, executioners, torturers, swindlers, adulterers, drug addicts... This is confirmed by the Russian writer, Alexander Solzhenitsyn, on the basis of his own experiences. Falsely accused by the NKVD for political transgressions he was sent to a Soviet labour camp for eight years. In his book *Gulag Archipelago* written when he was later freed, he recalls a friendship that he once had with a Red Army officer. They were like brothers sharing the same ideals, convictions and respecting the same values.

That was before Solzhenitsyn's arrest. After the war and after his release from the camp Solzhenitsyn found out that their ways had parted. Solzhenitsyn was fighting for his country's freedom, while his friend worked for the NKVD as an investigating judge – forcing confessions from innocent compatriots with the use of torture, condemning them to death or prison. Solzhenitsyn reflects that without the grace of God, he too could have gone astray like his friend if he found himself in the wrong place at the wrong time and if terrible pressure was put on him while being stupefied with a vision of a Utopian paradise on earth.

Solzhenitsyn came to the conclusion that as the gospels state there are not two categories of people – the good and the bad. Within all of us are the kernels of good and evil. Without the help of God "one and the same person, in this or some other period of his life, in differing circumstances, can become the embodiment of the devil or a saintly individual".

This conclusion of Solzhenitsyn was confirmed by a group of scientists who were taken aback by the extent of the genocide which occurred during World War II affecting the Jews, Poles, gypsies, Russians and others. The group examined what the circumstances are under which people are capable of performing such inhuman acts. They wanted to know what caused so many Germans, among whom were many learned, educated, family men who loved their wives and children, to commit the crime of genocide. They would murder thousands of prisoners and after their shift would return home to water the flowers, play with the dog and their children, talk with their wives, and listen to classical music as if nothing had happened – only to repeat the whole criminal process the next day. Solzhenitsyn and scientists point to a type of split reality – a form of schizophrenia of people working under the influence of criminal ideologies, such as German Fascism or Communism.

Solzhenitsyn and the scientists didn't say anything new which Christ had not already said turning to the accusers who wished to stone the adulteress: "*Let him who is without sin among you be the first to throw a* stone at her" (John 8,7). His disciple John writes in his letter to the early Christians, "If we say we have no sin, we deceive ourselves, and the truth is not in us" (I John 1,8). The Russian writer Fyodor Dostoyevsky, following his ordeal in Siberia, commented about those who try to organise a world without God, "If there is no God, everything is permissible."

On the ladder of Love

As I approach the end of my life I find great consolation in the truth that we are all the property of God, that He who is Love from the very nature of His Being, has "loved (us) with an everlasting love" (Jeremiah 31,3); that He created us for Himself as His children in His image and likeness. That is why "none of us lives to himself, and none of us dies to himself. If we live, we live to the Lord, and if we die, we die to the Lord; so then, whether we live or whether we die, we are the Lord's" (Romans 14,7).

The principle value – Love – the queen of virtues rules over life. But only authentic Love deserves to be described like this, a love which is unselfish and difficult to achieve. According to this principle life is the most beautiful of adventures, but also an arduous ascent, like climbing up a ladder. Evelyn Waugh in his novel Brideshead Revisited used the analogy of the ladder of Love and it was used again by George Weigel, a popular Catholic theologian and one of the main American commentators on religious and social life. This graphic depiction of life as a ladder of Love is simple and comprehensible to everyone. Whether we are conscious of it or not, we are climbing up the ladder towards God, ever higher and higher. The rungs are often creaky and break when our love is not all-embracing and authentic but just a poor substitute for the real thing. But God guides us to the top. For a substitute to true Love one can consider a love which is exclusively sexual, selfish and half-hearted in all its many variations. These are impoverished loves, wrongly aligned and acting as caricatures of true authentic Love. Ideologies often leave a false sense of love when they proclaim superiority of particular races, nations and social classes. Without reference to the True God they lead without fail to catastrophe. All religions preach about Love, and the founders of various religions were humans like Buddha, Mahomet and others, whereas the Christian faith was brought to us by God himself – Jesus Christ – who put on human nature in order to be able to talk to us in a human voice about how the Lord our God "feels" about us. Only He proclaimed and personified true, full and authentic Love. Christ, who offered the greatest sacrifice for our sins said, *"...and I, when I am lifted up from the earth, will draw all men to myself"* (John 12,32). I will conclude these reflections with a prayer by Dietrich Bonhoeffer –

O God, early in the morning I cry to you.
Help me to pray
And to concentrate my thoughts on you:
I cannot do this alone.
In me there is darkness,
But with you there is light;
I am lonely, but you do not leave me;
I am feeble in heart, but with you there is help;
I am restless, but with you there is peace.
In me there is bitterness, but with you there is patience;
I do not understand your ways,
But you know the way for me...

Part IX

America and The Radio Rosary Hour

The decision

In 1966 the provincial chapter of Conventual Franciscan friars in the USA appointed me as parish priest to the Polish Parish of Our Lady of Częstochowa in Montreal for another four years. A few days later the Father Provincial Jerzy Roskwitalski telephoned me with a problem. Father Kornelian Dende, director of the Franciscan radio station operating out of Buffalo in New York State, was disappointed that no one had been assigned as his secretary at the radio apostolate when Father Melchior Fryszkiewicz returned to Poland for health reasons. Although Father Provincial had suggested several American priests in Father Melchior's place, Father Dende did not approve of any of them. And then out of the blue he proposed me.

It was around this time that religious congregations and orders started to take into account the wishes of their members in certain situations when allocating apostolates, for example the nature of one's education or the particularities of the proposed new role. This was a departure from the centuries-old tradition connected with the vow of obedience. In this case Father Provincial asked me if I would agree to move over to the radio network. I replied that I would not want to make such a decision myself; I felt at home in the parish and all the debts had been paid off and the work was not an issue.

The practice of obedience has its merits, and many a time a friar discovers in himself dispositions that he didn't even know he possessed but which the superior was able to recognise in him. I left the decision with my superior. I drew upon military principles saying, "Father Provincial, for me you are like a military general in time of war. You know all aspects of the front, its strong and weak points and you therefore designate appropriate officers to particular posts, as required".

I think that Father Kornelian must have taken into account my literary accomplishments, my mastery of the Polish language and knowledge of its history, but above all my life experience. I gave my acquiescence. After two days I received my *obediencia*, the document ordering me to transfer to the radio station in Buffalo.

Another kind of missionary activity

After a more in-depth reflection upon my change of activity, I came to the conclusion that work in this area would actually be the fulfilment of my desire to be a missionary. This desire germinated while I was in the Junior Missionary Seminary in Niepokalanów and came to life again in Africa. But the missionary activity I was now about to start had a slightly different character from the more usually accepted idea of an overseas mission. Its target congregation was the far-flung Polish diaspora scattered all over Canada and the USA. The official name of the radio network was Father Justyn's Radio Holy Rosary Hour. The radio network took in all the major concentrations of Poles covering an area from Montreal to Vancouver in Canada and from the north down to Florida in the United States. My work consisted of writing radio-commentaries and answering listeners' letters. I was to work in the capacity of a ghost-writer – a faceless, nameless, anonymous person labouring in the background; the audience never heard my voice. The texts which I wrote were broadcast by the director of the network Father Kornelian Dende under his own name. I accepted this situation in the spirit of Franciscan humility.

I started work for the radio station in the Polish millennial year of 1966. Father Kornelian was the second director of the radio station. The founder of the programme had been Father Justyn Figas, who broadcast the Word of God for twenty-eight years while Father Kornelian continued for a further thirty-six years. They combined in their personalities the best characteristics of both Polish and American culture. One would need the writing skills of Sienkiewicz to describe their rich and varied personalities adequately. Sienkiewicz based the fictional characters for his historic epic *The Trilogy* – Zagłoba, Skrzetuski, Wołodyjowski and Podbipięta – on real-life people who were descendents of Polish officers exiled from their homeland after the collapse of the insurrections in Poland. These soldiers who later settled in California were prototypes for Father Justyn and Father Kornelian.

Both successive directors of the network made the programme so well-known that *L' Osservatore Romano* described The Rosary Hour as "the largest Polish-speaking pulpit in the world". During the radio's particularly fruitful period of expansion in the USA the Church in Poland was functioning under the harsh conditions of German and then later Soviet enslavement. Therefore there wasn't the slightest chance of establishing a Catholic radio station there. While referring to my experiences and what I lived through while working for The Radio Rosary Hour, I find it impossible to quantify the enormous work of these two great luminaries of Poland and the Polish diaspora.

Father Justyn – the founder of the network

Father Justyn's family made their way to the USA on the first wave of mass economic migration from Poland. They were lured by the statement engraved on the base of the Statue of Liberty in the Port of New York "*Give me your tired, your poor, your huddled masses yearning to breathe free...*"

The Figas family escaped from the Prussian occupation of the Wielkopolska region of Poland where they were forbidden to speak Polish. Like many Polish immigrants they settled down in the hilly countryside of Pennsylvania, where the father of the family found work in the coal mines. Michael, who later took the monastic name of Justyn, was the oldest of eleven children. He was ten years old when his mother died. From his family home he inherited a deep faith, a great love of people and an attachment to the land of his ancestors – Poland; bestowing no less a sentiment on America in turn. He was well-read in Polish and American literature. In his radio chats you could detect the picturesque language of the Polish writers Adam Mickiewicz, Henryk Sienkiewicz and Władysław Reymont. All his life he was an opponent of the American idea of the "melting-pot", that is the erasing of national characteristics of immigrants. He made sure that Polish children learnt not only the English language but also Polish. He would explain that the true Americans were the indigenous (American) Indians while the English, Germans and Poles were all merely settlers on the American continent. His talents and diligence contributed to his rise in managerial positions in the Polish province of the Conventual Franciscans in the USA. Six times he was called to the office of Provincial. His organisational talents came to the fore in setting up the structure of The Radio Rosary Hour and the building of a boys' school – Saint Francis's High School, in Athol Springs, New York State. He also constructed the novitiate in Ellicott City, Maryland, the Seminary of Saint Hyacinth in Granby, Massachusetts and Saint Joseph Intercommunity Hospital in Cheektowaga, near Buffalo.

Father Justyn first stood in front of the microphone when radio broadcasting was still in swaddling clothes. The first time was quite by chance, when a pair of broadcasters were discussing a moral problem which they couldn't quite present in an adequate way. One of them flippantly threw out the remark that they should consult Father Justyn – a well-known preacher by that time. He was duly invited to the studio. His performance was greeted with such enthusiasm by the listeners that they demanded that he should return to the microphone and continue with his wise and penetrating observations.

Father Justyn started to broadcast his own radio programme in 1931. His broadcasts became so popular that in a very short time a whole radio network was inaugurated taking in the largest concentrations of Polish speakers in the USA and then later in Canada. He rented air-time from seventy-nine radio-stations. It was at that time that he was named the "most popular Polish-American priest of the first half of the twentieth century".

There were many factors that helped in the expansion of the radio network. It was a time when the immigrants formed closed communities in order to preserve their national identity. In Buffalo, in New York State, where Father Justyn set up The Radio Rosary Hour headquarters, the poor immigrant Poles first built the church of Saint Stanisław (Stanislaus), Bishop and Martyr, and later the smaller church of Corpus Christi, in which the stained glass and wall paintings recorded the thousand-year history of Christianity in Poland. Around these and other Polish churches arose humble dwellings of Polish immigrants. On a Sunday afternoon the Polish district would come alive. The voice of Father Justyn could be heard from the open windows all along the street. One could see through the open windows whole families gathered around wireless-sets in a prayerful atmosphere – father, mother, children, grandparents and even invited guests. The programme would start with the hymn *Różaniec mój* (My rosary). The form of the time-honoured Slavic opening greeting directed at the listeners would always tug at their heart-strings: *"Praise be Lord Jesus Christ."* A half-hour catechesis session by Father Justyn would occupy the central part of the programme. It would be on various topics followed by a session of answers to questions which had been sent in by the listeners, often sprinkled with humour. The programme would end with the transmission of a Benediction service with the exposition of the Blessed Sacrament.

Testimony of an important listener

I will quote here the reminiscences of Cardinal Król, Archbishop of Philadelphia, who used to listen to The Rosary Hour in his youth.

"For many thousands of Poles The Rosary Hour is a programme which has accompanied them from their childhood. It formed the characters of our mothers and fathers, teaching them how to remain faithful to God and how to raise their children in a Godly fashion; it taught love for the country of our ancestors – from the banks of the Wisła, Warta, Odra, San and Bug. It raised the spirit, confirming faith in human dignity; it portrayed national values and encouraged the development of personal talents, strengths and abilities, which the new life in America required. It taught how to face the future boldly trusting in God and His Divine Providence... We all remember with what reverence our parents would switch on the wireless, tuning it to Father Justyn's programme. Those gathered around the sets would listen in the greatest of silence and concentration to the Word of God, flowing out in the beautiful native Polish tongue. We would wait impatiently for the no-nonsense and humorous responses of the speakers, singing hymns along with the choirs and then we would kneel down during the transmission of the Benediction service in front of the Most Holy Sacrament. As America is wide and long, every Sunday, almost every Pole would gather by the radio set, as if for a solemn feast, participating in a huge congress of The Radio Rosary Hour. I can confidently say that many years before Father Peyton threw out the catch-phrase "A family that prays together, stays together", the Polish immigrants were already putting this into practice, thanks to which they bonded as one heart and one soul."

The name of the radio programme

Listeners often wondered about the name of the radio programme: *The Radio Rosary Hour.* It is true that each programme started with the hymn about the rosary and during the programme there was often reference to the Blessed Virgin Mary but really the name itself was symbolic. The word *rosary* literally means a wreath of roses. The roses are the *Hail Marys* of the faithful. Just as roses are some of the most noble, beautiful and highly-scented flowers, so the Angelic salutation is the most pleasing to Our Blessed Mother, since it reminds her of the moment when she gave her assent – and God started to implement the salvation of the world. Allegorically, a special form of this wreath of roses – as an offering to Our Lady – was to be the community of the Polish immigrants, a part of the Polish nation transplanted from Europe to the land of George Washington. Many groups of Polish immigrants, both in Canada and the USA, united around their radio sets and like rosary beads, became one mystical chain forming a spiritual whole. Father Justyn, a Franciscan, was absolutely right. The easiest way to reach the Son of God is through His Mother – *through Mary to Jesus*. And this is the way which he always advocated.

Aid to Poland

Father Justyn really earned the title of *Father of Polish Immigrants* during the war. The immigrants painfully experienced the fourth partition of Poland between Hitler's Germany and the Soviet Union. Father Justyn was the first to reach out speedily with help to the stricken nation. With the permission and support of the US Department of State he made two trips to Europe. His first trip was in November 1939, with an eye to setting up centres on occupied territory to which funds collected in America could be sent. Unfortunately neither the Soviet nor German embassies would give him permission to enter occupied Poland. Neither was his attempt to cross into Polish lands through the forested and rural borders with Romania successful. Therefore Father Justyn remained in Romania visiting the camps of interned Polish soldiers, who numbered over forty-thousand and who had crossed the border with the intention of continuing the fight for Poland. He was witness to their hunger, misery and disease; to their despair and fear for the families they had left behind in their country.

In 1942 Father Justyn visited the Polish soldiers in England and Scotland, especially the famed airmen who had fought in the Battle of Britain. Next he made his way to Rome. During these trips he met with the highest authorities in the allied governments and with the chief of staff of the Polish armed forces, General Władysław Sikorski. He also met Cardinal August Hlond, Primate of Poland (1881-1948) whose canonisation process has been opened in 1992, and with the Superior General of the Jesuits Father Włodzimierz Ledóchowski (1866-1942) who came from a very distinguished and deeply religious family. One of Father Ledóchowski's sisters Julia Ledóchowska founded a new order of Ursuline sisters and was canonised in 2005 by Pope John Paul II as Saint Urszula Ledóchowska while his sister Maria Teresa founded a missionary congregation and was beatified in 1975 by Pope Paul VI. His uncle was Cardinal Mieczysław Ledóchowski (1822-1902). Father Justyn had meetings with various members of the hierarchy of the Catholic Church and several times met Pope Pius XII, and Monsignor Giovanni Battista Montini, later Pope Paul VI. He would often go back to the tragedy of the Polish nation in his radio chats reminding his listeners about the contribution of Polish culture to global heritage; he would often pray for Poland and encouraged people to support Polish activities with their sacrifices.

I met Father Justyn shortly before his death. Bed-ridden, time and again he would reach for his oxygen. He prepared his last programmes with great difficulty and asked that after his death the work of The Radio Rosary Hour should continue.

Rosary Hour Garden Parties

During Father Justyn's time The Rosary Hour was supported by voluntary contributions from listeners. Air-time was rented and the price quoted was dependent on the number of inhabitants living in a particular area. Larger metropolitan areas like New York, Chicago, Philadelphia and Montreal would bump up the price proportionally to the number of inhabitants, even though Poles constituted an insignificant percentage of the total number of people living there. In this situation the donations of the listeners did not cover the running costs and Father Justyn was always looking for other means of income such as garden parties, auctions, balls, lotteries, bingo and square dancing. The most popular were the garden parties which were organised on an enormous scale. They took place in Athol Springs, a suburb of Buffalo, on the open grounds belonging to the Franciscan school. A special train would operate connecting Buffalo with Athol Springs bringing in tens of thousands of listeners and sympathisers of The Rosary Hour. During the garden party the participants could watch folk-dancing and circus acts, they could take rides on merry-go-rounds, participate in games and go horse-riding. Orchestras contributed with dance music.

Father Kornelian Dende

The Franciscans chose as the successor to Father Justyn a no less providential and outstanding person – Father Kornelian Dende. He was the son of the editor of the Polish émigré newspaper *Republika-Górnik* in Scranton, Pennsylvania. His father shortened his childhood somewhat by insisting that he utilise every spare moment in learning something useful. Thanks to this approach he could play several musical instruments and could touch-type. He had been prepared for the radio apostolate through his studies in Lwów, Rome and Montreal. He had already drawn attention to himself even as a student – always coming top of the class in all his academic activities. After his ordination he worked for the Catholic Press Agency in New York City. Subsequently, for many years he was occupied as guardian of the order's Franciscan youth, both in the seminary and in the novitiate.

He was a person full of perseverance, of limitless energy and possessing a strong will; he was also quite demanding of his juniors. He started his work at the microphone by taking elocution lessons in order to acquire a fuller and more resonant pronunciation. His artistic sensitivities made him a patron of the arts, which I will describe later.

At the time of the death of Father Justyn The Rosary Hour network had seventy-nine stations. Father Kornelian reduced this number to fifty because some of the air-wave ranges overlapped each other, so that listeners could tune into the programme on two different stations. These changes were forced onto Father Kornelian by the high cost of renting radio air-time and yearly increases in the fees. By introducing these cuts expenses came down quite a bit, while the air coverage remained the same.

Father Kornelian was a great organiser, possessing many practical skills. He could repair electrical faults, work at the carpentry-bench, undertake plumbing jobs, get involved in printing processes and he could cook! What he wasn't familiar with he would learn with the help of expert text-books! He was also a demon for work, for example he would send out letters to listeners before novenas six times a year. The three of us, Father Kornelian, Father Eligiusz Kozak and myself would stuff envelopes from early morning to late at night. We had to send out sixty-five thousand letters, each one having four enclosures. In order to reduce expenses we would also sort the letters according to their postal codes and we would then pack them into mail bags marked for the main distribution centres so that the postal services could forward the letters onwards without delay. The entire project had to be completed within three days as other work would be beckoning.

Father Kornelian did not usually take holidays. A change of work was enough rest for him. He would relax during trips connected with some business commitment, for example when he went to the Annual Meeting of the Polish American Congress or when he went to Poland to receive an honorary doctorate from the Catholic University of Lublin, or when he travelled to deliver a talk to a Polish organisation. I did manage on three occasions to get him to go on a short holiday. The first time was to Poland. In Warsaw we paid a visit to the Primate of Poland Cardinal Stefan Wyszynski (whose canonisation process was opened in Poland at the request of Pope John Paul II in 1989) and who welcomed us in his warm embrace asking about our work and inviting us to take part in the Corpus Christi procession. We were allocated honorary positions right next to the baldachin while the Primate carried the monstrance.

Visiting the Primate of Poland, Servant of God Cardinal Stefan Wyszynski, 1972

After that we visited Niepokalanów, Częstochowa, Kraków, Oświęcim (Auschwitz) and also my family in Poznan.

The second time we went to Fatima and Lourdes; and the third trip was to California to see the Franciscan missions established by the famous Fra Juniper de Serra (1713-1784), even before the Americans had managed to lay claim to the territory. Pope John Paul II declared Fra Juniper blessed in 1988.

Franciscan poverty characterised Father Kornelian. Among other things this was noticeable when he would receive a gift which he would put away in a cupboard and when an appropriate occasion arose he would give it away. On one occasion he managed to give a couple celebrating their wedding anniversary the same present which they had offered to him many years before. The couple didn't know whether to laugh or be offended. From that time onwards Father Kornelian always marked on the gifts the date when he received them and the name of the donor. He was also very sensitive towards the plight of the poor and disabled, the fate of exiles, the wanderings of his compatriots and the sick and elderly. To those in need he was never short of words of encouragement in his letters, chats and in his prayers, and very often he would slip a few dollars into the envelope, especially in letters to Poland. He would discern the needs of the heart. It was enough for a listener to casually mention a forthcoming wedding anniversary and immediately he would obtain from Rome a Papal Blessing. He would send congratulations to families when a son or daughter was getting married and would import prayer books from Poland.

He was a lover of tradition. Most of his listeners were older people attached to the continuity of tradition so Father Kornelian did not change the format of the programmes; he only raised their standard and made them even better. He liked to remind his listeners of a cartoon of himself in a Chicago newspaper in which he is standing by the microphone with Father Justyn, the latter wagging his finger at him saying, "Don't forget that I will be watching you!" Father Kornelian's life motto was the principle: *Respond to a need.* Mostly these needs were spiritual and moral.

These are general character-sketches of the two directors of the radio programme. The first one I got to know mostly from accounts about him and from documents, the second one I got to know more closely from working with him and through living with him in a religious community. Both of them left an indelible mark on me. Both of them were role-models for me and for many others.

A new home for The Rosary Hour

Father Kornelian built a new centre for The Rosary Hour in Athol Springs, Buffalo, along the shores of Lake Erie, next to the parish church of Saint Francis and the High School of the same name. He designed and decorated the centre himself with works of art associated with Poland and the Polish diaspora. The works of art were produced by Polish artists. Firstly, Father Kornelian issued an invitation to the world-renowned artist Jan Henryk de Rosen (1891-1982), creator of the huge mosaic of Christ the King in the Basilica of the Immaculate Conception in Washington, DC. Rosen was a convert from Judaism. Prior to this he had completed the polychrome in the Armenian Cathedral in Lwów and in the chapel on Mount Kahlenberg, near Vienna, which commemorates the victory of King Jan Sobieski over the Turks in 1683. His paintings are to be found in the Vatican, in Poland and in many American museums. At the request of Father Kornelian he executed five splendid large paintings for The Rosary Hour chapel – representing Christ the King, Our Lady Queen of the Seraphic Order, the Stigmata of Saint Francis, Saint Bonaventure, Saint John the Baptist and the Conversion of Saint Paul. The second artist he invited was the muralist Józef Sławinski (1905-1983) from Warsaw, a specialist in *sgraffito,* a technique whereby a wall is covered in several layers of coloured plaster which are then scratched off to a particular design and to a required layer of colour. The work continues both day and night, while the artist's assistant sprinkles the plaster with water so that it does not solidify. This *sgraffito* art decorates the walls of the lobby of the High School and the chapel. There are scenes commemorating the Baptism of Poland, her one-thousand year fidelity to Christianity represented by the figure of Saint Maksymilian Kolbe and other great Polish Franciscans who have contributed to the welfare of Poles in America, like Father Leopold Moczygęba and Father Justyn Figas. Behind the altar in the chapel there is a scene representing the Coronation of the Blessed Virgin Mary.

The presence of Our Lady in The Rosary Hour programme and in the works of art and her spiritual patronage over the activity created an indefinable atmosphere. Great artists teach us to look at the beauty of the human face and at various aspects of nature from a different perspective. The paintings of the Polish artists Jan Matejko (1854-1929), Stanisław Wyspianski (1869-1907), Artur Grottger (1837-1867) and Jacek Malczewski (1854-1929) uncover before our eyes a new vision of beauty, because in transforming reality the artists also disclose to us something of their own personality. Similarly, we look upon a field differently once we have been informed that on this spot and against this particular landscape a battle raged, for example Grunwald where in 1410 the joint forces of the Poles and Lithuanians repelled the Teutonic Knights, or on the slopes of Monte Cassino where in 1944 during the concluding months of World War II the Poles and allied forces successfully fought the German army.

But where did Father Kornelian get his artistic inspiration from? Father Tadeusz Zastępa, a professor at the Catholic University of Lublin, who spent a whole year working at The Rosary Hour, was of the opinion that during Father Kornelian's studies in Rome he became enthralled by Michelangelo's *Pieta* in St Peter's Basilica. Father Kornelian wrote in his notes on the subject: "As soon as you look at the statue which constitutes an enigmatic whole, your eyes and thoughts are driven to meditating upon the all-encompassing peace and pain – but not resignation – on the face of the Virgin Mary. It took the genius of Michelangelo to capture and then preserve for future generations the radiant beauty of Our Lady, which was the external expression of her immaculate soul."

Father Kornelian himself had a not insignificant artistic talent. His paintings were eagerly sought. I much admired his free-hand doodles and landscapes which he executed on black sand during his long telephone conversations.

Contact with the family of the artists

Every time I happened to be in New York City, I would pay a visit to Mrs Wanda Styka, widow of the Polish painter Adam Styka (1890-1959). His father, Jan Styka (1858-1925), who had executed the monumental painting *The Crucifixion,* was the most notable of the whole family of painters. It is the largest religious panoramic painting in the world. I saw it in Forest Lawn Memorial Park in Glendale, California, where a special pavilion had been built to house it. Jan Styka was a student of the famous Polish artist Jan Matejko. Apart from the work *The Crucifixion* he also co-created the famous *Panorama Racławicka* now hanging in Wrocław, Poland. His son Adam made an unforgettable impression on me with his painting *The Homage of Angels.* The painting hung in Wanda's apartment where we had many of our conversations. Father Kornelian and I asked her to donate it to The Radio Rosary Hour, but she refused explaining that during her husband's lifetime, they would kneel in front of the painting every evening and pray together. The painting was for her a way of keeping in spiritual contact with him. But Father Kornelian, refusing to admit defeat, ordered a copy of the painting to be made, which later decorated the living-room of our Radio centre. In the house of the Sisters of the Holy Family of Nazareth, in Torresdale

288

near Philadelphia, I saw another equally moving picture by Adam Styka, representing the Nazi execution in Nowogródek of eleven Polish sisters of their congregation in 1943. Apparently the German soldier who conducted the execution asked for forgiveness before his death. The murdered sister Stella and her ten companions were beatified in 2000 by Pope John Paul II as martyrs. The colourful paintings by Adam and Tadeusz Styka (both artist sons of Jan Styka) were put on our calendars and sent to listeners of The Rosary Hour.

American Częstochowa

Many years before, during my time in Italy with the orphans, I met in Rome a young priest from the Pauline order, Father Michał Zembrzuski (1908-2003). At the time I found out from him that Stalin had ordered the closure of all religious houses in Hungary – both male and female congregations – where he had been working as a priest since 1934. The Communist regime ordered the secularisation of thousands of priests and sisters belonging to various congregations, forbidding them to wear religious habits and appropriating their properties. Cardinal József Mindszenty (1892-1975) was imprisoned, eventually seeking asylum in Austria. In this situation Father Zembrzuski was forced to leave Hungary. Cardinal Mindszenty's canonisation process was opened in October 1996.

Many years later I caught up with Father Zembrzuski in Doylestown, about twenty-six miles to the north of Philadelphia, where he built among the Pennsylvanian hills an American Częstochowa. Pauline superiors gave their blessing to Father Michał's initiative. He started by opening a chapel for the faithful made from a converted barn. Overcoming many difficulties and with the help of many Americans of Polish descent he managed to build a church in honour of Our Lady of Częstochowa. A beautiful streamlined church designed by the architect Jerzy Szeptycki was ready for use by the Polish millennium year of 1966. It was consecrated by Cardinal Jan Król of Philadelphia in the presence of the President of the USA Lyndon B Johnson. The president delivered a speech in front of a crowd of 130,000 Polish-Americans who had come from all over the United States. But the Communist government of Władysław Gomułka would not allow Cardinal Stefan Wyszynski to attend the celebrations. He was represented however by my friend Bishop Władysław Rubin.

Poland, which found itself under the yoke of Communism, was in no position to commemorate its thousand years of Christianity in 1966 with any major external monument. Neither had it managed to build the church of Divine Providence in thanksgiving for regaining its independence after the years of partition on the conclusion of the First World War in 1918. Therefore, the construction of American Częstochowa was to be the expression of gratitude to Our Lady for her maternal protection over the Polish state and its people scattered all over the world at the conclusion of the Second World War. Today, American Częstochowa is flourishing and is a magnet for pilgrims of various ethnic origins, and many Poles unable to return to their own country before their death have asked in their wills to be buried in the cemetery in Doylestown.

Cardinal Karol Wojtyła

Increasingly, around this time, the Cardinal of Kraków was being noticed on the international stage. I personally met him for the first time in Rome during the Second Vatican Council while staying in the Polish College in the Piazza Remuria. I was the guest of my friend from university days, Bishop Władysław Rubin, who at that time was the administrator of the house. Cardinal Wojtyła would leave the college each morning for the sessions at St Peter's Basilica where in front of 2,500 bishops from around the world he would address them to their great appreciation. But I saw the cardinal rarely, and I was even less likely to have an occasion to actually speak to him. Anyway, such meetings were not in my league. But I still remember very well the silhouette of his slightly bent shoulders as, lost in thought he would slip silently into the chapel to pray in the early mornings.

But later I did have other opportunities for contact with the cardinal. In 1969 I went up to Montreal for a five-yearly reunion with my orphans. Around the time that we were having our formal dinner Cardinal Wojtyła was being driven along the streets of Montreal for a meeting with officials from the Canadian Polish Congress. The guide who was accompanying him was none other than my old parishioner Mr Władysław Stępien, who said to him as an aside,

"Not far from here Father Łucjan Królikowski is celebrating a reunion with his orphans from Africa."

"Let's go to them!" said the cardinal, to which his secretary Father Stanisław Dziwisz responded,

"We don't have the time. We are already very late for the meeting with the delegates of the Polish Congress."

"Let's go to the orphans!" came the final words.

We were completely taken aback by the visit. I did not know at the time that the cardinal had been an orphan himself and as a result was particularly sensitive to the plight of orphans. A red blur loomed in the doorway. Someone unknown to us, surrounded by an entourage, was making his way in determined strides towards the microphone, where I was standing. I greeted him overcome with emotion. My one-time "charges" were completely bewildered when a cardinal from Poland started to talk to them. He reminded the orphans that they were to be ambassadors for Poland, and that the legacy of their culture and faith in Christ and the Church demanded allegiance from them in terms of the trials which their country was going through. The visit lasted no more than a quarter of an hour but it united us in spirit with our native country.

A longing

During this period I was becoming increasingly homesick for my family. I maintained only a tenuous correspondence with them in order not to implicate my father and siblings in any possible harassment or persecution by the officials – but this contact was not enough. Sometime after the death of my mother I devised a plan to meet up with my father and sister Władzia in France where two of my maternal uncles had settled and had married French women. They were Leon Tomiak who lived in Caen in Normandy, and Walerian Lewandowicz in Paris. My father and sister were to visit my uncle in Paris. The security agents most probably would not have issued them with passports had they been aware of the planned meeting with me – a known anti-Communist!

It is hard to describe the meeting with those so close to me after so many years of separation. The floodgates of emotion burst open. Only God and the angels saw what was really happening in our hearts. As a thanksgiving for the grace of the encounter we went to Lourdes, since our whole family has a great devotion to Our Lady and Saint Bernadette (1844-1879). That was to be my first trip to Lourdes. We also visited Uncle Leon in Caen, who in turn drove us to Lisieux, the home of Saint Thérèse of Lisieux (1873-1897). It brought back memories of reading Saint Thérèse's *Diary of a Soul.* The time with my uncles was spent in reminiscing – and there was a lot to recall and catch up on. We did not know that Uncle Leon in Caen and cousin Zbyszek Tomiak in England had taken part in the allied invasion of Normandy on 6 June 1944. My cousin Zbyszek was part of the tank corps and my uncle was a commando. They both took part in the successful battle of Falaise, where the Poles under the command of General Maczek (1892-1959) enclosed the advancing Germans in a pincer movement so that they could not progress any further.

Spiritual therapy

From 1969 we started to enrich our weekly radio programmes with prayers for the sick. I would assemble them from letters we received from the listeners who were going through difficult times in their lives, or who were ill or were suffering spiritually or physically. After a few years we published a little book *Prayers for the Sick* although a more appropriate title would have been *Prayers for Various Situations.* We were encouraged to publish the booklet after we heard from a listener who said, "I admire the literary creativity of the author who has composed so many prayers for the sick. It takes quite a writing talent to come up with one-hundred-and-eighty pearls of wisdom all on the same subject, but each of them in a slightly different way. I suppose this would be...the saddest book in the world! After all it would be a book about suffering, which of course no one greets with joy, even if they know how to carry their burden in a God-like fashion."

Mystics would not have agreed with the words of our listener. If he were right such books would never have been written. The prayers which I arranged were an expression of solicitude for the spiritual welfare of the sick and for those who were suffering. They were not ordinary prayers but prayers which were torn from the soul of lonely people, often depressed or on the brink of despair. The preface to one of the booklets was written by a friend of Cardinal Karol Wojtyła – Cardinal Andrzej Deskur – who has been wheelchair-bound for many years. The booklet was reprinted several times by the Marian Fathers based in Warsaw. One of my old pupils from the Tengeru Settlement Camp, who later became a religious sister at the Institute for the Blind in Laski near Warsaw, wrote to me: "Since we only have one copy of Prayers for the Sick (*Modlitwy Chorych*) we are copying it out by hand for ourselves." This little book of prayers is only available in Polish.

A Trip to my Homeland

During my time in Canada and later in the United States changes for the better were occurring in my country slowly but surely. Communism was beginning to crumble. The socialist economy was failing. However, people were still being persecuted and they still lived in poverty; there was neither bread nor freedom.

In spite of the danger I planned in 1969 to visit my country for the first time, but not without trepidation. Many people advised me against the trip. But I had appropriate documents and I undertook the decision to go. But I was terrified when after landing at Warsaw's Okęcie Airport the doors of the plane were not opened for a long time while the stewardess counted all the passengers on board at least three times. Then, after we descended onto the tarmac she organised us in pairs, and proceeded to escort us into the terminal building. The American passengers were muttering under their breath, "What sort of a place is this? Only cattle are counted and led away like this." The officer in the passport-cabin spent a long time reading from two books, one on his right hand and one on his left to find out who I was. I am sure that the Secret Police had a file on me in which they had written notes from informants. I should imagine that there was mention in it about the alleged "kidnapping" and how I had "abducted" the orphans to Canada. I sensed that he was trying to make up his mind how he should approach me – how to behave towards me. He asked about my occupation, and I said that I was a teacher; I didn't elaborate that I was a teacher of religion, of catechetics. He must have had a card in his hand which stated that I was a priest, but he still referred to me as "Mister". He asked me if I was carrying any letters for anyone. I answered, "Yes, but only to the Canadian Embassy informing them that I had landed in Warsaw and that should the need arise I would ask them for their help." After my passport was given back to me I was sent to a uniformed woman who checked my luggage. Behind her back I could see the smiling but somewhat nervous faces of my family – my sister and brother with his children, whom I hadn't yet met. They were holding a bouquet of flowers to welcome me. After checking the remaining documents I asked the official, 'What next?" A maternal smile spread over her serious face and she said, "Go to your family, of course." As I sank into the arms of my family the brakes that had held back the tears broke. I had waited so long for this meeting, and now for a long time I couldn't say a word. The greatest pain was that our mother was not with us. If God allows such things, she saw me from heaven.

First visit to Poland to visit family, 1969

An incredible encounter

While in Warsaw I went with my family to the Grand Theatre *(Teatr Wielki)* to see a production of the Polish composer Stanisław Moniuszko's opera "The Haunted Manor"*(Straszny Dwór)*. As the performance was sold out my brother Maryś tried to buy us some tickets from ticket-touts. Meanwhile I was standing with my family in the background patiently observing the tide of music-lovers making their way up the steps. All of a sudden from among the crowd I picked out the silhouette of a young man who resembled my friend Rysiek Jędrczak from the Second Corps, to whom I owe in no small measure my seminary days in Lebanon. We had been very close to each other but the Italian campaign in which he had taken part as an officer-cadet sapper, had separated us. Suddenly I had the thought that it might be him. He was even now mounting the stairs of the theatre, so I ran after him in order not to lose sight of him forever. I laid a hand on his shoulder, from behind. He spun around in fear thinking that the Security Police had become interested in him. I asked him if the name Królikowski meant anything to him.

"Zbyszek!" he exclaimed with joy, calling me by my religious name – a name which I had stopped using for all practical purposes after my Soviet slavery, but which he would still use when referring to me. We fell into each other's arms. He gave me his address. It turned out that he now lived in London and that he was visiting his mother whom he was seeing for the first time since the war.

The anniversary of "The Miracle by the Wisła River"

In 1970 The Rosary Hour joined Polish émigré celebrations commemorating the fiftieth anniversary of the Battle of Warsaw or, as the Poles refer to it "The Miracle by the Wisła" (*Cud nad Wisłą*). As the Red Army stood at the gates of Warsaw in August 1920, the Chief-of-Command for the Soviet armies Marshall Tuchachevsky, certain of victory, wrote in his order, "Let's march over Polish corpses and take the revolution to the whole of Europe." We know from history that by then the Polish forces had been retreating from Kiev for six weeks, in front of a million-strong enemy army. Tuchachevsky in his memoirs wrote about the collapse of morale among the Polish soldiers: "This was no longer an army with whom we should have been engaging. Complete demoralisation and complete lack of confidence in success undermined the will of the leaders as much as that of the masses of soldiers."

Despite this threat the Polish armies under the leadership of the charismatic Marshall Józef Piłsudski (1867-1935) pushed back the enemy from the gates of the capital. With this victory, once more Poland was confirmed in her traditional title as the bulwark of Christianity.

It might be appropriate here to explain why we have a right to call this victory a "miracle by the Wisła River". God never sets himself up as a competitor to human beings. His help does not take away from our human bravery or merit. But His help does depend on real co-operation between God and man – a situation well known to the farmer for whom the wheat grows spontaneously but only after he has ploughed the field and scattered the seeds, and thanks only to the sun, rain and wind. In that memorable year of 1920 the depressed nation was very aware that it might once again lose its newly-regained independence. Therefore while the Polish army was preparing to engage with the enemy the rest of the nation kept vigil at prayer. In all the churches throughout the length and breadth of the nation, people were cleansing their souls in the sacrament of reconciliation, and accepting God in Holy Communion; people were offering sacrifices and taking part in night vigils of prayer and song. In Częstochowa under the ramparts of Jasna Góra tens of thousands of women and children lay on the ground, in cruciform fashion, during a novena petitioning God to come to the rescue of their country. In the event that Warsaw should fall, Marshall Piłsudski had apparently chosen Częstochowa as the nation's capital to unite all the people and provide the impetus to continue to defend the country. Victory came on 15 August on the feast of the Assumption of the Blessed Virgin Mary. At the time no one could have had any conception of the uniqueness of the event, even though it was already the era of the Fatima apparitions – but these had not yet been formally affirmed by the church. In 1917, Our Lady in a message to three Portuguese children, warned the world about the dangers that were to come from the East, from atheist Russia. At the time she asked the world for prayer and for penance.

Beatification of Father Maksymilian Kolbe

The news that Pope Paul VI had taken the decision to beatify Father Maksymilian Kolbe, a Conventual Franciscan, filled Poles around the world with great joy. Having him officially declared Blessed was the fulfilment of the dreams of many who knew him. In the Roman curia of our order I have seen stacks of documents about his life and work – four volumes of letters and five volumes of articles, diaries and notes.

The beatification ceremony was appointed for 17 October 1971 and The Radio Rosary Hour organised a Franciscan pilgrimage to Rome to mark this event – the largest ever pilgrimage-group consisting of over 730 people. After the Vatican celebrations we visited Assisi, the spiritual home of the worldwide Franciscan movement, a movement which derives its spiritual inspiration from *Il poverello* of Assisi – The Little Pauper of Assisi. In his book *Assisi Chronicles* (*Kroniki Asyżu*) the Polish poet and writer Roman Brandstaetter – a convert from Judaism – made the following appropriate commentary for this auspicious occasion: "We keep watch for the fragile human figure holding up with superhuman effort the crumbling walls of our civilisation. When this person finally comes to us we will recognise him immediately by his ragged appearance and simple evangelical words...because he will explain to all people that hatred is a crime against God and humanity; and that the crime (of hatred) is the obliteration of human nature. Let him talk to murderers and those who are being murdered, to those who harm and to those who have been harmed and let him finally bring to the world the right to freedom and a peaceful death... All for the Love that moves the stars and the sun..."

A deep spiritual bond united Saint Francis with Father Maksymilian Kolbe. Both set their highest values on Love. Saint Francis would run down the alleys of Assisi calling out "Love is not being loved". Meanwhile his spiritual son, Father Maksymilian was to say seven hundred years later to his brothers who were forced to leave their monastery during the war, "Remember to Love". When he found himself in the pit of the human hell which was Auschwitz concentration camp, he still proclaimed that "Love is stronger than death".

Love without measure

While I was in Rome for the beatification ceremonies for Father Maksymilian I met a famous Polish missionary from Japan – Brother Zenon Żebrowski. He originally came from the Kurpie region of central Poland. His father had emigrated twice to the US in order to support his large family. Zenon decided to enter the Franciscan order. He was a good friar and a good carpenter-builder. In 1927 Father Maksymilian selected him to undertake the building of the chapel and the first barracks in Niepokalanów. Several years later Niepokalanów was to become the largest monastery in the world. In 1930 Father Maksymilian took Brother Zenon with him to Japan, where the second monastery and printing house called Garden of the Immaculate Mary (*Mugenzai no Sono*) was built in Nagasaki. Brother Zenon was instructed to oversee the supervision of the building works. He was also responsible for the distribution of the Japanese edition of the publication, Knight of the Blessed Virgin Mary (*Rycerz Niepokalanej*). Brother Zenon never really learnt to speak Japanese but he made contact with people with great ease. During the Second World War the Japanese authorities interned all foreigners except Brother Zenon on account of his exceptionally useful charity work, with which he earned the love of the inhabitants of the "Land of the flowering cherries". The Japanese associated his name with *zenno*, which in their language means "almighty". That was how he appeared to them when he begged clothing and food from the rich in order to distribute them among the poor. After the dropping of the atom bomb, Brother Zenon instigated care for the victims of the atomic conflagration in Nagasaki, opening an orphanage, a shelter for the homeless and in Hiroshima itself a centre for psychiatric patients. The Emperor decorated him with the highest order of the land for his activities. He was also offered a free travel warrant that was valid on any form of transportation. Just before his death, he was treated to an unusual form of recognition. During his pilgrimage to Japan, the Holy Father John Paul II visited the elderly brother, which moved him to tears. With an overwhelming feeling of gratitude he would repeat, "First Maksymilian, and now a Polish Pope." Japan honoured Brother Zenon by erecting an obelisk in the foothills of Mt Fujiyama with the inscription, *Brother Zenon – love without end.* Will Japanese Catholics ever ask the church to beatify him? Surely God has already recognised him as a saint.

Meeting with Brother Zenon Żebrowski, 1971

The highlight for a group of one-hundred-and-eighty participants in The Rosary Hour pilgrimage to Rome was a two-week visit to Poland. First the participants went to Niepokalanów and then to the defunct German concentration camp in Auschwitz. We were accompanied by an American bishop, Walter Curtis from Bridgeport in the state of Connecticut. In Niepokalanów we were greeted by two of the oldest brothers who had been companions of the Blessed Maksymilian; one was from the Polish and the other from the Japanese Niepokalanów.

In Niepokalanów, Front row 6th from R; 1971

In Auschwitz – the largest cemetery in the world, bigger even than all the Roman catacombs put together – we toured the barracks and the assembly point where Maksymilian Kolbe had asked for permission to take the place of the prisoner who had been sentenced to death by starvation. The pilgrims also visited the death-cell of the saint and the crematoria and looked reflectively at the fields surrounding the Harmęże village where the ashes of the burnt bodies of camp prisoners were scattered. Maksymilian once said that he wished to be pulverised into dust for the Immaculate Virgin Mary.

Maksymilian presents us with a great mystery, as does every saint. For example, the trajectory of the illness – tuberculosis – which he contracted shortly after his ordination, is still a mystery. The fact that he spent so much time in sanatoria was a cause of serious worry to his superiors. Sending him for convalescence to a quiet convent in the countryside they advised the local guardian to buy a plot in the cemetery! Meanwhile, Maksymilian, operating on only one functional lung, managed to establish two huge monasteries, one in Niepokalanów and the second in Nagasaki; whereas in the starvation-bunker he outlived everyone, preparing his companions for a Christian death. After two weeks of slow deterioration from lack of food and drink he was finally killed by a SS soldier with a lethal injection in order to make room in the bunker for other unfortunate souls. Maksymilian probably thought that he would win the martyr's crown in Japan, in a pagan country. In his vision of Our Lady she had presented him with two crowns, one red and one white. She had a different plan to that of her beloved Knight. He was to die in Europe to help stop the genocide conducted by the two totalitarian countries, Germany and Russia. With what joy Maksymilian reached for the red crown because, as he explained to the brothers in Niepokalanów, he had been promised heaven. In our customary focus on his death we are apt to forget that throughout his entire life he had been prepared by his many voluntary sacrifices for that final heroic impulse.

Many years later in 1990 a man named Franciszek Gajowniczek came to public notice in the United States; he was the former Auschwitz prisoner for whom Maksymilian Kolbe had given up his life in the starvation bunker. Mr Gajowniczek came to our Radio Centre and Father Kornelian conducted an interview with him. His testimony was shattering. He described the exchange of prisoners as follows:

"At an opportune moment during the harvest in late July 1941, one of the prisoners from Block 14 escaped from the camp. As a reprisal, during the evening roll-call there was a *decimation* (the calling out of ten prisoners to be starved to death) from my Block. I was among those who were called out. I said, 'I'm sorry for my wife and children whom I have just orphaned.' These words were overheard by Father Maksymilian Kolbe. He stepped out of his row and approaching the Deputy

Commandant of the camp, Carl Fritzsch, attempted to kiss his hand. Fritzsch asked the translator, 'What does the Polish pig want?' Father Maksymilian pointed at me, and declared his willingness to die in my place. Commandant Fritzsch with a motion of his hand and the word *Heraus* (Out!) ordered me to leave the line-up of condemned men while my place was taken by Father Maksymilian. At the time it was difficult for me to take on board the enormity of the event which had embraced me – a condemned man – who was to be allowed to live longer while someone else willingly and voluntarily offered his life for mine."

After Auschwitz the pilgrimage participants drove to Warsaw and admired how the city had been rebuilt. They also looked at the ruins of the notorious Pawiak prison where the German occupiers had taken Maksymilian before he was sent to Auschwitz.

On the way to Warsaw the route took us past Częstochowa, about which Cardinal Karol Wojtyła, the future Pope would say, "This is where the heart of Poland beats". For hundreds of years Polish kings, leaders of the nation, distinguished clergy and lay people, famous overseas guests and most numerously the ordinary Polish people have all gathered before the throne of the Blessed Virgin Mary, Queen of Poland. At the start of the famous Jasnogórski bugle-call, the trumpets blast out a fanfare and the drums roll. God had given us Mary as our mother, and from now on anyone who asks for her help will not be left abandoned. Blessed Maksymilian lived by this truth.

Worried about Poland

The Church in the socialist Democratic Republic of Poland was a Church of silence. From the time that the Communists took control of the government there had been constant persecutions. Because the Catholic Church formed a strong united organisation it was not easy for the enemies of the Church to break it up. Nonetheless, because of war time activities and the devastating Nazi occupation followed by Communist rule, the Church needed help. To this end, The Catholic League was established in the United States in 1973 and every year it would conduct a country-wide collection for the needs of the church in Poland. The Rosary Hour would join in the collection periodically, giving over the entire hour-long programme on all its stations in the USA and

Canada to support the effort, and the donations would be forwarded to the League's headquarters.

The biggest problem in the land of our ancestors was the lack of sufficient churches. In Warsaw, all the churches lay in ruins, having been destroyed by the Germans after the 1944 Uprising. Many churches in all parts of the country needed repairs. Most enclosed convents functioned in almost primitive conditions – without running water or central heating. Moreover, many poor families would additionally turn to these convents for help. Catholic hospitals, which were slowly being taken over by the state, were in need of medical supplies. The Catholic press was drastically reduced and almost all Catholic publishing houses were closed down. Even copies of the Bible, which are essential for catechesis, were almost impossible to obtain. Although there were numerous vocations to the priesthood the seminaries did not have adequate living and study facilities. Lectures took place in dining-rooms or the chapel. Libraries were often located in corridors.

My silver jubilee

1971 was the year of my silver jubilee of ordination. One should thank God for such a great blessing. With this in mind, I made my way to the Near East and first of all I went to the Holy Land. The last time I had been there was to say my first Mass, in the places sanctified by the life of Jesus and Mary. At that time, at the end of World War II, the Jews were fighting the Arabs country-wide.

My visit to Jerusalem coincided with a banquet given for Polish alumni of the Biblical Institute. There I met Father Pawłowski, of Jewish descent, who had been saved from the Holocaust by Polish religious sisters. He invited me to his parish community in the old town of Jaffa on the shores of the Mediterranean, where Saint Peter received the call of the Roman centurion Cornelius asking for baptism (see Acts 10). Father Pawłowski's community welcomed converts from other religions and consisted mostly of Polish women who had married Jews. Services were held in the French church. I heard confessions and celebrated a Mass with a homily. After that, we travelled around on a scooter for a week visiting holy places and Jewish co-operative farms (*Kibbutzim*) where the residents willingly explained to us their way of life. In Haifa I visited a

Carmelite Father Rufeisen, also a Jew, who for many years had been denied citizenship by the Israeli Parliament *(The Knesset)* because he had converted to Catholicism. He also evangelised amongst his own people. My companion Father Pawłowski spoke Hebrew which facilitated all sorts of contacts. In Tel Aviv I was not given a stamp in my passport, only on a loose piece of paper, so that I could later travel from Cyprus to Lebanon, because there was no direct communication between Israel and Arab states. In Beirut, the Maronite Patriarch was my old professor, Father Ziade. Thanks to him and with the help of a young priest I was able to visit my old haunts. It wasn't difficult as Lebanon is a small country. I didn't forget to visit the French Jesuits in the Bekaa Valley, in Tanail, and the Franciscan monastery in Baalbek, where later terrorist units of Hezbollah moved in. As a farewell gesture the Patriarch prepared a great surprise for me – he invited my fellow students from university to the Bishop's palace for dinner. But I barely recognised them, because in that climate people age quickly. In comparison to their beards and bushy hair – I still looked quite young!

International Eucharistic Congress

Our radio network provided its listeners with the full coverage of the forty-first Eucharistic Congress which took place in Philadelphia in 1976. The Congress was hosted by our own countryman, Cardinal Jan Król, Bishop of Philadelphia. The cardinal had been invited to The Rosary Hour programme earlier and he prepared his listeners to experience that public manifestation of faith in the real presence of Jesus, God-and-Man hidden in the Blessed Sacrament. The cardinal found his way into the hearts of Polish people because of his sensitivity to the trials and tribulations of contemporary society, especially within the broad range of ordinary folk – children and young people, workers and those who were suffering in any way.

World-wide representatives of local churches who took part in the Congress created a wonderful mosaic of the Universal Church through their distinct nationalities, languages, culture and race. Our director, Father Kornelian also participated in the Congress and a delegation of eighteen bishops came from Poland led by Cardinal Wojtyła. During the Congress the cardinal made a speech and I quote the relevant parts about the Eucharist and human hungers:

"This Eucharistic Congress reminds us that the hungers experienced by modern man, the hungers of the human family, are multi-faceted. There is in the world a great hunger for bread, which weighs down the consciences of nations, of whole societies around the world. There is in the world a great hunger for food in developing countries. And it is good that we are reminded of this, here in the very heart of a wealthy nation, the richest country in the world. This Congress reminds us also of other hungers, hungers of the human spirit: hunger for truth, hunger for understanding, hunger after freedom, hunger for justice and hunger for Love. It is as if we recognise in these many other hungers, the whole truth concerning contemporary man and the human family, about which we know too little and for which we feel insufficient mutual responsibility. The Eucharist is not only a Sacrament. It is also a summons."

After the Congress finished, the delegates of the Polish episcopacy visited the major Polish centres in America. Some of the bishops visited The Rosary Hour Centre in Athol Springs.

Cardinal Król visiting the Rosary Hour Radio Station 1975

Cardinal Wojtyła blesses The Rosary Hour Centre

Cardinal Wojtyła, together with Father Franciszek Macharski, Rector of the Kraków Seminary and a future cardinal himself, visited us separately. On that occasion he solemnly blessed the centre, looked at the works of art and acquainted himself with our work. It was Cardinal Wojtyła's second visit to North America – and the timing coincided with his increasing recognition in the Western world. As already noted, in 1969 he had been invited by the Canadian Polish Congress and it was then that he had unexpectedly paid a visit to my orphans during their reunion. At that time the cardinal visited almost all the Polish centres in Canada ranging from the St Lawrence River in the East to Vancouver in the West, one of the most beautiful towns in the world in its setting between the Rocky Mountains and the Pacific Ocean.

Apart from participating in the Eucharistic Congress, Cardinal Wojtyła also delivered lectures at four American universities, including the prestigious Harvard University. For one of my programmes I wrote:

"All of this (activity) may prove to be an occasion prompted by the Holy Spirit, so that future members of the conclave may have the opportunity to get a closer look at him and appreciate his love for the Church, his wisdom combined with true simplicity and humility, his warm relationships with people and his exceptional sense of humour."

Sparks of History

In that same year of 1976, The Rosary Hour produced a brochure entitled *Sparks of History* to commemorate the bicentennial anniversary of independence of the USA. It consisted of brief, concise, loosely-aligned talks, concerning two great Poles – General Tadeusz Kościuszko (1746-1817) and General Kazimierz Puławski (1745-1779) – and their role in the fight for freedom and independence of the United States. This activity of theirs was instrumental in securing for Polish immigrants the moral right to settle on American soil.

I gathered material for the *Sparks* from two sources – from literature and from a long journey around the battlegrounds of our two national heroes. The month-long visit produced a lot of rich material. I still vividly recall the landscapes of battle-fields and monuments built to honour our heroes. I particularly remember the history of the American victory at Saratoga in 1777 to which Tadeusz Kościuszko contributed so notably by choosing the battleground and by fortifying it. Echoes of the victory encircled the world, resulting in the French nation sending concrete help to the Americans.

With increasing nostalgia I toured West Point, an institution strategically located on a bend in the Hudson River, where our compatriot Kościuszko had built a garrison for over 2,500 soldiers. Today that site is the base of the famous Military Academy. Several heroes of World War II were alumni of that institution, such as Generals Eisenhower, MacArthur and Patton. The colourful uniforms of the West Point cadets greatly resemble the uniforms worn by Polish soldiers during the 1830 November insurrection in Poland.

I was bursting with pride when from the steps of Independence Hall in Philadelphia I imagined myself standing with Jefferson, Franklin and others – members of the revolutionary Congress – reviewing the parade of Puławski's Legion. The death penalty hung over all the signatories of the Declaration of Independence. Meanwhile, Congress was demanding a receipt for every horse, harness and uniform. Puławski however declared that he did not come to America to busy himself with bookkeeping but to fight for freedom!

In Savannah, Georgia, tears welled up in my eyes when I squeezed in my hand the grapeshot bullet which took the life of Puławski. In my mind's eye I could see the symbolic funeral procession which was organised by the city of Charleston, Virginia for its defender. His faithful black horse formed part of the funeral cortège. At the time of his death Puławski was thirty-three years old. He was the only general to die during the War of Independence.

I also visited the inn called Fraunces Tavern in New York City, where in the upstairs Long Room, George Washington bade farewell to his generals. General Kościuszko received from him the highest order possible – the Order of Cincinnati.

In Philadelphia, Polish Americans have saved Kościuszko's house from demolition and have made it into a museum. Kościuszko lived there in 1797 during his second stay in America. His arrival was greeted with a cannonade and his carriage was pulled by distinguished citizens of the town. It was at that time that the long friendship between Jefferson and Kościuszko started a friendship which lasted many years until the death of Kościuszko. At Jefferson's beautiful home at Monticello in Virginia, there is a portrait of Thomas Jefferson painted by Tadeusz Kościuszko.

It is interesting to note that the Committee for the Bi-Centenary Celebrations of the Declaration of Independence of the United States chose to mount their exhibition in three European cities – Paris, Warsaw and London. The exhibition entitled *The World of Benjamin Franklin* reflected the early history of America in a thoughtful and interesting way. This gesture was a token of gratitude towards the French, Polish and English for the role they had played in a dramatic period of the history of the American nation two hundred years ago.

The listeners to The Rosary Hour followed the deeds of our heroes on American soil with interest and then discussed them on our programme. They commented on them in their letters, recorded them on cassettes and asked for printed copies and transcripts. We were pleased with this interest as the heroic deeds of such great individuals belong to the national heritage and they help us all in our own development. Interestingly our listeners appeared to know less about Tadeusz Kościuszko than Kazimierz Puławski. Every year in New York City there is an impressive Puławski Parade. Perhaps if there was a parade in honour of Kościuszko this would ignite more interest among Americans in this historical figure. After all, his contributions towards America were far greater than those of Puławski. Upon hearing about the death of Kościuszko, Thomas Jefferson wrote:

"No country and no person can be touched more deeply by his death than I. I enjoyed his friendship and trust for the last twenty years. During the time that he spent in this country I had the opportunity to observe almost daily his beautiful character, warm heart and genuine love for the cause of freedom... He is the purest son of freedom I have ever known – that freedom which belongs to everyone, not only the select few or the exclusive right of the rich."

During the funeral ceremonies in Paris on 31 October 1817, another friend of Kościuszko and also a comrade-in-arms, General Marquis de Lafayette gave a beautiful testimony about our countryman:

"To talk about Kościuszko is to remember a man who even his enemies and the very monarchs against whom he fought, greatly respected. His name belongs to the whole civilised world and his virtues are the property of the whole of humanity. America considers him to be one of its most famous defenders, while Poland bemoans the loss of one of its greatest patriots, one whose whole life was dedicated to freedom and independence. France and Switzerland stand in awe over his ashes and pay homage to the memory of one of the greatest of human beings, a Christian and a friend of humanity. Even Russia respects in him that fearless man that disaster could not overcome. All Poles consider themselves to be his children and proudly present him to other nations."

American democracy

From the time that I arrived on the American continent I have been observing how Americans implement democratic principles in their own private lives, and we discussed these issues over the airwaves.

Democracy is not easy to implement because it is an expression of the collective love of one's neighbour, which if it is to be successful needs to be anchored in God, the source of all Goodness. Americans have shown themselves to be not completely successful in this venture. This becomes apparent in two cases – the case of American Indians and the case of Afro-Americans.

They deprived the Indians of their freedom by locking them up in reservations and killing off their bison – so that all that is left of some of the Indian tribes is a name. The tragedy of the Indians is poignantly described in a speech attributed to Seattle, the Chief of the Duwamish (the town of Seattle is named after him). It was directed at Isaac Stevenson, the Governor of Washington Territory in 1854.

"Your God is not our God! Your God loves your people and hates mine! He folds his strong protecting arms lovingly about the paleface and leads him by the hand as a father leads an infant son. But, He has forsaken His Red children, if they really are His. Our God, the Great Spirit, seems also to have forsaken us... Our people are ebbing away like a rapidly receding tide that will never return... If we have a common Heavenly Father He must be partial, for He came to His paleface children. We never saw Him... we are two distinct races with separate origins and separate destinies. There is little in common between us."

Today the American Indians are no longer rebelling, and no longer defending their rights; they are slowly dying out. Americans also failed the democracy test in respect to Afro-Americans, who were brought over from Africa in their hundreds of thousands to be engaged in slave labour first on tobacco plantations and later gathering cotton. President Abraham Lincoln, a great democrat, looked on with great sadness at the spilling of fraternal blood during the civil war in defence of the rights of African slaves. The slaves were emancipated and the president was assassinated. Lip service was paid to democratic slogans almost to the time of my arrival in the USA. In 1963, Dr Martin Luther King, the Black American leader, standing on the steps of the Lincoln Memorial in Washington, DC rallied the entire American nation:

"I have a dream that one day this nation will rise up and live out the true meaning of its creed. We hold these truths to be self-evident: that all men are created equal."

The German Catholic philosopher and theologian, Dietrich von Hilderbrand (1889-1977) reminds us that democracy will blossom so long as nations stay in touch with God, who is the source of the ideal, and so long as they hold firm to the Decalogue. Von Hilderbrand wrote:

"...Moral values are the highest among all natural values.
Goodness, purity, truthfulness, humility of man rank higher than genius;
brilliance, exuberant vitality, than the beauty of nature or of art – than the stability and power of a state.
What is realised and what shines forth
in an act of real forgiveness,
in a noble and generous renunciation;
in a burning and selfless love,
is more significant and more noble,
more important and more eternal,
than all cultural values.
Positive moral values are the focus of the world,
negative moral values the greatest evil,
worse than suffering, sickness, death, or the disintegration of a flourishing culture."

Would that the guiding principles for Americans were the words of Pope John Paul II addressed to the world in his encyclical *Centesimus Annus*:

"In a world without truth, freedom loses its foundation and man is exposed to the violence of passion and to manipulation, both open and hidden... Democracy without values can lose its soul."

America is still a very religious country and to this day America is concerned about her Christian heritage. The virtue of gratitude is still commonly practiced and one is struck by the endearing simplicity and courtesy of so many of its people. But these values which America owes to many different religions and cultures are now under serious threat.

In May 1978 Father Kornelian and I attend a conference in Toronto, the aim of which was to unite into one family the several-million-strong Polish diaspora (Polonia) – creating one global Polish family, a Worldwide Polonia. The catchword of the conference was "We are building the Polonia of tomorrow". One hundred and seventy-six Polish émigré delegates attended from countries as far apart as Argentina, Australia, Belgium, Brazil, Canada, Denmark, France, Germany, Great Britain, Italy, New Zealand, South Africa, Sweden, Switzerland, The Netherlands and the United States of America.

There were about four hundred and fifty observers at the conference, not counting the media. The declaration by the mayor of Toronto of a Polish Week became the context for the *World Congress of Polonia*. During this week cultural and artistic events took place in various districts of the city. There were also exhibitions, such as *The role of the church in the life of Polish émigrés*. The Radio Rosary Hour programme also participated in the exhibition.

The Congress decided once and for all to get rid of the classification of émigré Poles as economic migrants, political or ideological refugees. They decided to leave these distinctions to historians and sociologists. The Congress defined the aims of the Worldwide Polonia as keeping alive the values of Polish culture; taking part in the efforts of humanity in maintaining freedom and democracy; giving support to the Polish nation in its fight for full freedom and independence; fighting for the rights of Poles still living in the Soviet Union; and exchanging ideas, programmes and news about Poles living on all five continents of the world.

The Congress was against the concept of the "melting pot", in which there is an attempt to mix together the characteristics and values of various cultures – a subtle form of domination because the larger nations will always impose their own values and discriminate against others. A plant transferred into another garden does not lose its identity, it doesn't act as fertiliser for other plants but retains its own attributes enriching the garden with its shape, colour and fruit. So it is with people and that is the reason why we defend ourselves against the concept of assimilation.

The Congress sessions finished on Sunday 28 May with a solemn Mass of Thanksgiving led by Cardinal Jan Król. Con-celebrating with him were, among others Bishop Szczepan Wesoły from Rome, the delegate of the Polish primate for the pastoral care of Polish emigreés; Monsignor Zdzisław Peszkowski, from the Polish seminary in Orchard Lake; and Father Kornelian. After the Mass a procession left for the Monument of the Unknown Soldier to the accompaniment of two orchestras. A hundred flags were carried and many wreaths were laid at the monument.

Part X

The election of a Polish Pope and the fall of Communism

A Slavic Pope

I had kept up a correspondence with the writer Father Henryk Werynski from Kraków over many years. In one of his letters after the death of Pope Paul VI in 1978 he wrote to me about a strange dream. In the dream he saw the College of Cardinals electing as Pope Cardinal Karol Wojtyła, who chose for himself the name of John. When the Patriarch of Venice Albino Luciani was elected, I wrote back to him: "As a Pole I can only be sad that your dream has not come true".

But the newly-elected Pope John Paul I died shortly afterwards and the next conclave called Cardinal Wojtyła to the See of Peter. He chose for himself the name of John Paul II, showing that he wanted to continue in the footsteps of his three predecessors. This was the fulfilment of many a Polish dream, even though at the time it seemed to be completely unrealistic as for 455 years only Italians had been elected as Pope. A Pole would have seemed to have had even less chance as he came from the Eastern bloc. Apparently, 563 years previously the Archbishop of Gniezno, Mikołaj Trąba (1358-1422), adviser to King Jagiełło and head of the Polish delegation to the Council of Constance in 1415, also had a good chance of being elected to the See of Peter. In the event he was not elected as Pope because some of the cardinals said, "*Si Trąba papa – Cracovia Roma*" fearing he might move the See of Peter to Kraków.

In The Rosary Hour we had long believed that the "Spirit blows where it wills". In one of Father Kornelian's chats he expressed the conviction that "Cardinal Wojtyła took an active part in the Second Vatican Council and today is one of the Church's foremost and greatest theologians. It is not inconceivable that the Holy Spirit will desire to have him elected as the next Pope." However, when Cardinal Camillo Ruini, Vicar General of the Diocese of Rome, declared that the new Pope was a Pole, the news took our breath away. For us his compatriots, this reaction stemmed from a variety of reasons and we immediately recalled the harrowing poem about a Slavic Pope (*O Słowianskim Papierzu*) written in 1848 by Juliusz Słowacki. Examples of a few of its most powerful verses are:

God's bell the Conclave's petty strife has stilled:
    Its mighty tone
Brings news of Slavic hope fulfilled –
    The Papal Throne!
Pope who will not – Italian-like – take fright
    At sabre-thrust
But, brave as God himself, stand and give fight :
    His world – but dust!..

... To bear our load – this world by God designed –
    That power we need:
Our Slavic Pope, brother to all mankind,
    Is there to lead!

With balm from all the world, our souls' torment
    Is soothed by him;
About his flower-decked throne a regiment
    Of cherubim.
Love he dispenses as great powers today
    Distribute arms;
With sacramental power, his sole array,
    The world he charms!...
... From the world's wounds he laves corruption's blight,
    The maggots teeming;
Health he restores, fanning our love alight,
    The world redeeming.
Sweeps out our churches, makes the portals gleam –
    So that each one
May see his God within Creation's scheme,
    Bright as the sun!   [Translated by Noel Clark]

In The Book of Quotations from Polish Literature (*Księga cytatów z polskiej literatury pięknej*) the Communists would not even allow the poem to be included. It was considered to be too prophetic and atheists are often quite superstitious. I reflected that the Holy Spirit had been working for many years, through hundreds of people in various situations, to prepare Karol Wojtyła to serve on the throne of Peter. An example of this theory was the intervention of Cardinal Adam Sapiecha (1867-1951), Archbishop of Kraków, who is alleged to have said to the young Wojtyła who approached him in order to obtain a statement of good moral standing, in preparation for his entry into the Carmelite order, "You should not shut yourself away in a Carmelite monastery. You will be needed by the church." On the other hand Our Lady probably also had much to say, as she did in Cana in Galilee; after all, Poland had just finished celebrating the 600th anniversary of her presence on Jasna Góra in the icon of Our Lady of Częstochowa. She also knew about his priestly motto placed on his coat of arms under the sign of the cross – *Totus Tuus* – All yours.

The choice of Karol Wojtyła as representative of Christ occurred when the fight between good and evil – godless, organised and militant Communism – reached a culminating point. At the time my compatriots cheered themselves up by recalling the words of the Primate of Poland, Servant of God, August Hlond (1881-1948), "Poland, you have not perished! You have not perished because God is not dead... It is His will that you should rise up again and live happily, my dearest martyr – Poland."

In the radio chats on The Rosary Hour we would talk about our gratitude to God and pride, because we were bursting with joy to have lived to see the calling of a Pole to stand at the helm of Peter's boat. We were happy that John Paul II greeted the crowds gathered in St Peter's Square with the ancient Polish greeting "Praise be Lord Jesus Christ!" (*Niech będzie pochwalony Jesus Chrystus!*) albeit in Italian; and that although he came from a faraway country his faith and traditions could be understood by all.

He found a shattered world, torn apart and divided. But we intuitively felt that the pontificate of John Paul II would be significant, that the dominant characteristic of this distinguished theologian, philosopher, social activist, youth leader, mystic and Man of the Church would be love for every person because everyone is a masterpiece of God, and created out of Love. We also knew that just as Christ came to those who were disadvantaged, so His successor John Paul II would direct his gaze on ordinary people, the uncomplicated, the poor, the oppressed, those who suffered and the marginalised. We knew that his pastoral ministry would be a "service of love".

Audience with the Pope

For a number of years Dr Stefan Graczyk, a well known and respected physician and long-time professor of medicine at the University of Buffalo, provided various items of information for our radio programme. During the Second World War he had served at the front line as a physician in the American army in the rank of a colonel in North Africa, Italy and France. During the Second Vatican Council he held the position of physician to the council which is an indication of the extent of his reputation and qualifications. In the eighty-third year of his life he decided to retire from his busy professional career. To commemorate this occasion he wished to have a private audience with the Polish Pope. He had already had audiences with Pope Pius XII, John XXIII and Paul VI. He asked me to arrange an audience for him with John Paul II. This was no easy task bearing in mind that it had only been two months from the time of the election, but I was helped in this task by my friend from university days in Beirut, Bishop Władysław Rubin who at the time held the position of Pastoral Guardian to Polish émigrés on behalf of the Polish Primate.

The audience was set for 20 December 1978, and just before it Vatican Radio had an interview with him, after which we went to the general weekly audience in the Pope Paul VI Audience Hall. It was in this hall on 23 October of the same year, that a moving scene took place against the backdrop of the superb sculpture of the Risen Christ by Pericle Fazzini. Two friends – John Paul II and Cardinal Stefan Wyszynski – dissolved into each other's arms, and for a long moment were held in a brotherly embrace. Two shepherds of the people of God were united in the memory of suffering and persecution for the Faith and the fight for freedom of the Polish nation. With humility the new Pope thanked the distinguished Primate for his unswerving loyalty to Faith. The Italian priest Antonio Malberti, a witness to this event, wrote that it was a spiritual banquet. During that long embrace, he experienced in his heart an overpowering desire to "visit that wonderful Poland, from which have come examples and role models capable of illuminating the Faith of the nations of Europe. These nations I love and wish that they would form one united country, without divisions, barriers or borders; because boundaries don't make any sense, especially for true Catholics who consider themselves to be free children of God." As Father Malberti continued, "The Polish nation is closest to my heart because it has given us John Paul II. I consider Poland to be my adopted country."

At the General Audience the pilgrims sang for the Pope the Christmas carol, Sleep Baby Jesus (*Lulaj że Jezuniu*). The Pope, who was visibly touched, intoned the second verse and explained to the non-Polish guests that this was the favourite carol of the brilliant composer Chopin, which he later incorporated into one of his works, demonstrating in this way his longing for his country and for Polish traditions of Christmastide. People from the Polish highlands presented the Pope with a sapling Christmas tree from the mountains and also gave him a Polish crib for his apartments.

Private audience with Blessed Pope John Paul II, 1978

After the general audience Dr Graczyk and I were escorted to one of the adjacent rooms. We were accompanied by my friend Bishop Rubin. Before us in the queue was a diplomat from the Far East and a group of Bishops. When our time came the doors opened and the Holy Father approached us with energetic strides, kissed us on both cheeks and then listened with interest to what we had to say. How different was this audience from those of bygone years, when the bishop would introduce the pilgrim who would be kneeling without saying anything, waiting only for a blessing. This protocol was once famously broken by the Little St Thérèse of Lisieux. John Paul II was glad to meet us as workers on The Radio Rosary Hour. He said, "I remember you well. I was invited by Father Kornelian, whom I know personally, to speak several times to the listeners of The Rosary Hour. You are performing a very important radio apostolate and you must continue to proclaim the Word of God strongly and courageously. The world needs the healthy seed of the Word of God supported by examples of a good life." The Holy Father was very interested in my group of Polish orphans – "the little exiled-wanderers". I presented him with a copy of the previous year's radio chats, a cassette with the programme A Pole on the Throne of St Peter (*Polak na Tronie Świętego Piotra*) and The Rosary Hour calendar illustrated with works of art from our headquarters.

For his part the Holy Father spoke with Dr Graczyk after which he bestowed his apostolic blessing on the management team of the radio and all the listeners to The Rosary Hour, their families, the elderly and the sick. With his blessing the Holy Father also took in all of the Polish diaspora (Polonia) and my former exiled-wandering orphans. I had a few pangs of conscience that I had taken up so much time of the Holy Father, who had so much else to think about at the beginning of his pontificate.

John Paul II as a pilgrim

From the very beginning of his pontificate the charismatic new Pope met with enthusiastic acceptance from around the world. So it surprised us when one of our listeners, an educated and practising Catholic, asked the question: "Why does the Holy Father travel around the world so much? Barely a year has passed and he has already visited Mexico, Poland, Ireland, and the USA..."

I mention this question because previous generations of Christians and non-Christians were accustomed to the fact that the Pope did not leave the Vatican; after the loss of the Papal States Popes were even dubbed the "prisoners of the Vatican". The established protocol was also conducive to confirming this image of an imprisoned Pope. The faithful convinced themselves of an image of the papacy where the Pope was an unapproachable, untouchable and severe ruler – as if created from a different clay. Blessed Pope John XXIII broke with the imposed protocol. He arranged visits to the sick and visited prisons in the various districts of Rome. The world loved him for that and his death was mourned by many who had never even met him. He was a father to everyone. Other Popes followed his example. His successor took the name of Paul VI, wishing to follow in the footsteps of Saint Paul. For his coronation he used the traditional Tiara, but dispensed with it in later ceremonies, eventually selling it and distributing the monies to the poor. Additionally, he made missionary trips to the Holy Land, where he is remembered with extreme fondness to this day, and to Colombia in South America, to India, Australia and the Philippines. In 1966 he expressed the wish to be in Poland for the millennium celebrations of the Baptism of the Polish nation, but the Communist regime, prompted by Moscow, would not give him a visa.

Pope John Paul II followed in the footsteps of his predecessors. He was urged on by Christ who in His final request asked that they *Go therefore and make disciples of all nations... teaching them to observe all that I have commanded you...* (Matthew 28,19-20) and Saint Paul: *Woe to me if I do not preach the gospel!* (I Corinthians 9,16). The question why the Pope travelled so much was also asked by the enemies of the Church, who like Judas touched on the material side of pilgrimages. "How much do these papal visits cost? Would it not be better to put aside this money for the poor?"

The actual itinerary of the pilgrimages is the best response to this question. John Paul II met young people, scientists, artists, seminarians, priests, bishops, cardinals, theologians, delegates from various Christian denominations, religious sisters, diplomats, and above all with the sick and handicapped. He met with pleasure Jewish and Islamic leaders; in Mexico he solved the sensitive issue of liberation theology, while in Ireland he called for the cessation of fraternal fighting. He brought nations together, confirming them in their faith and raising their spirits. At the United Nations in New York he challenged the national representatives to eliminate hunger, poverty, torture and war, based on respect for human rights. I should think that in the matter of influence in the world, there was no other statesman who came even close to Pope John Paul II.

The Pope makes a hit in America

Americans keenly observed the momentum with which the new Pope approached his pontificate. There was great excitement in 1979 at the news that he planned a visit to the United States but the general opinion was that the Pope would have a far from easy time there. It is true that in 1965 Pope Paul VI had already paid a visit to the UN in New York, but the headquarters of that institution are by their nature situated on extraterritorial land. Therefore when it was announced that the Pope would visit Boston, New York, Philadelphia, Des Moines, Chicago and Washington, many people were uncertain how to respond. Many deeply-felt prejudices surfaced including animosity towards the Pope and the Catholic Church. After all, some Protestants still consider the Pope to be the Antichrist and the Catholic Church to be the whore of the Apocalypse.

The aggressive American atheist Madalyn Murray O'Hair (1919-1995) who had previously been involved in activities such as removing crosses from public schools and abolishing prayers and Bible reading, demanded that the US Supreme Court refuse permission for the Pope to celebrate Mass in public. The American Civil Liberties association protested that the State of Iowa had recognised the date of the Pope's visit to that state as a formal holiday. It was this same organisation which had defended a neo-Nazi organisation of Hitler sympathisers who wished to organise a march through the town of Skokie, Illinois. References were made to the Constitution which apparently guarantees complete separation of church and state. Americans recalled that in

1928 the Catholic Al Smith, although a popular, well-liked and respected candidate, lost the bid for the presidency of the USA due to his religion. Meanwhile Catholics remembered with embarrassment how in 1960 John F Kennedy who was then running for the presidency declared before a group of Protestant clergy that if elected as president he would listen to the voice of his conscience rather than the voice of the Pope.

There were also voices of cautious moderation. Walter Cronkite, a popular non-Catholic American TV commentator at that time, gently pointed out to his compatriots that even the Polish Communists allowed the Pope to speak publicly, and even though Poland had been ravaged by the war and by two occupations, it did not raise the question about the cost of the papal visit. Finally, the Supreme Court announced that the separation of Church and State was not absolute, and that both parties upheld the same cultural and social values and more often than not moral and spiritual beliefs.

When Pope John Paul II finally arrived in Boston, he kissed American soil, smiled and extended his arms widely to everyone saying, "I love you America". All remnants of antagonism fell by the wayside. The entire pilgrimage of the Pope turned into a triumphant march, resembling the entry of Christ into Jerusalem. Everywhere he went he brought joy, hope, a breath of fresh air and a sense of new energy. Everywhere he was greeted with enthusiasm. Of all the scenes the most memorable and poignant was the welcome ceremony with President Jimmy Carter and his wife Rosalynn on the steps of the White House, where he was then escorted inside, to be greeted by members of the Supreme Court, Congress and the Senate. It was emphasised that he had touched the deepest spiritual springs of the American nation; it was said that he surpassed politicians, rock-and-roll stars and evangelists like Billy Graham. *Time* magazine called him a superstar. As Pope he was not interested in fame or popularity but in uncovering the goodness in human hearts which the Creator had purposely placed there in order to promote peace, fraternity and justice. He was satisfied in being known by the title of the Servant of the Servants of God (*Servus Servorum Dei*), a title which had been used by Popes down the ages. The richness of his personality and his individual sanctity meant that the masses became fascinated with the Catholic Church. I am reminded of the words of G K Chesterton about the Church: "It's a real miracle that an institution so old and great can constantly evoke new sensations." Oh eternal beauty, ever new...

Solidarity

I went to Rome with a manuscript about the history and work of The Rosary Hour (*Książka o Godzinie Różancowej*) with the intention of having it published. When they realised I was Polish Italians would greet me joyfully, exclaiming in Polish, *Solidarność*! (Solidarity!) That was just one example in 1980 of the way in which Europeans were reacting to the news about the striking workers demanding recognition of their basic human rights in the Gdansk Shipyards. This spurt of activity towards regaining their freedom was regarded by the world as a form of tearing off the mask which had hitherto hidden the true face of the Soviet Union – a masked face which proclaimed to the world that the Communist system was truly the rule of workers and that workers under Communism were experiencing nothing less than heaven on earth. The dock workers demonstrated to everyone that this was a lie. Poles living in the West watched their television sets with tears in their eyes at the unprecedented sight of workers kneeling by confessional-grills; at the huge cross suspended over the dockyard; at the dockyard gates where someone had attached a picture of Our Lady of Częstochowa and hung a portrait of the Pope flanked by Polish and papal flags. During the Mass the dockers went up to the altar to receive the Blessed Sacrament.

The unusual pictures of praying and striking workers made quite an impression on an indifferent and secular world. Intellectuals, young people and manual workers gathered round in support of the workers. All sections of society joined the movement. In total, ten million workers joined Solidarity. A major characteristic of the strike was its peaceful nature. No one came out with a machine-gun in their hands, no one provoked the militia or secret police, no one threw themselves at a tank with a bottle of petrol, no one set fire to the headquarters of the secret police or built barricades. The workers clearly used evangelical methods as provided by Christ in the blessings enumerated on the Sermon on the Mount. It was a method of not resorting to force or rioting in the face of adversity; a form of non-violence which had so influenced the leader of the Hindus, Mahatma Gandhi, when he successfully practiced it in his own country. Our compatriots in Gdansk had remembered this. It is a way of overcoming evil with good, a method which contains within it the enemy's own disarming love, thereby giving the enemy a chance to come round and change his ways; it does not take away anyone's life or destroy cultural heritage or property. The application of the non-violent approach by the Polish dockers said a lot about the maturity of the organisers and the self-discipline of the participating workers and dockers.

The Golden Jubilee of The Rosary Hour

In 1981 The Rosary Hour celebrated its Golden Jubilee. Fifty years of broadcasting the word of God, half a century of preaching the Good News about salvation, about the present and eternal Kingdom of God, a Kingdom of truth and life, a Kingdom of justice, love and peace. Can there be a more privileged mission to undertake on earth? At the time we had around two million listeners. The Holy Father John Paul II awarded the *Pro Ecclesia et Pontifice* decoration to the whole team – that is to Father Kornelian, Father Eligiusz and myself and his Apostolic blessing to all the listeners in the United States of America and Canada.

In connection with the golden jubilee celebrations we hosted two professors from the Catholic University of Lublin in Poland who were gathering information about our radio apostolate. Thanks to their work two new publications appeared – a monograph of 500 pages by Father Dr Jan Książka entitled Father Justyn's Radio Rosary Hour *(Radiowa Godzina Różancowa Ojca Justyna)* and Father Dr Tadeusz Zastępa's Catechists of the Polish Émigré Radio Rosary Hour Programme *(Emigracyjni katecheci Radiowej Godziny Różancowej)*, a work about the directors of The Rosary Hour, Fathers Figas and Dende. Two small volumes of my prayers for the sick were also published at that time – Radio Prayers for the Sick (*Radiowe Modlitwy Chorych).*

The Third Secret of Fatima

Previous Popes had maintained a deep silence when asked about the third secret of Fatima. Only on 13 May 1981, when John Paul II fell victim to a terrorist attack, did we find out that the children of Fatima in their vision had seen a praying bishop, dressed in white robes, who was killed. The secret about this vision was known to the Popes, but for reasons of their own they did not want to make it public. Therefore the world stopped in its tracks, in stunned terror, when a Turkish assassin turned his weapon on John Paul II during his public audience in St Peter's Square. It seemed as if the bullets which seriously wounded the Vicar of Christ had struck at the very heart of humanity. The well-known American journalist Michael Novak asked Pope John Paul II during his visit to the USA if he had ever thought about the fact that when he was overseas he was continuously exposed to the assassin's bullet. The Pope replied that he was not afraid of anything since he was always in the hands of God, and even if such a thing were to happen it would happen in his own "backyard" – in St Peter's Square.

I must confess that I was not particularly surprised by the terrible news about the attack. The years of my mature life had fallen at the worst period in human history. I knew that one always had to be prepared for the worst to happen. I was aware of the extent of panic in the Soviet Union caused by the workers' strike in Gdansk and the activities of the Slavic Pope, especially the call to solidarity. I suspected that among the many enemies of the Catholic Church and the Pope the Kremlin was the chief antagonist and could be the main instigator of such an attack. All the corroborative evidence pointed to the fact that Mehmet Ali Ağca was not working alone. Soviet intelligence knew very well about his Turkish fanaticism, his hatred towards Christians and his conviction that the Pope together with the entire developed world stood at the helm of a new crusade against Islam. He wrote that he would "kill (this) masked leader of Crusades". Later on the day of the attack, the Italian police found a letter in his hotel room in which he stated that he would kill the Pope in order to "demonstrate before the world imperialist crimes..." Soviet spies knew that Ali Ağca had been shadowing the Pope in Turkey, with the intention of killing him. In this way the fears of the Soviets and Ağca's hatred came together. But Ağca did not realise that in the West there is no theocracy as in Islam and he did not know that there is a separation between religious and secular authority, between the Church and State. But the Kremlin held the trump card in harnessing the furious hatred of Ali Ağca, while concealing its own machinations.

For our radio programme I eagerly collected statements by prominent people on the subject of the assassination attempt. At the news of the attack the American Senate halted its proceedings and paid its respects to the courageous Pope, calling him a "true emissary of the gospels and justice; a Good Shepherd to the whole world". The prime minister of Canada Pierre Trudeau posed the rhetorical question "Have we become such a barbaric world that we are incapable of respecting the life of God's envoy, one who is bringing us peace?" While in Jerusalem a devout Jew commented: "To shoot at presidents is a matter of politics but to shoot at the Pope is like shooting at God Himself."

John Paul II was convinced that he owed his survival to Our Holy Mother. He was strengthened in this belief by the fact that the attack took place exactly on the sixty-fourth anniversary of the Fatima apparitions. Meanwhile, mindful of the words of Christ on the Cross *Father forgive them for they know not what they are doing* he was prompted to forgive his attacker. After the attack John Paul II went to visit him personally in his prison cell to forgive him. Ali Ağca was sure that he had aimed accurately and that the Pope should be dead; he was amazed and asked "Who is Our Lady of Fatima?"

Given for "special help and protection"

I cannot help but mention here the celebrations which were occupying the whole of Poland and the Polish diaspora (Polonia) around the world, including The Rosary Hour. The celebrations concerned the 650th anniversary of the Icon of Our Lady of Częstochowa's presence on Jasna Góra. Cardinal Stefan Wyszynski did not live to celebrate the occasion although he had been preparing for the event together with his bishops for six years. As a pupil of Saint Maksymilian Kolbe, who used to write letters to the Blessed Virgin Mary on her feast days, I will follow his example and do something similar but with a slight difference. I will offer to Our Lady a garland of the most beautiful Marian hymns. Our Lady is not only our mother, but for the last three hundred and fifty years by solemn decree of the Polish sovereign King Jan Kazimierz in 1656 in Lwów Cathedral, Our Lady has formally became Queen of the Polish state and of the Polish nation.

The first hymn to come down to us from our ancestors is the early medieval hymn to the Blessed Virgin Mary Mother of God, the *Bogurodzica* (*Theotokos*). Another hymn is reminiscent of an echo, repeating the words of the Blessed Virgin Mary. It is a hymn sung by pilgrims making their way from all parts of the country to Jasna Góra: *We have heard the graceful voice of Maria beckoning us, "Come to me my children, the time has come..."* Another hymn was probably composed at a time when the Polish nation, like Simon of Cyrene, was asked to help carry the Cross of Christ. It was a time of national humiliation and scorn: *Don't abandon us! Don't abandon us! Mother, do not leave us. Mother, console us for we are in tears. Show us the way or we will perish! Teach us to Love, even though we are suffering, teach us to suffer even though in silence. Mother, don't abandon us!* Another hymn etched itself even more deeply into my heart and mind, as I heard it so often when in East Africa, sung by the Polish children each morning just as the mists were rising: *Mother of Consolation, Lady of heaven and earth, To you we sinners bring our hearts as offerings, We give them to you for safe-keeping, As did our fathers before us. We give you homage and adoration. Holy Mother of Consolation, Don't abandon us.* To this garland of hymns I will also add the relatively new hymn in honour of Our Lady of Częstochowa, 'The Black Madonna' (*Czarna Madonna*) which aptly expresses the feelings of the whole nation:

Madonna, Black Madonna,
How good it is to be your child,
Oh allow us Black Madonna,
To find refuge in your arms.
In her care you will find peace,
And protection from all evil,
For she is tender towards all her children,
And has a loving heart.
She will protect you –
When you offer her your heart,
So joyfully repeat these words to her:
Madonna, Black Madonna...

There is never enough said about you, O Blessed Mother. Pope John Paul II, commented as a true son of Poland, "Jasna Góra is the Nation's Shrine. You should put your ear to this hallowed ground to hear the beating heart of the nation within her maternal heart. It beats to the echo of our lives. How many times in history did it pulsate to the cries of Polish suffering? But also to the shouts of joy, gratitude and victory." (Częstochowa, 4.06.1979)

In 1940 Dr Hans Frank (1900-1946) who was Hitler's representative and German governor of Poland wrote: "For Poles, the Church constitutes a central reference point which constantly radiates out in silence, thereby fulfilling the function of a sanctuary light. When all the lights in Poland went out, there was still the Holy One left in Częstochowa and in all the church sanctuaries. We should never forget that!" How well Sienkiewicz captured the main characteristics of the Polish spirit. In his novel *Potop* (The Deluge) he wrote: "The enemy jeers at us and treats us with contempt when he asks us what is left from the glorious old values? And I reply, 'They have all disappeared, but something is left behind because we still have the faith and love of the Blessed Virgin Mary; and on that foundation everything else can be rebuilt'."

The truth of Sienkiewicz's words is authenticated by a sign originating from the second half of the eighteenth century about the necessary attitude of pilgrims arriving at Jasna Góra: "No company or group, no matter how large or how small, is allowed into the church until they have all said sorry to each other and forgiven each other all injustices and grudges. There are many godly people, who on arriving at the church, before they make their way to the chapel of the Blessed Virgin will not even look at the Holy Icon until they have made a perfect confession of their sins... for this was an old custom and one well known to our fathers."

Canonisation of Blessed Father Maksymilian Kolbe

Almost ten years had passed since the beatification of Father Maksymilian Kolbe. The church wanted to present the example of his heroic love to the whole world. The message was aimed especially to the young during their developing years, so that is why I am mentioning it in my memoirs. Globally many nations still vividly remembered the Second World War and the scenes of total annihilation in concentration camps. On 10 October 1982 St Peter's Square was completely full. The presence of thirty cardinals and over two hundred bishops underlined the solemnity of the occasion. Especially notable was the attendance of Archbishop Joseph Hoeffner of Cologne, head of the German conference of bishops; Cardinal Jan Król, Archbishop of Philadelphia; and Mother Teresa of Calcutta, now herself counted among the Blessed of the Catholic Church. Also present was Franciszek Gajowniczek, who had been saved from death by starvation by Maksymilian Kolbe. He was sobbing throughout the ceremony which elevated his rescuer to the ranks of the saints. Only God knows what thoughts were passing through his mind. At the request of both German and Polish bishops, the Holy Father elevated Our Lady's knight – Maksymilian – to the roll of holy martyr saints.

From December 1981 Poland had been suffering under martial law and the Free Trade Union Solidarity (*Solidarność*) had had its right to legal existence taken away. Because of this sanction the Polish Primate Cardinal Józef Glemp was prevented from taking part in the canonisation ceremonies for his compatriot. The pain of the whole nation was focused that day on the heart of the Polish Pope. During the offertory procession an aged Salesian missionary Father Mario Aquistapece, who had spent seventy-six years in China, carried up to the altar the biography of the saint and a picture of the Blessed Virgin Mary.

In the saint's biography there is a particularly touching passage illustrating the extraordinary sensitivities of young Rajmund (Maksymilian's baptismal name). At home he was affectionately called Mundek. Eight-year-old Mundek discovered that Saint Francis of Assisi could talk to the birds, and he also wished to have a little brother or sister from the animal kingdom. In his neighbour's garden there was a chicken-coop and in it there were laying hens. He took an egg from his own house without his mother's permission and also without the knowledge of his neighbour and put the egg under a hen to incubate. He was so excited that he would have his own little chick, fluffy and yellow and full of life. But the ploy came to light and Mundek was devastated.

For consolation he stood in front of Our Lady's altar in the parish church of Pabianice and asked her, "What is too become of me?" Heaven could not leave such a heartfelt question unanswered and gave him an immediate reply. Our Blessed Lady appeared to him and looking at him lovingly held out two crowns, one red and one white. She asked him if he would like to have them. The white one symbolised chastity and the red one martyrdom. He nodded that he wanted both. He had entered into a contract with heaven.

His mother noticed that from that day he changed completely. He no longer lounged about with his friends as previously, but became quiet, more focused, perfectly obedient, even serious and was often found praying in front of their home shrine. His mother asked him for the reason for this change of behaviour, fearing the onset of some illness. She coaxed him saying, "There are no secrets withheld from your mother, as your mother is given to you by God." This convinced him. He told her his secret and she respected it. She only told the story to the Franciscans in Niepokalanów, three months after his death on 12 October 1941.

Martyr for the truth, Blessed Father Jerzy Popiełuszko

On 18 October 1984, while Poland was still under severe restrictions following martial law, three functionaries of the Polish Ministry of Internal Affairs beastially murdered the chaplain to the Free Trade Union Solidarity, Father Jerzy Popiełuszko (1947-1984).

I have seen enlarged coloured photographs of Father Jerzy's corpse. In all my life I have never seen such a terribly battered body – and that of a human being whose guiding motto was the Biblical quote 'Overcome evil with good'. To the question of how one human being could inflict such torture on another there can only be one reply, *Misterium iniquitatis* – the mystery of evil. The author of evil is the Blasphemer of the Cross and the Church, that is, Satan. According to Józef Michalik, Archbishop of Przemyśl, the fruit of Satan's work on Polish soil at that time comprised around three thousand instances of breaking-and-entering churches and presbyteries, the murder of seven priests and the desecration of two-hundred-and-seventy-one cemeteries.

Father Jerzy's sermons which were delivered at the monthly Masses-for-Poland at his parish church of Saint Stanisław Kostka in the Warsaw district of Żolibórz were beautiful and undefiled; without the slightest trace of animosity or enmity in regard to those who were hostile towards the ordinary people or towards Poland. One of the last things he said in his homily in Bydgoszcz, just a few hours before his death, sounds like his last testament:

"Life should be lived worthily because we only have one life. Today we need to talk a lot about the dignity of the individual person in order to really appreciate that the worth of any one individual must always rise above anything which can be found on earth, except God – even above all the collective wisdom of the world. Maintaining one's dignity so as to increase goodness and vanquish evil is to remain free on the inside even during times of external enslavement."

Not for the first time, the Communists were shown up for what they really were. The Polish Bishops said of the situation in the country at the time:

"The authorities are not guaranteeing that they will rule any differently than previously, reducing the nation to poverty and incurring incredible national debts... Without reforming the country they are enforcing upon the nation an old and discredited ideology ostensibly dressed up in the robes of progress. They are announcing the creation of a new State... but without God or the Decalogue." (Jasna Góra, 26.08.1984)

On 6 June 2010, His Holiness Pope Benedict XVI elevated Father Jerzy Popiełuszko into the ranks of the blessed martyrs of the Holy Roman Church.

Mother Angelika's television

The Rosary Hour building which was situated along the shores of Lake Erie resembled a lighthouse, of which there are many along the lakeside. The Rosary Hour programme sent out rays of light to its listeners by means of its auditions. It is impossible to list here all the subjects that were raised or the names of all the people, both religious and secular, who sat in front of the microphone, or to describe the many prayers which we said together with the listeners. Just like a lighthouse,

The Rosary Hour was an excellent observation platform. Thanks to the radio's interception of programmes in many languages, we were extremely well informed as to what was going on in the world – for example in Poland, in America and in the universal Church. We also watched a lot of television, especially Mother Angelika's Catholic station EWTN (Eternal Word Television Network).

Christ comes to the help of His Church, especially in stormy and difficult times in its history. The American church witnessed His help at the point when it was threatened with schism. The instrument of God's help was to be a quiet and humble woman, Rita Rizzo, known to the whole world as Mother Angelika. Her personality can be better appreciated after reading the words of Saint Paul:

For consider your call, brethren; not many of you were wise according to worldly standards, not many were powerful, not many were of noble birth; but God chose what is foolish in the world to shame the wise, God chose what is weak in the world to shame the strong, God chose what is low and despised in the world, even things that are not, to bring to nothing things that are, so that no human being might boast in the presence of God (I Corinthians 1,26-29).

Rita herself was the last person to expect to be called to great things. She entered a convent in Cleveland, Ohio, where she was given the name of Sister Angelika. Eventually she established a new order of contemplative nuns, and her first postulant was her own mother Mea Rizzo. Later others joined them. The nuns recognised in their superior great skills in interpersonal communication and her depth of religious knowledge. They advised her to share this wisdom outside the monastery walls for the benefit of everyone.

In time Mother Angelika started to produce her own television programmes and rapidly they attracted a sizeable following of viewers. As she was battling with debts the American Episcopal Church wanted to come to her aid but she was afraid of some of their more liberal tendencies and declined their offer of help. She remained independent throughout, relying solely on God's providence. When there is a need for help the nuns storm heaven with their petitions. Mother Angelika was always faithful to the *Magisterium* of the Church and the Pope. After an investigation by a Vatican emissary and after Pope John Paul II bestowed his blessing on the work, the television network started to expand rapidly. Today, Mother Angelika's programmes are transmitted twenty-four hours a day all over the globe.

The spirit of Solidarity

In November 1985, Father Dr Józef Tischner (1931-2000) visited our radio centre. He was a very well known priest originally from the Polish highlands, who became Dean of the Philosophy Department at the Papal Academy of Theology in Kraków. He was the author of many scholarly books and an adviser and spiritual director of the Solidarity movement. Few people realise that at this time there operated in Vienna an International Institute for the Philosophical Study of Interpersonal Experiences. This body conducted research into ways of preserving basic Christian values in the face of threats from Marxist-Leninist Communism. Father Tischner headed the staff of that institution. Our charming guest accepted our invitation to the microphone and he spoke to our Polish audience about the spirit of Poland in the 1980s. I include here some of his invaluable statements:

"Usually when one refers to Poland one is referring to her body – indicating that she is poor, weak and ill, and rather like a sick person in need of help. But Poland is not only a physical body – she is essentially, if not primarily, also a spirit... However, when we refer to the Polish spirit, suddenly everything is turned on its head. It would appear that it is not the Polish spirit that needs assistance, but the rest of the world including Europe which needs assistance from the Polish spirit... Poland is a country of free people. I can say categorically that nowhere have I seen so many free people in public places as in Poland... How is it that in a totalitarian state, ruled by a dictatorship, free people are moving along its paths and roads? Freedom is one of our basic values. For people to be really free they have to be able to be responsible for their actions... The past few years, especially the Solidarity years, were years of growth and maturity towards a sense of responsibility. All of a sudden people became responsible not only for their own personal affairs but also for public affairs; they became responsible for Poland ... When asked what he understood by the expression 'native country' the nineteenth-century poet Cyprian Norwid replied, 'Your native country is one huge collective responsibility.' What a beautiful expression. Your native country is not represented by meadows, fields, rivers or factories. It is not prosperity or poverty. Your country is not even the government or authority. Your country represents responsibility... one huge collective responsibility. It is what a person carries around in his heart and which connects that person to others – not in an emotional way but above all in a moral way, with higher values...

"In the Polish national anthem we sing 'Poland has not perished whilst *we* are still alive...' In some ways the poet was not concerned with whether or not Poland was on the map of the world. What was important to him was that the people were Polish, because it is not Poland that gives birth to Poles, but Poles who give birth to Poles. The concept of Poland stems from a sense of responsibility, a great collective responsibility felt inside everyone of us... It is not important what we are going through but how we come out at the other end. We need to come out with a deepened sense of duty and a more profound appreciation of our native country, for trials are necessary for this sense of responsibility to mature in us. If there were no challenges, our sense of responsibility would be immature. The more profound the sense of collective responsibility the greater it becomes and the greater the right to sing those words 'Poland has not perished whilst *we* are still alive'."

Concerns for the Post-Conciliar Church

By 1985 twenty-five years had passed since the conclusion of the Second Vatican Council. This was not a particularly long period of time in the scale of world events but very important to our generation and so it was also touched upon in our programmes. We were persuaded to raise the subject because rumours were still circulating to the effect that the calling of the council was a mistake, that the council undermined the authority of the Pope and bishops and brought about confusion and anxiety in the hearts and minds of the faithful. But this was a completely false assessment of the situation. The Church is a living organism and must constantly renew itself and develop to meet new challenges and needs. *Ecclesia semper reformanda* – the Church needs constantly to reform and renew itself. It is not afraid of crises of expansion. The assurance of its permanency is that the Church is God's institution, at whose head is Christ, and whose soul is the Holy Spirit. And the Holy Spirit blows where it wills. It certainly played a trick on the cardinals, who thought they were electing an elderly, transitional Pope, whose pontificate would be sufficiently short to give them the necessary time to look around for an appropriate successor for those crucial times. And it was precisely Blessed Pope John XXIII who became the instrument of the Holy Spirit. He accomplished no small feat.

One of the fruits of the Council was the banishment of the ancient and erroneous understanding that the *Church* meant the Pope, bishops and priests. Today, everybody knows that all of the faithful are responsible, each in his or her own way, for the work of the Church. The salvation of our neighbours is everybody's responsibility. The priest cannot reach everywhere. Each member of the faithful has therefore to bear witness to their faith and should be a "light to the world" – the "salt of the earth". The Prefect of the Congregation of Faith, Cardinal Joseph Ratzinger, later Pope Benedict XVI, observed that the reforms of the Second Vatican Council will be proven efficacious when a wave of saints passes through the Church. On Sunday 1 May 2011, in St Peter's Square, in the presence of over a million pilgrims from around the world, His Holiness Pope Benedict XVI proclaimed his immediate predecessor Pope John Paul II to be counted among the Blessed of the Roman Catholic Church.

Trust the young

During a train journey from France to Germany, I met some students in my compartment who sat up right through the night discussing amongst themselves with great animation their experiences from a week-long stay in the French village of Taizé in Burgundy. While the subject of their experiences was new to me, it filled me with great joy and interest. They told me that they had learnt to pray at Taizé and had encountered God in Jesus Christ; whereas their Christian parents had often been too busy making a living and chasing success to help them find God either by word or example. As a result the next generation had lost the sense of the purpose of life. Moreover, I was interested in their stories about this ecumenical community of monks who were attempting to repair their parents' shortcomings, while instilling in the young a sense of hope for the future – a fundamental requirement for any spiritual growth.

I therefore made my way to Taizé, for the purpose of collecting information for my radio talks about this remarkable place. At the railway station several groups of boys and girls got off laden down with rucksacks and rolled up sleeping-bags. They started walking the couple of kilometres in the direction of the village of Taizé and so I followed them. Once there, I was struck by a scene which reminded me of a scouting jamboree. Perhaps it was like this in Jerusalem during the descent of the Holy Spirit at Pentecost – as I could hear so many different languages being spoken. The monks had handed over to the young people the organisation of the camp life, which they did willingly and with enthusiasm.

There were several thousand young people present and this number has grown consistently to its current peak since the centre's inception in the 1940s. The participants gather for talks under the trees – endless discussions which cover such subjects as the return to the sources of Revelation, the truth which God has shown to mankind in His goodness and love, a return to prayer and an exchange of experiences between young people of different countries. The moderator, who is usually one of the monks, explains some of the more difficult issues and helps with problems. The monks prepare a full week's programme for the young people, the culmination of which is participation at a Catholic Mass on Sunday.

In the middle of the compound stands a church which has been built by young Germans in the spirit of expiation for the crimes of Hitler. I always found it full of young people at prayer. In Taizé, prayer is the axis around which everything else rotates. One of the more astounding facts is that the young people, for the most part, had come from homes where there had been no tradition of prayer. They had always found prayer tiresome but here for the first time in their lives they were praying with great ardour. Many of the young people would take off their shoes before entering the church, barefoot. Due to the vast numbers the church building was extended with a circus-like tent. From the depths of the church one could hear the rhythmical chanting of hundreds of youngsters sitting on the ground or on low stools. They would melodically repeat short excerpts of Latin verses from the Old and New Testaments, the tunes of which were based on Gregorian and Byzantine chants. I can still hear today the verse: *"Deus caritas est: qui manet in caritate, in Deo manet et Deus in eo"* – God is love, and he who abides in love abides in God, and God abides in him (I John 4,16-17) or "Make a joyful noise to the Lord, all the lands" (based on Psalm 100). In this way the monks sorted out the problem of many languages. The repetition of the verses gave the opportunity for reflection. On Fridays there is adoration of the Cross during which the young at heart unite in a spirit of solidarity with oppressed, hungry, persecuted and suffering members of Christ's mystical body.

I was presented to the founder and leader of the ecumenical community, Brother Roger Schutz (1915-2005). His charisma can be summarised in these words:

"To understand every person irrespective of their race, background or perspective; to understand their ideological and moral intricacies, to get to know their frustrations, fears and yearnings, and to uncover in them the goodness placed there by God – Father and Creator – but which so often is buried under ashes. Above all to trust young people, giving them a vote of confidence, while listening to what they wish to say to their elders, discovering in them the best part of their creative intuition."

When Brother Roger found out that I was Polish, he led me to the church before the icon of Our Lady of Częstochowa which had been placed not on the wall or an altar but on a low stool in the middle of a praying crowd. We both knelt down and at the suggestion of Brother Roger said aloud 'Hail Mary' in Latin for the persecuted Church in Poland.

I stayed in Taizé almost a week and found out more about the work which grew out of the embers of the Second World War. Roger Schutz was the son of a Protestant pastor in Switzerland and a French Protestant mother who with their hearts and minds overcame religious divisions in their longing for the unity of Christians. For some time Darwinist theories undermined the faith of young Roger, but he regained his faith and followed in his father's footsteps by studying theology. The atrocities of war shocked his conscience, because of the realisation that there were Christians fighting on both sides of the front. He asked himself: Where is the source of this evil which is so rampant in the world? The answer came in the writings of the English convert, novelist and man of letters, G K Chesterton: "The source lies within me". Paraphrasing these words Roger Schutz would say: "The source of evil lies in the disintegration of Christianity. This break-up leads people astray, distancing them from God. What can be done about this and how can this scandal be removed?" Roger Schutz curtailed his studies and in 1940 moved to France in order to look after refugees from various nations who had been affected by the war. On finding out about his work a resident of the Taizé village said to him: "It would be good if you could remain here with us. We are so poor and abandoned and times are so bad". He accepted this as the prompting of God himself. In 1949 he founded a community of brothers who accepted candidates of various Christian denominations. The Apostolic Nuncio in Paris, Cardinal Angelo Giuseppe Roncalli, later Blessed Pope John XXIII, gave permission for them to use the building of the village Catholic Church for prayers. And that was the start of the Holy Spirit's gust of wind.

The young people in Taizé asked the monks if they were trying to form a movement – an international organisation. The brothers replied, "No, we do not want to form a movement. God has given you to us for just a few days, and we do not wish to retain you for ourselves. We do not want to create a movement whose centre would be in Taizé. What God has given to us we wish to give to the whole world, following the example of the Blessed Virgin Mary who gave her Son to the whole world. Go back to your communities and parishes and don't enclose yourselves in small groups. Go out and courageously take part in the lives of your own parishes."

Cardinal Roncalli – a long-time supporter of the community – greeted the brothers of the Taizé community with the joyful words, "Oh Taizé, you little springtime" at the start of his meeting with them. Cardinal Roncalli put his complete trust in the brothers and talked about a future renewal of the Church. The Holy Spirit would blow again with this springtide wind when later Pope John Paul II started to organise meetings with millions of young people from around the world at International World Youth

Days. Brother Roger was tragically murdered by a confused psychiatrically-ill woman in front of his brothers and many young people while attending compline on 16 August 2005. At the same time Pope Benedict XVI was attending the Twentieth World Youth Day in Cologne, Germany.

Not far from Taizé lie the ruins of the famous Benedictine Abbey of Cluny, founded in 910AD, just before the birth of my own country. The Benedictine community of Cluny contributed to the expansion of faith in Europe and it also had an effect on the young fledgling church in Poland. I also visited this historic site.

The Third of May Constitution – Pride of the Polish nation

In 1991, Poles around the world celebrated the two hundredth anniversary of the Third of May 1791 Constitution. Professor Franciszek Adamski, a sociologist from the Jagiellonian University in Kraków, gave a talk on its subject over our radio. He reminded our listeners that the constitution was the second such document in the world after the American Constitution which was declared in Philadelphia on 17 September 1787. The Polish 1791 constitution is sometimes referred to as "the last testament of the dying nation", as shortly afterwards in 1792 Prussia, Russia and Austria started to partition our country. The Third of May constitution engraved itself onto the hearts of Poles and is their great pride. Thomas Jefferson, as president of his country and as a democrat and signatory to the Declaration of Independence of the United States of America and a friend of Tadeusz Kościuszko wrote that the world at that time had received three constitutions worthy of remembrance and respect. They were in order of their proclamation, the American, the Polish and the French.

The values contained in the constitution stem directly from an understanding of Natural Law and have been already interpreted for us in the Gospels. Therefore, the first paragraph of the text of the constitution starts by describing the special role of Roman Catholicism in shaping the social, legal and cultural principles of the New Order in Poland: "The national religion in Poland is and will be the Holy Roman Catholic Faith with all of her laws..." In the very next sentence, as if to emphasise the Polish tradition of tolerance: "Freedom is assured to believers of all faiths due to the love of our neighbour as a consequence of our Christianity".

The values espoused in the constitution call us to a constant review of our conscience to examine if we are faithful to them. We are also obliged to defend those values as people nowadays – especially in the West – have a mistaken notion about freedom, and an unjust social order has divided people into rich and poor, into extremely rich and appallingly impoverished, into first class and second class citizens. Poland offers the world her faithfulness to the principles of the Constitution of the Third of May.

The word of God on the air waves

According to tradition every year the new season of The Radio Rosary Hour was opened by an ecclesiastical dignitary, either from Poland or from another country. Sometimes it was the Primate of Poland Cardinal Stefan Wyszynski, several times it was Cardinal Karol Wojtyła from Kraków, or Cardinal Władysław Rubin – initially in his capacity as a representative of the Polish primate for pastoral care of Polish émigrés around the world and later as Secretary to the Congregation for Oriental Churches. Among many other bishops, Cardinal Jan Król of Philadelphia also spoke several times to the listeners. On one occasion the President of the Catholic University of Lublin, the Reverend Professor Mieczysław Krąpiec, a Dominican, made his unique contribution. The university was the only Catholic university in Poland which continued to operate throughout the Communist era. He spoke about the university compiling a *Catholic Encyclopaedia* and a project to produce an *Encyclopaedia of Philosophy*.

The subject matter of the radio programmes was varied and touched upon aspects of personal life, family issues, social, national and universal concerns. Examples of some of the titles of the talks were:

Everyday spirituality – Sienkiewicz, a bard of family life – The Bible's approach to suffering – Renewal in the Spirit – Women's Liberation – Love your neighbours – We crucified the Lord – Humility, the Queen of virtues – Communism, a blessing or a curse? – Christ in death-throes till the end of the world – Sex education for children and young people – Muslims – Reincarnation – Purgatory – Heaven – Hell – Gossip, backbiting and slander – The responsibilities of freedom - The strange book of the Bible – Dr Mengele of Auschwitz and the camp midwife Servant of God Stanisława Leszczynska .

The titles on their own do not say much about the content or worth of the programmes, so I will let the listeners say what they thought about the sessions.

Handing over to the listeners

In their letters the listeners acknowledged The Radio Rosary Hour as a great gift from God and evidence of divine providence. A few examples of testimonials from letters kept in the radio archives are as follows:-

"I was in such a chaotic state and beset with so many difficulties that I couldn't see any way forward. Father's talk about Divine Providence settled my fears. Difficulties still remained, but I was no longer afraid of them. I now know that with God's help I will be able to overcome them."

A newcomer from Poland wrote: "The Communist authorities gag the Church, so that one does not hear religious programmes over the radio... The Rosary Hour helped me to become acquainted with and understand better the teachings of the Church and has thereby enriched my personality."

Another person wrote: "How many souls all over the country have been fed by the beautiful and profound talks presented by Father Kornelian. Every word falls on my dead soul and brings it back to life. I had been psychologically and morally despondent for five years. Today I am a completely different person."

In order for The Rosary Hour programme to reach those Polish émigrés who found themselves beyond the reach of the radio-waves, and above all in order to reach the sick and house-bound, we started to print the talks and chats and to produce them on magnetic tapes which were sent out on request. A Franciscan sister of St Felix, a subscriber to the printed version of the talks, confided in me: "I read the talks, or rather I discuss them with God. In each sentence one feels the strength of conviction, the light of faith; so every so often I have to pause for a moment of silence... The loneliness which I feel in my life helps me to appreciate the loneliness that God experiences in the wasteland of human hearts."

The voice of the clergy

Both American and Polish clergy expressed a high opinion about our radio apostolate. The bishop of the Diocese of Buffalo, Father William Turner wrote to Father Justyn, "You're not even aware of how much good your work is accomplishing and the effects of The Rosary Hour. As bishops we have daily evidence of that! It would be an irreparable loss to our Faith if The Rosary Hour fell silent." While Cardinal Król wrote: "Not many works, equally great and beautiful, have imprinted on them the stamp of God, and certainly not for such a long time."

A pastor from Chicago, Monsignor Ilinski working with the Polonia noted, "An awesome activity, this radio apostolate... Your talks are well researched. They do not mislead or contain personal, often hazy, concepts of self-styled theologians, but preach and explain the truths which were taught by Jesus Christ." While Father Kazimierz Żuchowski wrote, "I often meet people who have obtained almost all their religious knowledge from The Rosary Hour". The President of the Catholic University of Lublin, the Reverend Dr Marian Krąpiec, made the comment that The Rosary Hour is a "...living source of culture and contact should be made with it".

The effects of any pastoral work, by its very nature, will sometimes elude detection, since its main focus is the hidden, interior spiritual life. All the supernatural harvest from pastoral work, by the will of God, is deposited in heaven as directed by Christ: *"...provide yourselves with purses that do not grow old, with a treasure in the heavens that does not fail, where no thief approaches and no moth destroys"* (Luke 12,33).

Mary Jung

It seems appropriate here to pay homage to a petite woman, who was an exceptional, selfless and highly respected worker at The Radio

Rosary Hour – Maria Jung. The Buffalo Polonia, in particular the inhabitants of Broadway and Fillmore districts, affectionately referred to her by the diminutive form of her name – Marysia. She never wanted to draw attention to herself. The Americans have a very good word for someone of such a retiring nature. It is *self-effacing* – someone who wishes to stay in the background, in the shade, obliterating their tracks. But this was not as a result of low self-esteem. Marysia was perfectly aware of her worth and talents, but she preferred to keep a low profile. She never sought recognition, and when she was praised she had the knack of turning the words around in such a way that the person who praised her felt in turn to be appreciated. That was part of her charm and one of the reasons why she was so highly regarded.

At the age of seventeen, freshly out of a secretarial school, she decided to work for the radio apostolate, which she served almost up to the time of her death. She was fluent in both Polish and English and she was familiar with Polish history and literature. Marysia knew everything about The Rosary Hour. During the life of Father Kornelian her main task was taking down dictated radio talks and the answers to listeners' questions. Marysia never counted the hours at work and was always willing to undertake new projects. I listened with amazement when she recounted how during the huge Rosary Hour picnics (garden parties) she would buy an admission ticket to enter the grounds, even though as an employee of the radio programme she could have got in free!

She loved Poland, even though when I first met her she had not as yet visited the country. I was surprised that she had never been there; but the reason lay in her voluntarily chosen simple life-style. From her own modest income she supported various charitable organisations, both American and Polish. I managed to persuade her to put aside some savings every month towards a trip to Poland; and she finally made the journey. Because she had the ability to make contact with people easily and quickly she felt as much at home in Poland as in Buffalo.

Once, Marysia was attacked by a thief as she was going up the steps to the radio station. He tried to grab her handbag, but because she was holding onto it tightly he lifted her up in anger and slammed her down onto the steps. She broke her pelvis and for the first time in her life she was hospitalised. Not long after she came out of hospital a burglar broke into her apartment at night and demanded money. Marysia couldn't get out of bed because her crutches were out of reach, so she calmly pointed to a plate in the kitchen with her milk money, telling him to take it. While the thief was ransacking the apartment in the belief that he had found a wealthy woman's residence, Marysia was trying to talk to his conscience, explaining to him the spiritual benefits which accompany the practice of honesty!

The Death of Father Kornelian

The American government appreciated the contribution of Father Kornelian to American life and on 21 September 1964 he was invited to the White House by President Lyndon Johnson. On 6 February 1978 he was also invited by President Jimmy Carter shortly after his visit to Poland and I accompanied Father Kornelian to the White House on that occasion. Leading members of the American Polonia were also present. President Carter, a deeply religious man, thanked Father Kornelian for consistently preaching the word of God. He made the point that overall peace, rule of law and security in the world could only be based on respect for human and Divine laws. The evening was enhanced by a recital given by the Polish-American pianist Artur Rubinstein (1887-1982), a Polish Jew, who was one of the world's most accomplished pianists. The Catholic University of Lublin honoured Father Kornelian in 1984 with the Medal of Merit and bestowed on him an honorary doctorate for his contribution to promoting Polish culture on American radio.

On 31 August 1996 God called Father Kornelian Dende home to heaven – a gain for heaven but a great loss for those of us still on earth, especially in America and Canada. The word *success*, which in America is treated as possessing magical qualities from birth to old age, simply did not exist for him. The priesthood was his life's work and service. He was the soul of the radio programme. He died of a haematological cancer, having intended to continue his work to the end, ignoring any physical ailments.

In my eulogy at his funeral I said that he was "an exceptional individual, of great intellectual and spiritual calibre, a person with vision. He can be characterised by the very words he himself preached as a newly ordained priest, 'If I were an artist I would paint a Catholic priest as a person of enormous proportions, with huge feet firmly entrenched in the soil, but with his head reaching far above the clouds. Only in this way, it seems to me, could I represent to you the work of a priest as mediator between God and humanity, between heaven and earth.' This concise and symbolic vision of the priesthood was recognisable throughout his life, in his spirituality and pastoral work, especially in his radio apostolate."

Because his service at the radio station occurred over the period of the Second Vatican Council, which called for the spiritual and moral renewal of the Church, he turned this evocation into the mission for the radio apostolate. In the chapel of the radio headquarters he placed a reproduction of the cross from the San Damiano church in Assisi from which Christ spoke to Saint Francis saying, "Go, repair my Church". The listeners missed Father Kornelian, as they had the founder and the first director of The Rosary Hour, Father Justyn.

The decline of The Rosary Hour

After the death of Father Kornelian the directorship of The Rosary Hour changed several times, and its light started to dim. Despite this situation and despite the increasing financial difficulties, the Franciscan Rosary Hour bravely continues to offer its loyal listeners Polish language Catholic broadcasts but unfortunately only on a few radio stations because air-time is very expensive and the programmes can also be heard via the Internet.

The seventy-fifth anniversary of The Rosary Hour passed by without any great celebration. In our Franciscan Polish province based in the USA there were increasingly fewer priests of Polish descent and people were asking "would it not be better to have radio programmes in English? After all, we are in America." All I could think of was the metaphor of the melting-pot, where cultural characteristics of individual countries become lost in the dominant culture.

In this situation, I am therefore grateful that even in America one can now tune into religious programmes transmitted directly from Poland such as *Radio Maryja* (Radio Maria) and *Telewizja Trwam* (Television Faithful). I can only trust that God will send providential people of the same stature as Father Justyn and Father Kornelian to carry on the work among American Poles. America and Polish-Americans deserve to have priests of their calibre.

Parting with radio work

In 1999 I said goodbye to my radio work which I had been engaged in for over thirty-four years. A new generation was taking over. I was directed towards pastoral work in the Polish-American parish of Saint Stanisław (Stanislaus), Bishop and Martyr, in Chicopee, Massachusetts, located about three-quarters of an hour by car to the west of Boston. This change of work came as a result of a great longing I had for such pastoral activity – work for which my life experiences in a Siberian labour camp, the army, youth work in Africa and Canada and at the radio apostolate – had all adequately prepared me.

The State of Massachusetts is part of New England. It was from here that the English colonial expansionists moved southwards and westwards. It is a charming part of the American continent, somewhat resembling the Podkarpacki region, the area incorporating the foothills of the Carpathian and Bieszczady Mountains in the South East of Poland. The town of Chicopee borders its larger neighbour, Springfield, Massachusetts just as Praga once bordered the larger town of Warsaw. Springfield lies within the State of Connecticut rather than Massachusetts.

I have grown to like Chicopee which has over 54,000 inhabitants representing a vast array of countries. Poles constitute the largest group, followed by the French, Irish, Portuguese, Germans and Jews. In the near future the number of Latinos who are mostly from Mexico, will increase. In Chicopee I decided to improve my knowledge of the English language, since in the Province of Quebec, the French language had been sufficient, while during my radio apostolate I spoke and wrote exclusively in Polish. The pastoral work in Chicopee is conducted

346

basically in two languages, but in reality English is the dominant language.

Celebrating my jubilee of ordination with the old "Africans" and orphans, Chicopee, Massachusetts 2006

Apart from regular pastoral duties I was also given the spiritual care of the Padre Pio Prayer Group and the Beautiful Years Club for older parishioners. I teach religion in the parish primary school, though in reality religion is taught to the children by religious education teachers, while I just go to visit the children on occasions, so that they become accustomed to the sight of a priest! The parish forms a proud close-knit community. In 2006 the parish organised festivities for my diamond jubilee of priesthood – sixty years since my ordination – in which many of my past pupils and refugee contacts also took part.

The mystery of the small coffin

While in Chicopee I heard a harrowing story about one of my young charges, who was ten years old when I brought him over to Canada from Africa. His name was Andrzej Nowakowski. From the photograph taken in Germany an almost baby-like face looks out, with blond hair and grey eyes. He was always considered to be a complete orphan, without a living mother or father. He left the Soviet Union amidst a wave of other small exiled-wanderers when General Anders gave the order that the army should evacuate as many small Polish children as possible, especially orphans. At the time Andrzej would have been two years old. All that was known about him was his name and date of birth, but no one knew who had handed over those details. In the speed with which one had to leave the Soviet "paradise" there wasn't the time for verification of such fine details.

No one ever sought out Andrzej and for his part he never asked after his family, convinced that they had all perished. In Canada the boy was much loved, being a bit of a "sweetie" – an affectionate child. There were even futile attempts to adopt him, which never came to anything but certainly not from any fault with Andrzej. After finishing school he decided to enter the Canadian army. They demanded an identity card, but he did not possess one. They asked about his nationality and how he came to be in Canada. He told them that he was Polish and that he had been brought to Canada by Father Królikowski, via Africa. The amazement of the army officials steadily increased and reached its zenith when he enumerated for them the countries he had been to during the first ten years of his life – Russia, Persia (Iran), Kenya, Tanzania, Italy, Germany and Canada. He had arrived in the land of the maple leaf with the orphanage. Although he did not have any documents, which was unheard of in the West, the army kept the recruit, because the boy was healthy, well-built and intelligent.

But his life story awoke suspicions that maybe he was a "mole", a Soviet spy. Just such types of individuals, street-wise yet on the surface apparently naive, could make good spies. They therefore started to find out about him without his knowledge, checking the information he had supplied, writing to the embassies of countries he had named, to the Red Cross and to the International Tracing Service. Their suspicions that he might be a spy were totally unfounded.

During his military service Andrzej married a French teacher named Jeannine. When the military wanted to negotiate a new contract to transfer him overseas or to other Canadian provinces, his wife was understandably distressed at the prospect of his prolonged absences. She said, "I will be pining away here waiting for you, while you will be flying around the world." Loving his wife and being of a sensitive disposition Andrzej resigned from further service in the army. When he was demobilised he was handed the file of papers concerning his identity. He did not destroy them but neither was he particularly interested in them.

Sometime later, he handed over to a compatriot friend of his, Łucjan Stępien, an asylum seeker from Nowy Sącz (in Southern Poland), the file of papers saying, "Here, have them. See what you can make of them." Łucjan, who was grateful to Andrzej for his help and hospitality took the request seriously and started to analyse the papers with detective precision. He filled in the gaps in the work started by the Canadian army as he wanted to trace the family roots of his friend. His search covered all over Poland, and he was finally put onto the right track by information contained in the Polish Forestry Veterans' Almanac (*Almanach Leśników Polskich - Kombatantów*). This large tome contained thousands of names. He looked up the Nowakowski family in Eastern Poland, from where they had been deported to Siberia. And a miracle happened. Among the names he found the entire Nowakowski family, with the names of the parents, father Jan and mother Irena, four daughters and two sons with all their dates of birth. The date of the youngest son's birth agreed with that which the Canadian army had discovered for Andrzej. The information in the Almanac was accompanied by an annotation to the effect that the family had been deported to the USSR on the 20 June 1941 from Pinsk. They also mentioned that before the war Jan and Irena Nowakowska and their children, Elżbieta, Irena, Maria, Danuta, Jan and Andrzej had lived in Forestry accommodation in the State Forest of Moroczno in the Polesie region of Poland (now in the Ukraine). This information had been handed over to the Almanac by Maria Nowakowska, who had managed to avoid being captured and sent to Siberia. She also gave the editors of the book her telephone number. Łucjan Stępien contacted her by telephone and she proved to be Andzrej's sister!

After the declaration of the so-called amnesty the Nowakowski family had the right to return to Poland from the Soviet Union as members of a military family. On release from prison the father had enlisted in General Anders's army. But unfortunately the rest of the family did not make it from the farthest reaches of Siberia in time to catch the last transport to Iran. To make matters worse, little Andrzej caught typhus and was sent to a hospital. After some time they informed his mother that her son had died giving her a small closed box and informing her not to open it for fear of contagion. Little Andrzej was buried and was mourned.

In 1946, the Nowakowski family finally returned to Poland from Uzbekistan and settled in Warsaw, later moving to Celestynów and Otwock. A year later, at the conclusion of the Italian Campaign, the father rejoined the rest of the family, but sadly died shortly afterwards.

On returning to Poland from Canada in 2001, Łucjan Stępien telephoned the Nowakowski family. The mother, Irena, was still alive at that time. He asked about Andrzej. Old wounds were re-opened. Someone at the other end of the receiver answered curtly that "Andrzej is dead. We buried him in Uzbekistan." But after this telephone call the family became restless and started to analyse the matter further. Questions started to be raised as to why they were told not to open the small chest. Did it really contain the remains of little Andrzej? What could have been inside it? Was the body of little Andrzej really in the small chest? Perhaps by mistake it was exchanged with a little Russian child? It was even feasible that in the small chest there had been no human remains at all but only a rock or a piece of wood. Perhaps some evil person was the perpetrator of this macabre situation? Perhaps it was some form of foul play and if so, who could have done such a thing? Who would have had the audacity to steal a live child from a mother and abducting it, present it as their own in order to get out from that inhuman land? The small chest buried a long time ago in Uzbekistan still held onto its secrets.

But if it was some form of foul play, at least the perpetrator had an ounce of decent honesty, by handing over little Andrzej to the orphanage in Teheran, thereby enabling reconnection with the family, albeit sixty years later. By the dictates of Divine Providence Andrzej had found his family. Shortly after Stępien had made contact with the family, Andrzej went to Poland for a meeting with his family. But his mother did not survive long enough to meet her son; she died three weeks before he was reunited with his family. But she died happy in the knowledge that she would meet her son in heaven. At Warsaw airport his closest relatives had no problem recognising him from among the crowd of passengers streaming out, due to his striking resemblance to other male members of his family!

There are no such things as chance encounters

Whenever I visited Poland, as a rule I would visit Niepokalanów, my spiritual home. On several occasions I met an American, Claude R Foster, Professor of History at West Chester University in Pennsylvania. For thirteen years he had been collecting material for a monograph about Saint Maksymilian Kolbe, taking statements from eye witnesses such as Franciscan brothers in both the Polish and Japanese Niepokalanów, but mainly from Father Kolbe's secretary, Brother Hieronim Wierzba. Professor Foster, a Protestant, presented the biography of the saint in his book entitled *Mary's Knight* within the context of the history of the twentieth century. He particularly placed an emphasis on the example given by Saint Maksymilian, in giving up his own life for his neighbour's. In this way Maksymilian has become "the patron of our difficult times, patron of the twentieth century" as Pope John Paul II said. According to Brother Hieronim, the saint put particular stress on fulfilling the will of God, that is, on conforming his will to the will of our Creator, following the example of the Immaculate Virgin Mary. I became friendly with Professor Foster, who is now spreading the word about Saint Maksymilian in Germany and in the United States.

Our bond – a spiritual homeland

In spite of my various activities connected with the radio and later with parish work in Chicopee I have never lost touch with my former charges. The five-yearly meetings of the whole group have never seemed sufficient. We would exchange letters, telephone each other and from time to time I managed to get to Montreal or Toronto, where the largest number of them lived. I would always notify them in advance about my arrival. The meetings in Montreal usually took place in the home of Staszek and Bogusia Szymanska. In Toronto we would meet in the parish hall of Saint Maksymilian Kolbe Church in Mississauga. In keeping with Canadian custom the women would bring the food and drink. I would start the meetings by giving them some spiritual encouragement asking them not to lose the heritage which had been bestowed on them in the past and urging them to deepen the values which they had received in Africa. In the early years they would ask about Father Caron who was always close to their hearts, and also after Father Dostaler, but not so frequently after Father Larame as he had been with them for only a few weeks when they had first arrived in Canada. They were always eager to hear news from Poland. They were always willing to hear about their friends who had moved to other Canadian provinces looking for work and who lived in Ontario, Windsor, Kitchener, Sault, Ste Marie and on the farms past Sherbrooke. Contact with those far flung friends was much harder. After that, a family atmosphere would prevail and as we were together again enjoying each other's company we could fondly reminisce about Africa. We would also exchange new information and current news, sharing perspectives and observations.

Over the passage of time the ties between us have become stronger. That was and still is – our family. I cannot over-emphasise the strength of the ties that connect me with those now grown-up former-refugee children. In spite of passing years, uneasy childhood and dispersal around the globe we are still very close to each other. That bond is our spiritual homeland. It is similar to the intimate bond experienced by soldiers who have gone through combat together. We have a common language and share similar experiences and memories. Moreover we don't share these experiences readily with strangers because not everyone will understand us.

I still maintain contact with Izabela Choroś in New Zealand, who is a delegate to the World Congress of Polonia. She was twelve years old when she and her mother were deported to Siberia. She still remembers that during the arrest her father was shot in the courtyard. The children of Izabela who were all born in the antipodes converse in beautiful Polish. Another former refugee now living in New Zealand with whom I have maintained a correspondence over many years is Malwina Rubisz-Schwieters, a poet and social activist. Her brother died in Katyn. In England, the United States of America and Canada my inspiration has been Hela Chojnacka-Boguniewicz, who for the last quarter of a century has been conducting summer camps for the Polish brownies in American Częstochowa (Doylestown, Pennsylvania) and educating senior cadres of the Polish guiding movement. In England similar work was conducted for many years by Luna Boniewicz-Golinska. I must also mention here Małgosia Bejnarowicz-Niwczyk, an example of one of the many wonderful members of the Polish scouting movement working tirelessly around the world for the benefit of young people.

Krystyna Serafin-Pryjomko, who lived for many years in England and has recently moved back to Poland, built a children's home near Arusha in Tanzania. She collects money for this cause from her many contacts – the so-called "old Africans" – that is, the Polish refugee children exiled to Siberia who had found a temporary home and refuge in Africa. A school is now being built for orphaned African children near Tengeru. The charity she set up – The St Gabriel Home Foundation – has a website with more information on it about their work. As she says, "The beauty and warmth of Africa and its compassionate people gave me back my stolen childhood. Now, I intend to repay this priceless blessing by providing some of Africa's remarkable children with this most precious gift…" I could never find enough time to list all the splendid, socially-active refugee "children" I am in contact with. But all of them are conscious that God sees them and loves them very much. And His love is the greatest gift of all.

Many of the former-refugee children dream about returning at least once in their lifetime to the places from which they were deported to Siberia; to see their homes, wander around inside and to remind themselves once more how it was when the enemy terrorised the family in the middle of the night and ordered them to leave within the hour with their bundles in their hands. They want to remind themselves of the sound of the whining of their pet dogs who ran after the horse-wagons begging to be taken along as well. They want to recreate what is beginning to disappear from their memories, which they never truly understood in the first place, especially what their mothers were going through when they were separated from their husbands.

In their imagination their thoughts turn towards their homeland where they grew up, where they were educated and where they spent their childhood. They want to see once more the houses, fields, orchards and streams which they knew long ago in their childhood. But many who managed to return to their old family haunts have experienced distress. They have been unable to locate their family homes, and they have found that orchards have been chopped down and parental fields turned into pastureland. All traces of their previous lives have been obliterated; only in rare instances have small churches remained to bear witness to the marks of war against God and religion.

Reunion of "Africans" and Tengeru orphans in Fawley Court, England 1997

The President of Poland and refugee children

In 2007 I received an invitation from the Polish government to attend a conference in Warsaw on 8 November in the Belweder Palace. The honorary patron of the conference dedicated to *The Wanderings of Polish Refugee Children 1939-1950* was the President of Poland, Lech Kaczynski (2005-2010). Participants in the conference were some of the ambassadors of the countries which had offered hospitality to the Polish children evacuated from the USSR during the war years – Iran, the Republic of South Africa, Mexico, New Zealand and Canada. The conference started with a con-celebration of the Holy Mass, and the chief celebrant was the Army Bishop for the Polish forces, the Most Reverend General Professor Tadeusz Płoski. (The bishop together with the President of Poland – Lech Kaczynski – was to die tragically in an airline crash over Smolensk in April 2010.) Several historians took part in the conference and among the audience were many who had also lived in refugee settlements in the countries represented. The topic of my presentation was *The Odyssey of the Tengeru Orphans.* The day was unforgettable and full of emotion. When I recalled the hymn which was considered to be the wandering refugee children's anthem, *O Lord, who art in heaven, lend to us your hand... and crush the sword that has ravaged our land. Lead us back to a free Poland...* the entire auditorium stood to attention and sang all the verses of the hymn. Tears gathered in my eyes making it difficult for me to continue speaking. I saw again in front of me the little orphaned children of Karkin Batash singing, *Out of our pain and toil Poland will rise up to live again.* After my presentation and a hearty applause they sang again the hymn *O Lord, who art in heaven.*

Three days after the conference, on 11 November 2007 – the occasion of the Polish state holiday of National Independence – I was decorated at a ceremony in the Presidential Palace by President Lech Kaczynski with the Commander's Cross of the Order of Restitution of Poland. Previously, in 1966, I had received the Cavalier's Cross of the same Order from the Polish Government-in-exile! As at the conference, there passed in front of my mind's eye pictures of the ranks of guardians who had looked after the welfare of the children and offered them a helping hand. In many cases there has been no formal expression of thanks in this life but God will express his gratitude.

On the back of my photograph taken with President Kaczynski, which I sent out to many of the refugee "children" in New Zealand, Australia, England, Canada and the USA, I wrote: "I believe that the Polish nation, cleansing itself from the Communist plague has at last turned its attention for the first time in sixty-six years to the plight of the refugee orphans, using my person to do so."

In the Presidential Palace, in 2007, with the President of Poland, Lech Kaczynski and Solidarity activist Anna Walentynowicz. They both died tragically in an airline crash over Smolensk in 2010.

By way of a rationale

These memoirs arose in much the same way as my book *Stolen Childhood.* The "children" asked me to fill in the gaps which they had identified in their wandering lives. After many years readers of the children's saga encouraged me to write down my own memories of subsequent events by posing the question, "Whatever became of the orphans Father brought over to Canada? How did they accept their status as exiles and their betrayal by the allied forces which stopped them from returning home; how did they adapt to life in a highly organised society after spending several years in the African jungle?" My memoirs are an answer to those questions and a rebuttal of the slander directed at me by the Communist regime for kidnapping the children. It also exposes the faulty thesis of the Communist propaganda which had said that the boys would be taken into slavery by Canadian millionaires, while the girls would be handed over for prostitution.

I was also prompted to write this memoir by the conviction that the case of the wandering refugee "children" scattered around the globe is part of the history of the Polish nation. It is also my great responsibility, having lived through such a wealth of experiences, to share these with my readers as a warning that nations should never allow themselves to be ruled by maniacal ideologues again. For all these reasons these memories needed to be preserved from oblivion.

It is hard to summarise these events as the memoirs constitute the narrative of my own fate. They are about my experiences and meetings with interesting people in various countries, but also about the fate of those orphaned refugees. One of my nephews, amazed at the sheer variety and number of interesting events in which I had participated, said that it is as if in my one life are contained three lives. But I did not intend to write solely about myself. The contemporary Polish poet Father Jan Twardowski (who died in 2006) wisely put as the sub-title of his autobiography, "Thoughts – not only about myself. It's important that memoirs be not only about oneself." We are very aware that "no man is an island".

Apologies

I apologise to God and to mankind for all of my faults and causes for misgiving, especially my sin of negligence while looking after the orphans. I consider reaching the understanding that we should lead our life in accordance with God's wishes and that we should be mindful of His commandments – uniting our will with the will of God – to be a singular grace. We pray every day for the accordance of our will with the will of God with the words taught us by Christ, "*Thy will be done on earth as it is in heaven...*" Often an obstacle standing in the way of our acceptance of the will of God is our arrogance, and also pride and mistrust that God may want to deprive us of the freedom which He Himself has given to us. But He gave us freedom so that we could choose Him as the greatest Good, and love Him. God does not want to have slaves. Slowly I came to the realisation that what God wishes most of all is the harmonisation of our human will with His Divine will. How simple, sensible and uplifting this is and at the same time how ennobling. God – Creator and Artist – awaits my co-operation, because He knows what will serve my best interests, my development and personality and what will gain eternal joy for me. Agreeing with the will of God does not mean losing your own volition but ensuring that it accords with the will of God and co-operating with God, just as an apprentice works with his master. The saints understood this very well. Saint Maksymilian Kolbe always taught that the small "w" of our will should be in accordance with the big "W" of God's Will. Fulfilling the will of God and co-operating with Him bestows on humans the greatest honour and distinction possible, which no human person can ever bestow on another.

Acknowledgements

Above all I wish to thank God for the freely bestowed gift of my life. No one asks for that gift. Life is a gift from God, who of His very nature is full of Love. The Bible confirms that God has *"... loved you with an everlasting love"* (Jeremiah 31,3). I am anchored in His love. I belong to God. He is my Father. There is no other explanation. Anyone who refers to Him differently would be like an orphan, because his life would be empty and lacking in meaning.

It is God who planned my life in time and space. He chose my parents making them the channels of my life. Despite our betrayals the core of our humanity is God's masterpiece. God also arranged that my spirit was fed with thousand-year-old Polish Christian and cultural values.

I thank God for the gift of my vocation to religious and priestly life as a Franciscan and for all the graces associated with this way of life. It still amazes me that He chose me for His service. I was the "useless servant", but Christ chose me in order that He might work through me. I was to become His clumsy tool.

I also thank God for the gift of faith which was fostered within me by my beloved mother through her prayers and the example of her saintly life. I kept faithful to that faith in spite of various moral and ideological crises in the world and in spite of my own failings. My faith is the faith of a child who is aware that God is leading him by the hand through the jungle of life. Yet at the same time I am surprised that so many people turn away from God and abandon their faith in Him; while on a daily basis they are prepared to put their trust in humans, placing their confidence in their nearest and dearest; wives trust their husbands, children trust their parents, friends trust each other.

Finally, as most of my life has been connected with the fate of refugee children, I thank God that He entrusted them to my care. I consider them to be my family. They are my greatest joy. In spite of being dispersed around the world we constitute one large family.

I want to include here several sentences from a letter sent to me by one of my "African" pupils, Irena Rzewucka-Sucha, the content of which is typical of those refugee children. Today's young people may find it difficult to understand her sensitivities and her way of experiencing the world, but this letter is an accurate summary of everything that happened to those refugee children in their wandering lives all those decades ago:

"I am writing to you Reverend Father as I would to my own father, about what pains me and what gives me joy. You are too young to be my real father but I have known you longer than my real father. I only knew my father for a short time in Poland, when I was still quite young. Then, on 10 February 1940 we were taken to the heart of Russia. There we had a constant battle not to die of hunger, so there was no time to get to know my father better and in more depth. And when my brother Władek and my father enlisted in the Polish army my mother and I were left alone. Life was constantly separating us. In Teheran our father was with the army while we were in a civilian camp living in tents. From Teheran the army left for Egypt and onwards to Italy to fight against the Germans, while we left for Africa. Therefore I write everything to you as I would to my father. Maybe I shouldn't think like this but you are like a father to me, and that is why I write to you about everything, since I trust you. We know each other and have been corresponding with each other for many years now. I am happy that I can write to you..."

May Irena's letter serve as the crowning of my reminiscences, my labours and cares, my hopes and love. With each passing year I become more frail but I consider it the greatest grace to be able to still celebrate the Most Holy Sacrifice, the most perfect act which throws into insignificance all human choices, decisions or activities. It is an event which unites heaven and earth; therefore I try to celebrate the Holy Mass with great concentration and with much love since it is a sign of the New Covenant between God and His people. With increasing pace time is bringing me closer to the end of my life. I wish to continue living for the greater glory of God, making good use of every remaining moment – as a committed and content Franciscan friar. *Pax et Bonum*!

The End

Epilogue

A discussion of Homer's mythological *Odyssey* evokes in us a high school student's desire for some adventure. This idea started to attract me when I entered the Franciscan Order and pronounced my simple vows before Father Maksymilian Kolbe, known today as a Saint and a martyr of the Auschwitz Concentration Camp. But, when I reached the age of twenty-one ominous events began to unfold in my life, as if two of Homer's mythological monsters were replaced by two very real ones – Hitler who invaded my country from the West and Stalin who attacked Poland from the East. They both had the same intention – to erase Poland from the map of the world. They began a "new order" by killing the intelligentsia. As for the ordinary people, the Nazis intended to use them as slaves in their newly acquired *Lebensraum* (colony). Communists, on the other hand, intended to "re-educate" the Poles and make them *"homo sovieticus"* – people without a homeland, history, religion or culture.

My personal odyssey began in a boxcar travelling to a Siberian concentration camp, commonly known as a *gulag*. When the war was over, miraculously I became a free man, but like many of my compatriots, I could not return to my homeland which had been given over to Stalin as a "reward" by the victorious Allies for helping them defeat Hitler's panzer-divisions. It was a heartbreaking experience for myself and all the Polish soldiers who were also Allies and had fought on all fronts from the first encounter of the war to the last. I was forced then, as many of my compatriots were, to continue my wanderings through various continents and countries of the world. At the age of 91, I have still not entirely settled down.

All of my experiences and trials have taught me two important things. The first is that ideologies like Communism and National Socialism — ideologies without a belief in God — always end up in disaster. These Utopian doctrines bring misery and death to millions of innocent people. The second is the value of love. It would be impossible to survive the Soviet concentration camp without encountering love from other inmates and from all the people I later met in the free world. These good ordinary people were, and still are for me, evidence of God's Providence. I never doubted it, but when tempted to think that the Lord could have left me when I needed him most, an answer came to my mind in the form of the well-known story about Divine and mortal footprints in the sand which concludes with the Lord explaining, "When you saw only one set of footprints in the sand it was then that I was carrying you."

Thank you, God. I am learning to love you more and more.

Father Łucjan Z Królikowski, OFM Conv
Chicopee, Massachusetts, Lent 2012

Made in the USA
Charleston, SC
13 October 2012